Slow Travel and Tourism

Tourism, Environment and Development Series

Series Editor: Richard Sharpley
School of Sport, Tourism & The Outdoors, University of
Central Lancashire, UK

Editorial Board: Chris Cooper, Oxford Brookes University, UK;
Andrew Holden, University of Bedfordshire, UK; Bob McKercher,
Hong Kong Polytechnic University; Chris Ryan, University of Waikato,
New Zealand; David Telfer, Brock University, Canada

Slow Travel and Tourism
Janet Dickinson and Les Lumsdon

Tourism and Poverty Reduction
Pathways to Prosperity
Jonathan Mitchell and Caroline Ashley

Tourism Development and the Environment: Beyond Sustainability?
Richard Sharpley

Title in preparation

Sustainable Tourism in Island Destinations
Sonya Graci and Rachel Dodds

Please contact the Series Editor to discuss new proposals at
rajsharpley@uclan.ac.uk

Slow Travel and Tourism

Janet Dickinson and Les Lumsdon

publishing for a sustainable future

London • Washington, DC

First published in 2010 by Earthscan

Earthscan Ltd, Dunstan House, 14a St Cross Street, London EC1N 8XA, UK
Earthscan LLC, 1616 P Street, NW, Washington, DC 20036, USA
Earthscan publishes in association with the International Institute for Environment and Development

For more information on Earthscan publications, see www.earthscan.co.uk or write to earthinfo@earthscan.co.uk

ISBN: 978-1-84971-112-8 hardback
ISBN: 978-1-84971-113-5 paperback

Typeset by 4word Ltd, Bristol
Cover design by Yvonne Booth

A catalogue record for this book is available from the British Library

Library of Congress Cataloging-in-Publication Data

Dickinson, Janet
  Slow travel and tourism / Janet Dickinson and Les Lumsdon.
    p. cm.
  Includes bibliographical references and index.
  ISBN 978-1-84971-112-8 (hbk.) – ISBN 978-1-84971-113-5 (pbk.)
  1. Sustainable – tourism. 2. Tourism – Environmental aspects. 3. Bus travel. 4. Railroad travel. I. Lumsdon, Les. II. Title
  G156.5.E26D54 2010
  338.4'791–dc22
                            2010003762

Printed and bound in the UK by TJ International, an ISO 14001 accredited company. The paper used is FSC certified and the inks are vegetable based

FSC
Mixed Sources
Product group from well-managed forests and other controlled sources
Cert no. SGS-COC-2482
www.fsc.org
© 1996 Forest Stewardship Council

Contents

List of Figures and Tables

Figures

Tables

Acknowledgements

The authors greatly acknowledge the help of Peter McGrath, Derek Robbins, Nigel Underwood and Richard Sharpley in the provision of useful advice and in editing of the drafts of the final text. Their interest and support for our endeavours is much appreciated.

List of Acronyms and Abbreviations

AONB	Area of Outstanding Natural Beauty
CAGR	compound annual growth rate
CO_2	carbon dioxide
EEA	European Environment Agency
EU	European Union
EU-25	Schengen Agreement countries
EU27	the enlarged European Union
EU ETS	EU Emissions Trading Scheme
EUROSTAT	EU Statistical Office
EuroVelo	European cycle network
GDP	gross domestic product
GHG	greenhouse gas
HST	high-speed train
IAPT	International Association of Public Transport
IPPC	Intergovernmental Panel on Climate Change
LDCs	least developed countries
LPG	liquefied petroleum gas
Mt CO_2	million metric tonnes of CO_2
NO_X	oxides of nitrogen
pkm	passenger km
ppmv	parts per million by volume
SBB	Swiss National Railway
SO_2	sulphur dioxide
UNCED	United Nations Conference on Environment and Development, otherwise known as the Earth Summit, in Rio de Janeiro
UNEP	United Nations Environment Programme
UNWTO	United Nations World Tourism Organization
Velib	Vélo Liberté
WTO	World Tourism Organization

1
The Emergence of Slow Travel

Our treatise is a simple one. From its roots in the slow food movement of the 1980s, with concern for locality, ecology and quality of life, slow travel has gained momentum over the past decade. It will continue to grow as the need to reduce our carbon footprint becomes central to our lifestyles. Characterized by shorter distances, low-carbon consumption and a greater emphasis on the travel experience, slow travel heralds a fundamentally different approach to tourism. We contend that it will become more widespread in future decades. The aim of this book is to define slow travel and to discuss how some of its underlying values are likely to pervade new forms of sustainable tourism development. The book also aims to provide insights into the travel experience; these are explored in several chapters that bring new knowledge about sustainable tourism transport from across the world.

In recent years slow travel has emerged as a topic of discussion in a number of academic, tourism sector and media contexts. In academia, slow travel, and associated terms such as slow tourism, slow mobility and soft mobility, have increasingly been associated with low-carbon travel (Hall, 2007a). For example, Matos-Wasem (cited in Ceron and Dubois, 2007) refers to 'le tourisme lent', and Dubois and Ceron (2006a) have referred to rail tourism as 'slow tourism'. Dickinson et al (2010a) have defined slow travel as follows:

> *Slow travel is an emerging conceptual framework which offers an alternative to air and car travel, where people travel to destinations more slowly overland, stay longer and travel less.*

The idea also encompasses more experiential elements such as:

> *the importance of the travel experience to, and within, a destination, engagement with the mode(s) of transport, associations*

*with slow food and beverages, exploration of localities in rela-
tion to patrimony and culture at a slower pace and, what might
best be described as, support for the environment. (Dickinson et
al, 2010b)*

The implicit conceptual framework on which the discussion focuses is that of
slow consumption, a counter-cultural wave against the plethora of products
and services that emphasize speed and convenience over quality of experience
(Honoré, 2004). The rationale underpinning this emerging work is that slow
ways of doing things bring more meaning, understanding and pleasure to any
given form of activity, whether it be food or travel. It is a conceptual alternative to speed as one of the driving forces in the lives of people living in western
cultures (Germann Molz, 2009). It takes forward the notion that Peters (2006,
p1) refers to when he comments:

*... I will challenge the basic assumption underlying this line of
thinking, the idea that time spent travelling can be reduced to a
neutral and measured unity which can be saved if we speed up.
The core of my argument is that travel not only takes time, but
it also makes time.*

To a lesser extent the discussion has also extended to the role of the supply
sectors. Several commentators, for example, have turned their attention to a
critique of food supply. In particular, they discuss the ecological justice or otherwise of global food production systems. They ask how it can be ethically
right to produce 50 per cent of crops in order to feed animals and 10 per cent
to fuel vehicles, while starvation exists in many parts of the developing world
(Fonte, 2006; Pollan, 2007). Is there not a parallel with tourism? How can we
move towards more equitable and sustainable forms of travel? How might
such new forms of tourism flourish in a world that is changing to meet the
strictures of the ecological limits to growth? These are fundamental issues
which tourism scholars need to address; this book seeks to offer a contribution to the discussion.

Slow travel has many parallels with slow food. Nilsson et al (2007) discuss the development of slow food and the interfaces with slow cities
(Cittáslow) in terms of improving quality of life, principally for residents, but
also coincidentally for the tourist. The authors refer to the emergence of slow
food as a response to 'globalised homogenisation' and Cittáslow as a reaction
to the 'globalization of our townscapes' (Nilsson et al, 2007, p2). The threads
of the argument are similar. There is a resistance to an economic domain
which prioritizes globalization, standardization and rationality. Instead, the
focus, it is argued, should be on the vernacular, local distinctiveness and place-
based knowledge. Individuality and diversity are essential for the health of
towns and for tourism.

It is interesting to note that in a series of in-depth interviews with participants from Cittáslow towns in Italy, Nilsson and his colleagues discerned a
cautionary approach to tourism. The concern was about exploitation.

Encouragement of the tourism sector might overwhelm the small-scale nature of development in their localities, especially in relation to their heritage and gastronomy. Nevertheless, authors argue that there is a place for tourism in Cittáslow towns; there are linkages that can be progressed to good effect. The authors translate a paragraph of the work of Frykman to capture the essence of time and spatial distance, central to what he termed slow tourism, as being:

> *An indicator of a wider process – a reaction in that time and space is compressed in the fast society. The hunting of seconds tends to wipe out the peculiarities of place and persons ... Therefore, places in contemporary Europe have put their continuity and history to the front. Slowness has become one of the many ways to express such peculiarity. (Frykman, 2000, p37)*

The word 'fast' is recurrent in the tourism and hospitality literature. The analysis of the fast food concept by Ritzer (1993) explains why the quest for rationality, efficiency, control and predictability in the hospitality sector may not necessarily be beneficial for society. Ritzer's book, more importantly, offers a reflection on the cultural drift towards fast as the dominant way of life in North American society. The approach, exemplified by the McDonald's organization, is symbolic of several wider dehumanizing processes pervading society:

> *McDonaldization refers to the process by which the principles of the fast-food restaurant are coming to dominate more and more sectors of American society as well as the rest of the world. (Ritzer, 1993, p3)*

This influential work has spawned a literature on the word 'fast' that focuses on the cultural processes which ensue in tourism (Bryman, 1999; Weaver, 2005). It presents a vision of tourism which is increasingly disengaged from its roots in education, religion and exploration (Walton, 2009). It is symptomatic, it is argued, of a tourism that is 'sucking the difference out of the difference' (MacCannell, 1989). In the context of travel, Høyer (2009) argues that conference tourism is a classic example; in his view, it is a corridor of nothingness that results in little meaning and heavy environmental impact. The outcome, he notes, is part of the process of 'grobalization', a term first introduced by Ritzer (2004). This refers to the organizational need to increase sales and profits without recourse to factors such as local culture in production and environmental externalities in costing structures. It has an affiliation with the concept of McDonaldization:

> *Grobalization leads to an increasing dominance of nothing in the form of non-places, non-things, non-people, and non-service, all at the expense of something on a nothing-something continuum ... Non-places of late-modernity are, for example, major*

highway crossings, highway motels and international airports.
(Høyer, 2009, p65)

The guiding philosophy of slow then is partly an antithesis to fast, but there is also a connectedness with ecology and sustainable development which comes from an interest in locality and place as well as from strands of green travel. This is not articulated in any way as a school of thought to which we might refer. The ideas have been unfolded by an eclectic mix of writers, advocates and scholars during the past two decades. Nevertheless, there are several recurrent themes and values present in the literature that can be summarized as:

1 slow equates to quality time
2 it is about physically slowing down to enjoy what is on offer
3 a quality experience
4 meaning and engagement
5 in tune with ecology and diversity.

Other characteristics relating to slow travel include the avoidance of staged authenticity, if that is ever possible, for some would argue that tourism is about performance and contestation of space (Mordue, 2005). In the moving space, slow travel is also about a critical appreciation of the journey and with an underlying value that travel need not impact heavily on the environment. Some of these elements have been codified as a set of guiding principles for the tourist, such as one provided by Jenner and Smith (2008). This is an example of several books which exhort the tourist to adopt green travel modes, but also encourage the reader to enjoy a place by taking on the mindset of the slow traveller: it is a perception about how to engage with both the travel element and the destination. For example, tourists are encouraged to choose destinations nearer to home, to travel by environmentally sensitive modes and select accommodation that has minimal environmental impact.

MacCannell (1989), in his seminal work, *The Tourist*, recollects that all tourists seek much the same, regardless of the form of tourism, although he makes little reference to environmental consciousness. But do they? Segmentation is more prevalent than hitherto; there is a multitude of values in the market and this renders it more difficult to portray the tourist in a set of neat typologies. Even the slow traveller cannot be categorized as one discrete market segment; there are shades of green (Dickinson et al, 2010a). Some tourists look for more than others, and with an intensity of experience that is widely different to the most casual holiday participant. Those seeking slowness in their holidays have been described as a niche market, prevalent in Europe (especially in Italy), and North America, but it is far more widespread than this.

As discussed before, the concept of slow has been considered more widely in the context of gastronomy and cultural heritage than in relation to the act of travel per se. The early work was pioneered in the 1980s by Petrini, the founder of the Slow Food movement located in Italy, but the concept has now expanded across Europe and to a lesser extent in North America (Pietryowski, 2004). There are numerous examples of food and beverage production as an important element of destination development where local provenance and authenticity fit well. Many ecotourism companies have taken advantage of this; they offer exploration holidays (experiential in nature and also often marketed as being pro-poor) that embrace the culinary arts of different communities with which they engage (Bessiere, 1998). Thus, whilst there is a strong European strand of thought, the art of slow food and locality retains a presence at destinations across the globe, in spite of the globalization of agro-food and much of the hospitality sector. This is a diversity which facilitates differentiation, as much a hallmark of slow food as is enjoyment of locality and the commonplace in slow travel (Halager and Richards, 2002).

There is also emerging a literature base that explores the relationship between transport and tourism (Lumsdon and Page, 2004). Much of the work relates to transport as a means of destination development and as an enabler of tourism where speed, access and travel cost are key elements (Prideaux, 2000). However, there is a conspicuous lack of research on slow travel or, for that matter, green travel (Page, 1999). There is a distinction. Green travel focuses on the transport element only, especially in terms of resource use and carbon dioxide (CO_2) emissions per capita per trip, whereas the journey to and around the destination is an important concept within slow travel, and slow travel refers to the whole tourist experience. However, in the discussion of the components of tourism, a relative lack of attention is given to the actual travel element. Some writers have questioned whether there are differences between travel and tourism, but these have focused, for the most part, on the world of the travel writer in defining the roles of the traveller and tourist (Dann, 1998). There is also the concept of transport as tourism, which Lumsdon and Page (2004, p6) explain as:

> designed or in use mainly for the visitor market only, is often indirect as it seeks to offer a different perspective of a destination, and is rarely fast. The travel cost model does not apply in this context. The expenditure of time or duration of travel is the prime purpose of the trip and is the main benefit.

The emphasis appears to be on transport as a form of tourism at the destination, or as Bull (1991, p32) refers to it: 'more properly a form of attraction than transport'. This narrows the interpretation somewhat. Transport to the destination is also part of slow travel, and equally it can have high intrinsic value (Walton, 2009).

Fast travel is often associated with the journey to the destination, and involves intensive energy consumption leading to high levels of CO_2 emissions. Thus, our interpretation of slow travel is that it is a counter-balance to this fundamental and negative factor; the mindset of the slow traveller therefore includes not only an experiential element, but it is also interlaced with a degree of environmental consciousness that leads to an avoidance of heavy environmental impacts. It is the difference between travelling as transit and travelling as a journey (Peters, 2006).

Thus, we exclude from slow travel the three main transport modes associated with contemporary tourism development: the car, the cruise liner and the aeroplane, as they are the major users of finite resources and generate CO_2 emissions and other pollutants in an unsustainable manner.

The tourism system

The slow travel approach signifies a different model to mainstream tourism development as advanced in most tourism textbooks (see, for example, Duval, 2007). Mainstream tourism is based on the principles of the supply chain, and supply-led consumer demand, maximizing the flow of tourists in relation to transport, accommodation and destination capacity. The aim of the tourism system is, therefore, to provide an adequate throughput of visitors (and their expenditure) in any given country or destination so as to meet the needs of the suppliers who put the elements together for profitable gain (Mill and Morrison, 1985). This is commonly referred to as mass tourism, as there is a need for substantial flows of demand, and it has been the main thrust of development since the middle decades of the 20th century.

Krippendorf (1984, pxv) explains the social stimulus for the tourism system as a form of ephemeral escapism from urban life:

> *All this falls into a kind of cycle, which may be termed recreation cycle of man in industrial society: we travel in order to recharge the batteries, to restore our physical and mental strength. On our trip we consume climate, nature and landscapes, the culture and people in the places we visit, which become 'therapy zones' for the purpose. We then return home, more or less fit to defy everyday life until next time ... but the wish to leave again and even more often is soon with us again ...*

In order for the system to work efficiently there is a need for fast, price-sensitive and direct travel to the destination from originating markets. Despite the decline in the popularity of the heavily packaged holiday and the rise of the internet as a main distribution intermediary, the structural elements of the supply chain have not changed radically. The process remains an essentially industrial one based on batch production of air travel, intense utilization of perishable accommodation stock at the destination and the creation of large-scale infrastructure, such as highways, car parking and hospitality outlets, to support the tourist flows stimulated through the marketing efforts of suppliers in a world of cascading substitutes (Lumsdon, 1997).

Krippendorf's work, however, points to the flaws in the system, especially in terms of learned cultural values that the system perpetuates. He suggests that values such as owning possessions, egoism, wealth and consumption have been propagated over community, moderation and honesty, and that the former are reflected in tourism consumption. He also points to the widespread increase in the globalization of supply over the multitude of local small business sectors and the increasing encroachment of government in the provision of services and infrastructure to meet the needs of mass tourism. Finally, he expresses a concern that resources for tourism are being used as if they were inexhaustible and that, somehow, the side effects of economic growth can be readily fixed by technology. Thus, for Krippendorf, the tourism system and mass tourism have many flaws; tourism as an escape from everyday life contains the seeds of its own destruction.

Trends and the environmental impact of tourism

Domestic tourism (overnight stays, rather than day visits) remains the most important element of demand in most countries. Despite this, there are relatively few studies which focus on this aspect (Cooper et al, 2008). Bigano et al (2004), however, have undertaken a comparison of domestic and international tourism. This illuminating work indicates that for most countries, domestic tourism accounts for the majority of tourist trips. For example, in the mature USA market there are an estimated total number of 1059 million tourist trips per annum, of which 999 million are domestic (i.e. some 94 per cent of all trips). In emergent markets such as China, India and Brazil, some 98–99 per cent of all tourist trips are domestic.

In most countries the number of domestic trips per annum remains less than the total population, indicating that people are taking less than one holiday trip per year. However, in 22 affluent countries, residents take more holiday trips than this. For example, in Sweden the average holiday trip ratio is 4.8 trips per person per annum. In the USA, the average is 3.7 trips per person per annum. It is, however, essential to note that domestic tourism is far more prevalent than international tourism; the estimate by Bigano et al (2004) is that it is five times larger. They also note that developing economies such as Brazil, China, India and Indonesia have important tourist markets which tend to be underestimated in size and potential for growth.

International trips tend to be the focus of most tourism texts. Even allowing for a margin of error in the calculation of global arrivals, the figures provided by the United Nations World Tourism Organization (UNWTO) are substantial. In 2008, there were 924 million international arrivals (UNWTO, 2009c). This is in comparison to a base figure of 25 million recorded in 1950. The rate of change has until recently been accelerating at a considerable pace; the total arrivals figure has doubled since 1990. The upward trend has been impressive and this has sustained a vision of growth through development across the world. The UNWTO projection is that intraregional trips will grow by 3.8 per cent per annum, and long-haul trips by 5.4 per cent per annum, thus giving 1.6 billion international arrivals per annum by 2020. Arrivals refer to the registration of a person entering a country for tourism purposes. Thus, it does not equate to a trip which may include arrivals at several different countries. It is nevertheless a firm indication of the scale of international tourism.

An examination of the major flows of arrivals, however, illustrates that intraregional trips dominate, accounting for a predicted 1.2 billion of the overall estimated 1.6 billion trips. Much of this is actually cross-border tourism between near countries such as the USA and Mexico. Most tourists simply visit countries near to their place of domicile. For example, France, which is the most popular receiving country in the world, accounts for 77 million arrivals per annum; most visitors arrive from near countries such as Germany, the Netherlands and the UK. Spain follows France, with 52 million arrivals, whereas the USA stands at 42 million. As most international tourism is by road, this requires a substantial commitment to infrastructure; although airborne tourism was, until 2008, enjoying a growing share in this short-haul market.

There are several environmental impacts ensuing from the development and scale of tourism; these are discussed more fully in Chapter 2. The major issues relate to use of energy, and in particular oil and CO_2 emissions. Becken and Hay (2007) argue that the predicted level of demand for tourist trips will not be feasible, given the level of existing oil supplies. Current forms of transport are almost entirely dependent on fossil fuels, principally oil, and this presents a major problem for the tourism sector. It is especially the case with the most popular mode, the car, as well as cruise liner and air travel. As oil supplies have now peaked, or are about to peak, the trend price of oil is likely to increase, as it becomes a much scarcer resource than hitherto (Greene et al, 2006). Transport to the destination and whilst at the destination relies primarily on oil: over 90 per cent of tourism transport is oil dependent. The main consumption of oil in tourism occurs in the origin–destination element of a tourist trip, and in the likely event of fuel scarcity there will be a radical change in the structure of the tourism market, a matter which we address in the final chapter.

The tourism sector is currently responsible for an estimated 5 per cent of total greenhouse gas (GHG) emissions worldwide, which at first glance seems modest. Tourism is, nevertheless, by no means a small player. It stands alongside total emissions derived from the world's commercial buildings (United Nations Environment Programme (UNEP), 2009). Furthermore, a main concern relates to the growth of the sector and hence an increase in the use of natural finite resources. Tourism is a reactive sector which has, for the most part, moved grudgingly to adapt rather than to mitigate the effects of climatic change. Not that slow travel is a panacea for all of the energy and climatic change impacts; all forms of tourism bring impacts. It is, however, a part of the wider sustainable tourism development framework.

The explanation as to why the travel element is worthy of development is compelling. If travel accounts for between 75 and 90 per cent of all of the carbon emissions accruing from tourism, then the issues of spatial distance and energy intensity of mode of transport are key factors in any strategy to reduce impacts (Gössling, 2002). Therefore, the focus of this book is on the travel element. As Becken and Hay (2007, p114) comment:

The dependency of most forms of tourism on motorised transport (and resulting greenhouse gas emissions) is a major impediment to achieving sustainable tourism.

The fundamental question is whether or not tourism can prosper within a new paradigm, signified by a lower consumption of resources and substantially reduced environmental impact. This is the major challenge, one which the tourism sector is slow to address. Even in times of temporary retrenchment, the mantra has always been one of resilience and a return to growth; media releases from the major institutional tourism sectors are replete with such phrases. Some argue that such a recovery in the second decade of the 21st century is perfectly feasible, given a growing global population of 7 billion people, rising middle classes in the developing economies and a supply sector hungry for trade. But how does this square with the knowledge that oil production has peaked and that the world's scientists are predicting the inevitability of major negative impacts accruing from global warming under current trajectories (Intergovernmental Panel on Climate Change (IPCC), 2007)?

There is mounting pressure for governments to address the major challenges of climatic change. The tourism system will, therefore, not only be affected by governmental regulation to encourage emissions reduction across all sectors, but also by market behaviour tempered by a need to reduce consumption of fossil fuels. This change will be stimulated principally by higher prices, but also partly by increasing awareness of the consequences of current travel patterns. A realignment of the market might already be in progress. Given the enormity of the challenges faced with regard to anthropogenic climatic change and the partial collapse of the world banking system in 2008, governments, destinations and transport and tourism providers are faced with a new set of market conditions than those pertaining in recent decades according to the UNWTO (2009a, p2):

> *future operational patterns for global economies will be vastly different from the past; the very nature of consumerism will be changed and so will our markets and prospects.*

Nevertheless, it is argued that tourism will remain as an integral part of our cultural existence; it is a quintessential product of affluence. The inextricable links to family commitments, friendship patterns and the gratification of consumption of products has rendered these strong cultural threads as essential in most societies. Tourism is one of many dimensions of a complexity of contemporary communication described as mobilities which pervade our patterns of living (Hannam et al, 2006, p1):

> *The concept of mobilities encompasses both the large scale movements of people, objects, capital and information across the world, as well as more local processes of daily transportation, movement through public space and the travel of material things within everyday life.*

Tourism is, therefore, in one sense a microcosm of this wider network of transport and communication including the prevalence of the mobile telephone and internet, as well as actual travel between and within places. The interface between the informational world and cultural values that ensue from changes to technology could well intensify in a world that is less confident about the future based on automobility and aeromobility (Cwerner, 2009; Dennis and Urry, 2009).

An analysis of past trends, therefore, may not provide the answers to future development. There is perhaps a need to refresh our thinking. How will tourism develop in a world constrained by dwindling finite resources and increasing pollution? A number of scenarios have been proposed. Butler (2008), for example, reasons that tourism will, for the most part, follow a similar pattern to recent decades. He notes that there will be some change, however, notably a decline in long-haul tourism, concluding that:

> Long haul travel is likely to suffer most as short and medium distance travel can be undertaken by other means than flying. One scenario would see the remote and distant destinations become even more the purviews of the affluent than at present, with the mass market being concentrated closer to home. (Butler, 2008, p350)

There is a degree of consensus aligned to support this view in the wider literature; that is, long-haul tourism will be the first market sector to witness decline (Peeters and Schouten, 2006; Yeoman et al, 2007). This will affect markets from the northern hemisphere and destinations in the south.

Some predict that there will still be a major growth pattern in Asia, Africa and Latin America, in terms of both intra- and inter-regional travel. This seems unlikely, however, in view of the lack of agency on the part of many of the countries involved, limited resource availability and increased impacts of climatic change. For many tourists in the southern hemisphere slow travel is, in physical terms, a way of life, as a combination of coach, train or ferries and walking are still primary modes. Whether or not there also exists a slow travel mindset, in relation to the travel experience and environmental conservation, is not known. These are simply the accessible modes available to some of the population; others have severely limited mobility. But even in the poorest economies of the world the use of the car is being encouraged, infrastructure provided and increasing consumption of finite resources given over to automobility.

Most developing countries aspire to modernize, and this currently involves increased mobility by car and two-wheeled powered vehicles. This includes the world's two giant developing economies, India and China. Not surprisingly, Chamon et al (2008) forecast rapid rises in car ownership in China and India that will change the face of domestic tourism in these countries. The current low levels of 15.8 cars per 1000 population in China, they predict, will increase to 411.6 in 2050; this compares with the current average in advanced economies of 482.4.

However, the car is currently not an affordable option for the majority of people living in developing countries. Nor do they take regular holidays; only a small percentage of the population have disposable income and the aptitude to travel. Travel to near-to-home destinations or to visit friends and relatives is, however, more commonplace now than in previous decades. The rapid increase in economic migration to cities in the late decades of the last century has also brought an increase in domestic travel. This is driven by family ties and commitments, many of which are a consequence of economic and political displacement (MacCannell, 1989). There are, of course, traditional patterns of holidaymaking in localities throughout the world. For example, the citizens of Buenos Aires in Argentina favour beach holidays in neighbouring Uruguay across the waters of the River Plata by ferry or by air. These cross-border trips count for a large proportion of the international arrivals to Uruguay (Lumsdon and Swift, 2001).

The pilgrimage remains a form of slow travel which has flourished through the centuries (Murray and Graham, 1997). Visits to holy places such as Jerusalem, Mecca and Medina in the Middle East, and to the holy rivers and high grounds of India, remain as examples of the traditional pilgrimage. Many still undertake these journeys on foot. The pilgrimage is increasingly being supplemented, however, by core elements of contemporary tourism, and new secular forms are emerging such as volunteerism or New Age travel (Collins-Kriener and Kliot, 2000; Dignance, 2006; Mustonen, 2006). The balance seems to be tipped more towards tourism than pilgrimage, rather than the equilibrium noted by Turner and Turner (1978) in earlier decades.

In terms of international travel, only a small minority of the wealthier sections of society in developing countries seek long-haul travel to other continents. The growth in recent years has been stimulated by tourism markets in developed economies in the south. The scenario which sees increases in outbound tourism is perhaps unduly optimistic. Several researchers predict that inter-regional tourism will decline in the face of dwindling resources, but in the realm of total tourism trip-making it accounts for less than 3 per cent of the world's travel (Becken and Hay, 2007; Bramwell and Lane, 2008).

The morphology

The future of tourism is inextricably bound to the future of transport in the global economy. Transport is the key issue, and one which governments and the private sector are currently failing to address, other than in short-term investment, much of which is associated with predicted long-term negative environmental effects. Medium- and long-haul tourism, for example, is clearly unsustainable in its present form, and despite the protestations of the aviation sector, technological improvements are likely to be marginal at best and outstripped by current growth predictions in the market (Gössling and Upham, 2009). Other forms of tourism, given the sheer scale of impacts modelled to date, will also need to make a contribution to the reduction of carbon, for example, in relation to travel by car for short- and medium-distance travel.

For some time now the 'business as usual scenario' has been increasingly subject to critical review (Hall, 2009). The traditional tourism growth model, with the recent additional mix of mitigation and adaptation policies, will not, as things stand, help to avoid serious predicted impacts of climatic change. The response to the climate change challenge relates not only to a legacy of previous inadequate strategies, but is as much about future development and the consequent increasing impact on the world's ecological systems (Parry, 2009). It is therefore timely that several authors have begun to reappraise sustainable tourism development, for this has helped to refine a conceptual framework on which to review and build a tourism system that will survive the present century (Sharpley, 2009).

The morphology from mass tourism to newer forms of tourism has been mooted by several authors. For example, Krippendorf (1984, p138) envisaged a 'more human tourism', where the supply sector becomes more educational and inspirational than simply selling tourist products. He envisaged that consumers will become increasingly aware of their personal impact and more ethical in their approach to travel. He also argued that we will need to prepare for more locally-based recreation near to our homes, envisaging a time when long-distance travel will be less fashionable. Fayos-Sola (1996) discussed the transformation of mass tourism to a market characterized by a high degree of segmentation, new technologies, a differentiation of products and more experienced consumers aware of social and environmental impacts. He identified a number of key trends in relation to increased mobilities, but in the main was concerned about a lack of policy-making to account for these developing trends.

Poon (1993), on the other hand, seemed more assured in her analysis; she presented a new tourism paradigm which differed markedly from the old tourism. She concluded that a new form of tourism would gain ascendancy; tourists would become more discerning and would want to blend their work and leisure life together into a more flexible lifestyle pattern. Thus, she argued, there would be a transition in the tourism system which would be characterized by being more competitive, flexible and aided by a rapidly changing impact of technology to meet the complex needs of new customers (i.e. their changed values and lifestyles and ready access to information). She envisaged a scenario where standardized mass tourism would give way to an innovative tourism paradigm, based on efficient use of technology to serve the needs of a marketplace no longer satisfied by a Fordian system of delivery of tourism packages. Poon also noted that the heavy environmental impacts of tourism would continue to degrade the environment before reaching a turning point. A tourism system which respects the environment would then emerge with the development of the new tourism. Seemingly, we have not as yet reached that point.

These authors have provided insights into the way in which contemporary tourism might change in the coming decades. Much of the new tourism that Poon and Fayos-Sola predicted is in the making. They recognized the changing nature of the market and the rapid pace of technology which has helped to shape not only tourism but all mobilities in the 21st century (Sheller and

Urry, 2006). Krippendorf (1984), in contrast, has provided insight into the way of slow travel and of the conscious traveller and balanced tourism development. Habitual behaviour in traditional markets and the resolve of the supply sector to make good their long-term investments means that the pace of change, however, has been piecemeal. Butler (2008) has described how tourism development thrives on a curious mix of dynamism and inertia. In his book, tourism is here to stay; there will be no terminal decline. On that count there is likely to be consensus.

There is a fundamental change envisaged, however, in the two worlds described by Poon – the dichotomy between old and new tourism. The new tourism, she argued, would be based on market information and mobilities. These are now pervasive in western cultures. Extending this scenario would mean that consumer markets will have a greater stake in shaping the future, in contrast to the past when the key players in the globalized tourism sector (e.g. development companies, hotel chains and airlines) have traditionally dominated transitory routes and destinations. However, as Mowforth and Munt (2009, p371) comment:

> Factors such as a structural shift from a Fordist to a post-Fordist mode of production, accompanied by cultural shifts characterised as moving from modernism to postmodernism, and a growing environmentalism, help explain the increase in the number of new forms of tourism. Independent travel has sought to distance itself from mass tourism, and a variety of benevolent terms (appropriate, alternative, acceptable, pro-poor, responsible, sustainable and so on) have been employed in an attempt to assert that it is these forms of tourism that provide an ethical and practically acceptable response to 'development' and to the structure of disadvantage of the Third World.

Slow travel is not, as we see it, an addition to the list of 'benevolent terms', nor is it primarily about tourism in developing countries. It is a term which brings together two preconditions for tourism in the future, namely carbon reduction in transport and a changed pattern of behaviour en route to and at the destination; in other words, the travel experience assumes a higher priority. This is not necessarily how all commentators view it, however. Some argue that slow travel is currently a form of holiday-making which focuses on what happens at the destination only. They argue that the travel element is external to the core element of the holiday. It is difficult to reconcile these seemingly contradictory conceptual elements, that is, that you can travel across the world by airliner, to then consume a destination at a slow pace. The positioning of several slow travel websites which advocate this approach may be no more than 'greenwash' (Peattie, 1999); they are in reality advocating more travel without recourse to any reduction of environmental impact.

There is another issue which this book seeks to address. Slow travel can be construed, in its narrowest sense, as a form of travel that is ascribed to by a niche market ready to combine green travel with a propensity to savour all that is cultural at the destination. This is only one interpretation. Another approach is to take the principles of slow travel (see Chapter 4) and evaluate the extent to which all tourists might adhere to them in different cultural and contextual situations. Following this line of thought implies that the principles of slow travel are as applicable to modified mass tourism as to other forms described as a new tourism.

The transition from a high-carbon tourism sector to a low-carbon one will take time and depends on a number of interfacing factors: price of travel, fashion, supply sector vision, and the availability of a wide range of substitutes in the leisure market (such as staying at home, virtual reality holidays). Mass tourism is likely to remain the cornerstone of future development in the short term, but destinations are well equipped to re-model their offer in order to meet the needs of a lower carbon economy. This will also allow them to compete more effectively for a greater share of local and primarily domestic markets. Slow travel will be more widespread than hitherto as a particular form of holiday-making. The pace and scale of this change will depend on the location and vision of each respective destination in response to the constraints of a post oil-based society, and more probably as a result of compounding external impacts.

One consequence is that this may result in a reduction in the scale of tourism consumption, as the nature of economic activity matches resource constraints. A related concept is de-growth, which in reality is a reduction in what the supply sectors offer. This is likely to be construed as a major threat to the current business-as-usual scenario. Hall (2009) has termed the current approach as 'economism', a policy framework which focuses on growth as represented by gross domestic product (GDP) and employment, rather than on human and social costs and benefits associated with tourism development. Slow travel is thus likely to be a response to a reduction in the tourism sector. In this context it is a generic term used to encompass the elements of sustainable consumption, the nature of the travel experience and a reconfiguration of destination management.

Slow travel presents an opportunity for tourism to flourish within a world economic order constrained by limits to growth. In this context, the principles of slow travel meet a prerequisite for low-carbon development. It also offers an opportunity to reduce current CO_2 emissions, perhaps by as much as 50 per cent. Is it a practicable form of tourism development? The book seeks to respond to this question.

The structure of the book

The scenario discussed thus far suggests that the tourism sector has an uncertain future, and will need to respond to complex problems in the face of climate change. The preceding sections provide an essence of slow travel and how it represents a 'new tourism' that offers a pathway for sector innovation. Of course, in many parts of the world, slow travel is already a way of life, and there is nothing exceptional in our thesis. However, in the developed world, slow travel represents a marked reappraisal of contemporary tourism travel.

The primary aim of this book is to define and establish the concept of slow travel. This will, no doubt, continue to be the subject of debate for some time: the following chapters set out key contextual issues, identify the primary ingredients of slow travel and provide case studies of slow travel.

The book begins with a reappraisal of the impacts of transport for tourism in Chapter 2. It provides an overview of the literature on tourism impact studies. The chapter explores the extent to which tourism is a force for good, or whether we have failed to register the negatives sufficiently. While there are widespread benefits achieved through tourism development, it is evident that these do not always materialize. It is also clear that there are many impacts. At the same time, there is some doubt that the benefits of tourism are equitably apportioned across the world, and this chapter spends some time unpicking tourism's claims to alleviate poverty. The chapter then focuses more specifically on transport impacts and draws attention to the impacts of travel to destinations which have been more or less ignored until recently. Transport has long been recognized as a cause of destination-based impacts; however, when set in a more global as opposed to local context, the impacts of transport for tourism become more significant due to GHG emissions and their role in climate change.

Tourism is affected by climate change, through the climate-sensitive nature of the tourism resource base; and is a major contributor to climate change, through the production of GHG emissions. The range of international climate change policy instruments are discussed, together with examples of responses at a national level. The chapter then analyses a low-carbon industry strategy that has arisen in response to policy and assesses the likely success of measures. It is clear from our analysis that the sector has a long way to go to achieve the reduction in GHG emissions currently proposed in international and national legislative frameworks. Finally, the chapter reflects on tourism impacts at both a local and global level, and critiques the concept of sustainable tourism development. It seems that while adopted in a wide range of documentation, sustainable tourism development is far harder to achieve. This is especially the case when impacts are assessed globally as well as locally.

Chapter 3 explores what drives tourism and travel. It examines theoretical perspectives from the social sciences that offer explanations for tourist demand. This begins with a discussion of tourism travel choice as a rational decision process and follows with an examination of the theory applied to the study of pro-environmental behaviour in order to offer an explanation for slow travel. However, while providing many insights into travel behaviour, much of this theory has been questioned by more recent perspectives to emerge from a variety of social science disciplines. In particular there is an exploration of the critiques provided by social representations theory and discourse analysis. The chapter discusses what these approaches might have to offer the study of slow travel.

More recently, two theoretical perspectives of significance to tourism have emerged from sociology: social practice theory and the new mobilities paradigm. Social practice theory provides a further critique of pro-environmental behaviour theory. It specifically questions the focus on individual agency, while excluding wider societal structures and the context of consumption. A social practices approach provides a framework with which to analyse institutionally embedded tourism practice. The new mobilities paradigm, on the other hand, provides at least a partial explanation of the increasing demand for tourism with its reflection on the relationship between mobility and society. Chapter 3 also considers the transport experience and insight from work on the consumption experience. Finally, various studies have alluded to the importance of identity in the tourism transport decision-making process. The chapter ends with a section exploring the potential role of self-identity and the need for further research to develop this area.

Our main thesis, the ingredients of slow travel, is set out in Chapter 4. The term slow travel has emerged, along with others, in a variety of academic, industry, media and internet mediated contexts. To set our ideas in context, the origins of the term are explored, especially in relation to slow food. Then the core ingredients, low-carbon, mode, travel and destination experience and environmental concerns are set out. This will not be the final discussion on slow travel; we propose a description for the purposes of debate. Our analysis has highlighted a number of aspects that we specifically seek to qualify: car- and water-based travel, distance, time, speed and cost. Finally the chapter sets out how the market for slow travel might be segmented, and explains how slow travel is different to mainstream tourism.

Having achieved this key aim, the following four chapters provide more detailed analysis of the primary travel modes which are integral to slow travel. Chapter 5 focuses on railway travel, Chapter 6 walking, Chapter 7 cycling, Chapter 8 bus and coach travel, and Chapter 9 water-based travel. Each of these chapters sets out the background to each form of slow travel, explores the experience offered, analyses the environmental issues and, in some cases, the health benefits. Each chapter concludes with a case study which provides a practical example of slow travel.

The final chapter revisits the current tourism system and the challenges faced by the tourism sector. It is evident that the 'business as usual' scenario is threatened, and the development path enjoyed by tourism in previous decades is no longer viable in its present form. The chapter explores the signs of transition to slow travel evident in policy, rising travel costs and changing travel behaviour. Three scenarios for slow travel are apparent: slow travel as a niche market predominantly focused on the middle class in western contexts; the emergence of slow travel localities; and slow travel as a guiding principle for all tourism. Finally we explore the coherence of a tourism system based on a new paradigm of slow travel.

2
The Impacts of Transport for Tourism

Slow travel, like other forms of tourism, has an impact on transitory routes and destinations. The extent to which positive impacts can be nurtured and negative impacts minimized is the major issue for tourism planners seeking to achieve sustainable development. As with other forms of tourism, evaluation of such impacts, and especially the transport element, is crucial in a wider context of the destination planning process and in terms of ecological footprint analysis (for a fuller explanation, see Peeters and Schouten, 2006; Wackernagel and Rees, 1996).

The traditional approach to tourism development, as discussed in the literature for the past three decades, has been grounded on the assumption that tourism delivers economic gain (Lea, 1988; Lee and Chang, 2008). In the context of developing countries this approach is now aligned to sustainable tourism, although researchers are increasingly reporting that the trade-off between the socio-economic impacts and economic delivery is complex (Tosun, 2001). Thus, the extent to which direct economic gains from tourism development outweigh, or are outweighed by, social and environmental costs is rarely assessed in the round.

The positive benefits that tourism delivers, and the efficacy of different development approaches, have been the subject of discussion by several authors (Chok et al, 2007; Gössling, Hall and Lane, 2008; Hall, 2007b; Nawijn et al, 2008; Scheyvens, 2009) and there are undeniably a range of associated negative impacts (Hall and Page, 2006; Sharpley, 2009). This chapter aims to present a more nuanced understanding of tourism impacts and a critique of the common view of tourism as a relatively benign service sector. In reality, tourism makes a significant contribution to climate change at the global level and this has been consistently ignored in destination-based impact analyses (Hunter, 2002).

The analysis refers to tourism impact studies that explore the triple bottom line framework of economic, socio-cultural and environmental impacts initially developed to guide companies towards providing a positive account in all three dimensions (Elkington, 1997). It then considers tourism's claims to alleviate poverty and the potential of pro-poor tourism, as these issues have become more prominent in recent years. The focus then switches to transport more specifically and the climate change impacts of tourism. Climate change is first introduced into this context, before setting out the relationship between tourism and climate change. Having set out the issues, there follows an analysis of current policy directions that have implications for tourism transport and potential low-carbon tourism strategies. The chapter concludes with a critique of sustainable tourism.

Tourism impact analyses

Most of the early studies on tourism impacts focused on economic outcomes. In particular, researchers set out to quantify economic impacts, and a variety of economic models and evaluation tools were developed (Archer and Fletcher, 1996; Fleming and Toepper, 1990). However, researchers increasingly recognized that there were negative impacts, and studies began to focus on the impacts on residents and the environment (Bramwell and Lane, 1993). The assumption, for many policy-makers and researchers, was that any such negative impacts could be managed to make tourism more sustainable (Lea, 1988). Given that many studies start from this perspective, that is, identifying a range of positive and negative impacts categories, it is not surprising that they have tended to find what they were looking for. Impact studies have also been limited by the range of impacts they have attempted to evaluate. The impacts investigated are often derived from previous tourism impact studies, and it is relatively rare for studies to explore stakeholder views to draw up context-specific lists (Pearce et al, 1996).

The structure used to investigate tourism impacts has, in recent years, been generally based on the triple bottom line framework. This approach has been adapted from the earlier work of Elkington (2004) in relation to companies, corporate social responsibility and sustainable development. It has been influential as a heuristic device to encourage organizations to evaluate all of their activities in a more comprehensive way, although the assumption that social and environmental performance can be measured in a similar way to financial and economic indicators has been the subject of criticism (Norman and MacDonald, 2003). Studies typically show positive economic benefits and negative socio-cultural and environmental impacts (Andereck et al, 2005; Ap, 1990; Gursoy et al, 2002; Hall and Page, 2006). While acknowledging that tourism can bring benefits, this section reviews the existing body of knowledge that summarize its key impacts and issues.

Economic benefits of tourism are accrued at a national level, through foreign exchange earnings and taxation. At a local level the benefits are associated with both increased investment in an area by government and commercial organizations and consumer spending in the local tourism economy. This leads to economic development through improved infrastructure (e.g. roads, water supply, energy supply) and job opportunities created by companies responding to increased visitor spending, both directly and indirectly related to tourism. However, the level of benefits can be questioned on a number of counts. For instance, infrastructure provision may be geared to serve tourists only; for example, the building of an integrated resort with improved highways and airport to serve it. At the same time, local people may still lack access to basic needs such as access to local markets or clean water. Where natural resources are in short supply, visitors can compete with residents for access to them. In many destinations in developing countries the main issue relates to water: should it be for tourists and golf courses, or the development of local agriculture (Essex et al, 2004)?

There are also limitations with the nature of job opportunities that arise through tourism. Jobs may not be desirable (Lankford, 1994); they can be part-time, seasonal, low-skilled, poorly paid and with little prospect of career development (Mason, 2003). In some places labour is brought in from elsewhere, or labour migrates from other regions, bringing other problems for a destination area (Croall, 1995).

Tourism may be developed by external organizations, often owned by foreign nationals, thus leading to leakage; that is, the money spent by tourists is drawn out of the local economy to other regions and countries (Gössling, Peeters and Scott, 2008). All-inclusive resorts are a prime example of this phenomenon. Such resorts are often owned by large international organizations and there is limited community involvement in their development (Sharpley, 2009). Tourists pay for an all-inclusive package. They can even be persuaded not to leave the complex, because of concerns expressed about crime and poor localities (Sheridan and Teal, 2006). Such resort complexes often import food and labour, and thus little money finds its way into the local economy. A similar diagnosis has been applied to the cruise economy in the Caribbean (Klein, 2005).

As well as questioning economic benefits, many studies identify a variety of negative economic impacts, such as localized inflation, increased house prices and housing costs, increased cost of living and increased local taxes (Ap, 1990; Hall and Page, 2006; Jafari et al, 1990; Johnson et al, 1994; Mason, 2003). Given the problems described in a growing number of studies, some have questioned the value of tourism as the most appropriate and successful economic development tool where there are better alternative investments available in many cases (Gössling and Hall, 2006; Gössling, Peeters and Scott, 2008; Nawijn et al, 2008). Sharpley (2009) argues that sustainable tourism development strategies rarely consider alternatives to tourism. This raises concerns, as economic development is both the main driver of positive socio-cultural and environmental benefits, and the main justification for negative impacts.

Tourism offers a number of potential socio-cultural benefits. Typically these include: enhanced international recognition of the destination region; increased availability of recreation facilities for local people; improved police and fire protection; improved quality of life; encouragement of cultural activities by local people; and preservation of cultural identity of the host population (Hall and Page, 2006; Pearce, 1998; Sharpley, 1999). However, there are also a substantial number of negative socio-cultural impacts, many of which depend on the destination context (Mason, 2003). Generally, where there is a large development gap between the host and visitor population, the impacts are greater (Smith, 1989). This is especially so where hosts have to adapt to western visitors (Nawijn et al, 2008). Socio-cultural changes may lead to a breakdown in community structure and a variety of social problems.

With respect to environmental issues, the main claim of tourism is that it helps to develop new facilities and conserves heritage of either a built or natural form (Mason, 2003). Development of new facilities can be linked directly to economic development and spending on infrastructure provision. Therefore, should economic benefits fail to accrue, such facilities will not materialize or subsequent funding for management and maintenance will not be available. Conservation of heritage is assumed to result from its recognition as being important for tourism. However, the natural heritage, in particular, can be highly contested, with local groups laying claim to various rights, such as hunting, that are in direct conflict with tourism. Where such rights are bound up with local livelihoods, tourism can threaten local jobs and subsistence (Tao and Wall, 2009).

Tourism was once heralded as the green sector for developing countries to adopt, but a plethora of studies show the extent of environmental damage that can be caused (Hall and Page, 2002; Mason, 2003; Mathieson and Wall, 2006; Page et al, 2001; Sharpley, 1999; Wearing, 2001). The negative environmental impacts of tourism, for example, physical damage, increased traffic problems, noise pollution, litter, overcrowding and destruction of heritage, have been the subject of numerous studies (Hall and Page, 2006; Johnson et al, 1994; Mason, 2003). Until the last decade, the focus was typically on the local environment, predominantly using environmental impact studies in relation to ecosystems. This is perhaps because tourism depends on high-quality environments and therefore studies provide insights into how to manage such problems. Assuming impacts are minimal and that they can be readily managed provides the basis for a good development opportunity. This remains a contested area, especially in relation to land use (Mckercher, 1992).

Poverty alleviation

The UNWTO highlights the tourism sector as a major player in poverty alleviation (UNWTO, 2005). In response to the United Nations Millennium Development Goal[1] to eradicate extreme poverty by 2015, the UNWTO established the Sustainable Tourism–Eliminating Poverty (STEP) initiative in 2002. The UNWTO (2009b) states:

> The potential for tourism to play a significant role in the alleviation of poverty is increasingly recognised by international bodies and national governments. Its geographical expansion and labour intensive nature support a spread of employment and can be particularly relevant in remote and rural areas where many of the poor live. UNWTO statistics show the growing strength of the tourism industry for developing countries.

> *In 2005, international tourism receipts for developing countries (low income, lower and upper middle income countries) amounted to US$203 billion. Tourism is one of the major export sectors of developing countries, and is the primary source of foreign exchange earnings in 46 of the 49 Least Developed Countries.*

This claim for poverty alleviation is particularly significant to concerns about the climate change impact of tourism, as it is often used as a justification of high-impact long-haul flights between source countries and destinations in the least developed countries (LDCs), as, for example, in the Gambia (Torres and Momsen, 2007). This has led some to question whether pro-poor tourism is an appropriate justification for continued growth in aviation (Nawjin et al, 2008). The argument in support of pro-poor tourism has been used to undermine attempts to increase the costs of flying through taxation or other measures (Gössling, Peeters and Scott, 2008). However, the relationship between poverty alleviation and tourism remains poorly understood and mostly contested in the literature (Hall, 2007b; Zhao and Brent Ritchie, 2007).

Pro-poor tourism has emerged as a strategy to increase the benefits of tourism for poor people (Pro-Poor Tourism Partnership, 2009). Whilst the concept is accepted uncritically in some quarters, several authors have explored the tourism potential for poverty alleviation in the LDCs and drawn a number of negative conclusions (Nawijn et al, 2008; Scheyvens, 2009). Whilst international tourism has been growing, the LDCs have experienced much slower growth, or even negative growth rates, and the overall share of international tourism in LDCs was less than 1 per cent of global tourism receipts in 2003 (Nawijn et al, 2008). In reality, most international tourism involves western visitors travelling to other western countries, particularly in Europe (Hall, 2007b; Scheyvens, 2009; Urry, 2000; World Tourism Organization, 2008). Hall (2007b) therefore questions the development potential of tourism without significant shifts in tourism flows to the LDCs.

LDCs frequently fail to provide the stable economic and political climate needed for sustained tourism development (Nawijn et al, 2008). Thus, while tourism may lead to economic development in a destination area, there is evidence that governments, particularly in the LDCs, find it difficult to redistribute this wealth (Nawijn et al, 2008). Tourism businesses, with the exception of a few niche enterprises, are not aiming to alleviate poverty but to make reasonable financial returns, and this might be at the expense of LDCs (Scheyvens, 2009). This is particularly given the huge global diversity of destinations LDCs tend to compete on cost; thus, tourism in LDCs is essentially dependent on wealth inequities between the West and the South (Nawijn et al, 2008; Scheyvens, 2009). Thus, in a global context, very little of the economic benefits of tourism accrue where they are most needed to alleviate poverty.

This is by no means an extensive review, but the fundamental argument remains. There needs to be a much more nuanced understanding of poverty alleviation and it cannot be a 'catch-all' justification for continuing business as usual. There is a need to review tourism development in the light of the wider systemic problems that face many LDCs. Given that the claim of poverty alleviation is most important in the developing world, and this is where the socio-cultural differences between host and guest are greatest, there is much potential for social-cultural changes to cause further poverty. This can arise as the host population, whilst lacking the skills to develop tourism opportunities, may be exploited as cheap labour. In addition, the exposure to western cultures may lead to a breakdown of local traditions and systems of mutual support. As with the economic development argument, this brings into question poverty alleviation claims:

> *Tourism is too often regarded as a panacea – an economic, social and environmental 'cure-all'. Globally, there is a lack of convincing empirical evidence to justify the claim that increased tourism development will lead to significant benefits for the poor. (Chok et al, 2007, p146)*

However, there are studies that show how tourism can be a positive force for development (see, for example, Gursoy and Rutherford, 2004; Hall and Page, 2006; Meyer, 2009), but the benefits are not universal. Poverty has many complex dimensions, and it is important to understand relative power relations of key tourism actors (Zhao and Brent Ritchie, 2007) and consider that the rich may gain most from tourism in the developing world (Hall, 2007b; Schilcher, 2007). It is also the case that the vast majority of studies, until relatively recently, have focused on local rather than global issues (Gössling and Hall, 2006); therefore, some of the most significant environmental, social and economic impacts of tourism have been overlooked. Such impacts accrue from travel, which is seen as an inevitable component of tourism (Dickinson et al, 2010b), although the inevitability of travel is the subject of further analysis in Chapter 4. Slow travel as a way of growing domestic markets in LDCs might well be an appropriate option for development.

In summary, there is a limitation to the triple bottom line approach as applied to tourism. The failings led the Davos Declaration to suggest a quadruple bottom line approach (UNWTO, 2007), incorporating *climate*, economic, social and environmental considerations. This is not the first time that there have been calls to add other dimensions to the triple bottom line, with health, spirituality and governance also being suggested in addition to the three core elements (Mahoney and Potter, 2004). O'Connor (2006) argues that a simultaneous balance between factors will be unlikely, and that it is imperative to refer to the integrity within any system as well as to appraise the ethics associated with it.

If a global analysis of tourism impacts is conducted, then claims of poverty alleviation will continue to be contested on the grounds of climate change (Nawijn et al, 2008; Peeters, 2009). It is therefore important that the tourism sector clarifies the extent to which development potential exists, and this should be on the basis of something akin to the quadruple bottom line evaluation. Perhaps there needs to be a more sophisticated appraisal, in line with the work of O'Connor (2006), a comprehensive evaluation including an analysis of the dilemmas afforded by contradictory positions, for example, between economic gain and environmental impact.

Transport for tourism

Within the triple bottom line framework described above, local tourism transport impacts are widely identified as negative impacts (e.g. increased accidents) rather than as benefits (such as improved access to locations, time savings and other indicators), all of which are factors measured in transport studies. The predominant issue is the negative outputs associated with the dominant mode of travel at the destination, the private car (Andereck et al, 2005; Dickinson et al, 2009; King et al, 1993; Lindberg and Johnson, 1997; Liu et al, 1987; McCool and Martin, 1994; Perdue et al, 1990; Vaughan et al, 2000). Transport impacts encompass parameters that are environmental (e.g. pollution, noise), social (e.g. reduced social space for children) and economic (e.g. congestion, parking problems).

Until recently, the focus of transport impact analysis related to destinations only. To a lesser extent, there was recognition of congestion on roads to access destination areas as a secondary issue (Holding, 2001). The focus has also been on land-based transport, especially car use. While some positive impacts have been identified, for example, improved infrastructure and tourism support of local public transport, tourism travel is one of the few aspects of tourism to be presented consistently as a problem (Høyer, 2000).

Until the last decade, international travel to access destination areas was largely excluded from the debate, aside from work focusing on major infrastructure projects, such as airports, where again much analysis centred on impacts local to the development. Studies have focused on local issues which, in the context of climate change, exclude a large share of the impacts accrued due to tourism arrivals (Gössling, 2002; Gössling and Hall, 2006; Lamers and Amelung, 2007). In particular, transport to access destinations, especially international air travel, has largely been excluded.

Recent studies have drawn attention to the fourth dimension of the quadruple bottom line; that is, the climate change impacts of tourism (see, for example, Becken et al, 2003a; Dubois and Ceron, 2006a; Gössling, 2002; Peeters et al, 2007). These studies imply that the boundaries of the tourism system need to be redrawn to encompass origin-to-destination travel. Gössling and Hall (2006) argue such a shift is vital if we are to reflect on the reality of tourist transport subsystems that are almost entirely oil-dependent. This type of analysis alters the balance. Tourism ceases to be a relatively green activity, to become one of the more energy intensive and polluting sectors of the world economy. The integration of transport and tourism in the form of slow travel will, of course, require a more refined approach to the monitoring of travel impacts during an entire holiday. The following section sets out the climate change impacts of tourism as determined by the quadruple bottom line analysis.

Climate change: implications for tourism

Defining climate change

The IPPC (2007, p30) defines climate change as 'any change in climate over time, whether due to natural variability or as a result of human activity', although it usually refers to anthropogenic changes since the early 1900s (Met Office, 2009). While there has previously been much debate about climate change, recent scientific study now confirms that 'warming of the climate system is unequivocal' (IPCC, 2007, p30) and there is a high confidence level (>90 per cent) that this is due to human activity. Global average temperature has risen by 0.7°C over the last 100 years (IPCC, 2007) and mid-range estimates project a 2–3.5°C rise this century (Met Office, 2009). The driver for this change is GHG production. GHGs arise from a variety of sources, with the burning of fossil fuel accounting for 56.6 per cent (Gössling and Upham, 2009). Other sources include deforestation (17.3 per cent), methane (14.3 per cent) and nitrous oxide (7.9 per cent) (IPCC, 2007). CO_2 is the main anthropogenic GHG. Its annual emissions grew by about 80 per cent between 1970 and 2004 (IPCC, 2007).

The impacts of climate change will be global, although the effects will be differentiated, with greater impacts in some regions and on some activities. Impacts are difficult to predict, but include sea-level rise and changes to wind, temperature and precipitation patterns. Such changes to environmental conditions also have significant consequences for socio-economic systems (Stern, 2006). Poorer parts of the world will be affected first (Ravindranath and Sathaye, 2002) and, ironically, on the whole, those countries producing the most GHG emissions seem likely to be affected least. The impacts on developing countries are driven by three factors: geographical position (they are most at risk from climate change); dependence on agriculture, the most climate-sensitive sector; and low income, resulting in low adaptive capacity (Stern, 2006). The IPCC (2007) identify the following regions as most at threat:

- the Arctic
- Africa
- small islands
- Asian and African mega-deltas.

Climate change is therefore much more than an environmental disaster. For example, declining crop yields will threaten the food supply of hundreds of millions of people in Africa (Parry et al, 2004), and there is potential for water stress in many regions of the world. According to the Met Office (2009), 1.5 billion people currently live in water-stressed regions, but that could increase to 7 billion by the 2050s. This will lead to large-scale migration and poverty, and 'over the next half-century, climate change could impede achievement of the Millennium Development Goals' (IPCC, 2007, p70).

Tourism and climate change

Tourism is both a climate-sensitive sector, which will be affected by changes to the climate in the future, and a contributor to climate change. There has been awareness of climate sensitivity in key sectors of the tourism industry for some time. For example, much research has focused on climate change impacts on Alpine ski resorts due to reduced snow and shorter ski seasons (see, for example, Moen and Fredman, 2007; Scott et al, 2003). However, it has taken the sector longer to address tourism as a significant contributor to climate change through its use of fossil fuels. Now, a growing body of studies highlight the high-carbon nature of tourism. Thus, while tourism is likely to be affected by climate change, it is also part of the problem and will therefore also be impacted by climate change mitigation measures implemented by governments.

To summarize, the issues for tourism are three-fold and interrelated:

1   Climate change will directly affect the tourism resource base through long-term changing climatic conditions, unusual weather patterns and sea-level changes, among other things.
2   Tourism is part of the problem and a cause of climate change through use of fossil fuel and production of GHG emissions.
3   As a result, international and national climate change mitigation measures will impact tourism activities indirectly through regulatory processes and fiscal measures.

This has triggered a recent wave of research examining: levels of GHG emissions associated with travel (see, for example, Becken, 2002; Ceron and Dubois, 2007; Peeters et al, 2007), accommodation (see, for example, Becken and Patterson, 2006; Gössling, 2002) and activities (see, for example, Becken and Simmons, 2002; Chan and Lam, 2003; Gössling, 2002); industry and tourist understanding of the issues (Barr et al, 2010; Becken, 2004; Hares et al, 2010); and mitigation and adaptation strategies (Gössling et al, 2002; Hunter and Shaw, 2007; World Wildlife Fund-UK, 2002). To date there have been various, rather limited, attempts within the tourism sector to reduce the tourism carbon footprint (see, for example, Caribsave, 2009; South West Climate Change Impacts Partnership, 2008; The Travel Foundation, 2006), but overall emissions from tourism are growing (Peeters et al, 2006).

Climate change impact on the tourism resource

As awareness of climate change has grown, the most pressing issue for tourism has been the impact on climate-sensitive resource bases. Early studies examined the potential, and actual, changes in tourism flows due to changing climatic conditions. Such studies have related to the likelihood of warmer summers both in destination areas (that are now potentially too hot for visitors) and origin market regions (potentially improved tourism conditions). They also related to the impact of reduced snow cover due to observed poor snow conditions over several seasons (see, for example, Breiling and Charamza, 1999). Studies examined specific regions, and a number of destinations commissioned specific reports (Aspen Global Change Institute, 2006). The wider literature on climate change highlights the following ecosystems that will be, and are already being, affected (IPCC, 2007):

- terrestrial: tundra, boreal forest and mountain regions because of sensitivity to warming; Mediterranean-type ecosystems because of reduction in rainfall; and tropical rainforests where precipitation declines
- coastal: mangroves and salt marshes, due to multiple stresses
- marine: coral reefs due to multiple stresses; the sea ice biome because of sensitivity to warming.

Such impacts will change the tourism resource base, and have a differentially greater impact on some destinations through biodiversity loss; however, there has been less work on this in the tourism area. For example, studies report that coral reefs will be one of the early casualties of climate change (Hoegh-Guldberg, 1999), and this has significant implications for destinations such as the Great Barrier Reef in Australia.

Climate change will modify the competitiveness of some destinations. There are some research studies that have adapted tourism climate indexes to examined potential for modified visitation patterns. The most popular index to date is the Mieczkowski tourism climatic index (Amelung and Viner, 2006), although it has been subject to some critical review for the lack of meaning attached to the quantitative climatic measures (de Freitas, 2003). Studies that have applied the tourism climatic index to tourism flows in Europe and the Mediterranean region, in particular, note the likelihood of a shift in northern European visitation patterns (Amelung and Viner, 2006). Ultimately, this may lead to shorter origin to destination travel patterns, as northern Europeans will have to travel less far to find tourism-compatible climatic conditions. However, this is not an exact science and there remains some uncertainty with regard to future climate changes across the world's regions.

A number of integrated studies highlight the linkages between regions affected by climate change with a recognition that tourism is contributing to global warming. The Alpine Pearls project is one such example. This Alpine initiative in Europe seeks to manage high-quality environments, providing quality tourist experiences but in a more sustainable way. It adopts a slow travel approach both to and at the destination (Verbeek, 2009). However, such linkages to tourism's impact on climate change are less common at a destination level, and tourism organizations have been slow to engage with climate change (Becken and Hay, 2007).

Tourism impacts on climate change

All components of tourism may contribute to climate change through GHG emissions from transport, accommodation and activities (Gössling, 2002). It is estimated that tourism contributed between 4 and 6 per cent of global GHG emissions in 2005 (UNWTO, 2007). It is now widely accepted that transport is responsible for the largest share of tourism emissions, estimated to be between 75 and 90 per cent of the total emissions of any tourist trip (Gössling,

2002). Air travel is a principal causal factor (Peeters et al, 2006), contributing 40 per cent of tourism CO_2 emissions (UNWTO, 2007) in 2005, despite accounting for just 17 per cent of tourist trips worldwide (Bows et al, 2009b). On the other hand, coach and rail travel, while accounting for 34 per cent of all tourism trips, contribute only 13 per cent of CO_2 emissions (UNWTO, 2007). Within the EU, the impact of tourist air travel is even higher.

Aviation

While air travel is the prime transport mode for just 20 per cent of trips, it accounts for 55 per cent of passenger km and 50 per cent of EU tourism CO_2 emissions (Bows et al, 2009b). Peeters concludes that 'air transport accounts for a rather small share of tourism trips, while causing the majority of GHG emissions' (2007, p15). Given that mitigation efforts should focus on areas with greatest impact, the UNWTO (2007) suggests that the focus should therefore be on a minority of tourism trips. The figures indicate this should be aviation-based tourism. There are some other concerns. While other industry sectors are working on reducing GHG impacts, emissions from the tourism sector are projected to grow.

It is also worth recognizing that whilst the current tourism contribution to emissions seems small, it is estimated that only 2 to 3 per cent of the world's population take international flights (Gössling, Ceron, Dubois and Hall, 2009; Simpson et al, 2008). Similarly, Brand and Boardman (2008), in a study of personal travel in the UK, found that air travel accounts for 70.2 per cent of GHG emissions from personal travel; the top 10 per cent of emitters are responsible for 43 per cent of GHG emissions. Adams (1997) used the term 'hypermobility' to describe the growing and almost obsessive demand for travel for all purposes. Gössling, Ceron, Dubois and Hall (2009, p132) describe it as the 'vast growth in temporary mobility by a relatively small number of individuals'. Their study at Gothenburg airport in Sweden provides evidence of some highly mobile people, taking over 50 return flights per year, with 3.8 per cent of hypermobiles accounting for 27 per cent of all trips.

Peeters (2007) also points out that the current growth in aviation will lead to the airline industry being responsible for a much greater share of emissions in the future, as other industry sectors continue to cut emissions. Current European targets are for an 80 per cent reduction in CO_2 emissions by 2050, yet aviation alone could account for the total emissions envisaged in this target (Bows et al, 2009b). On a global level, growth in demand for international travel from India and China will also exacerbate the problem. Given the significant role of transport in tourism GHG emissions, and its importance for slow travel, it is the focus of further analysis here.

Taken as a whole, the transport sector accounts for around 13 per cent of GHG emissions (Gössling and Upham, 2009), with the largest share attributed to road transport (Chapman, 2007). Thus, it is argued in some quarters that transport for tourism is responsible for a relatively small share of emissions, with the whole aviation industry contributing 2 per cent of global CO_2 emissions (IATA, 2008b) and in total 3.5 per cent of the anthropogenic greenhouse effect (Becken and Hay, 2007). However, this type of comparison with other sectors of the economy underplays the contribution of aviation:

> *The same basis of analysis would suggest that the UK's total transport and power station emissions are not major sources when compared with global totals; similarly the emissions from nations such as Belgium, Portugal and the Netherlands are too small to be the focus of concerted low-carbon action. Unfortunately, this view is all too prevalent in discussions over climate change... All emissions are inevitably the aggregate of smaller percentages; using this as an excuse for relative inaction will collectively lead to individual, sectoral, national and, ultimately, global apathy. (Bows et al, 2009a, pp105–6)*

The airline industry acknowledges that emissions are set to grow (IATA, 2008b). Tourist travel in Europe is both increasing in volume and shifting to less energy-efficient modes (van Goeverden, 2007), as 'budget airlines have compressed Europe's cities into a transnational network of cheap and accessible playgrounds' (Larsen et al, 2006, p101). As Nilsson (2009, p126) indicates, 'from a global, environmental perspective the development of low-cost aviation is nothing less than disastrous'. In the EU, Bows et al (2009b) predict that the aviation share of tourism trips may increase to 30 per cent within two decades and be responsible for a 75 per cent share of CO_2 emissions in tourism. This reflects an overall trend of people taking more holidays and travelling further.

There is also the question of aircraft emissions at altitude. Due to the altitude at which aeroplanes fly, their NOx emissions undergo a variety of complex interactions with other compounds, leading to a much greater impact than that of CO_2 alone (Bows and Anderson, 2007). This leads to additional radiative forcing; that is, the human modification of the natural greenhouse effect in the upper atmosphere (the troposphere). While there is still some uncertainty over the science, it is estimated that the radiative forcing of air travel is two to four times the effect of CO_2 emissions (Becken and Hay, 2007; Chapman, 2007). Therefore, closer attention needs to be paid to the climate change impacts of aviation emissions.

Car-based tourism

While air travel causes significant climate change impacts, attention also needs to be paid to land-based travel, especially car-based tourism (Sharpley, 2009). Leisure-related travel (a broad category) accounts for between 40 and 50 per cent of all travel in industrialized countries (Becken and Hay, 2007; Holden, 2007). In the UK, leisure-related travel accounts for half of all journeys and 53 per cent of mileage if shopping is included, or 31 per cent of journeys and 40 per cent of mileage with shopping excluded (Department for Transport, 2009), while in Germany it is estimated leisure trips account for 48 per cent of mileage (Schlich et al, 2004). In the USA, leisure accounts for 57 per cent of long-distance trips (round trip of over 100 miles or 160km), of which 30 per cent is to visit friends and relatives and 27 per cent for other leisure purposes, including sightseeing, the outdoors and relaxation (Bureau of Transportation Statistics, 1995).

Car dependency is high for leisure travel (greater than 70 per cent of trips in the UK; Department for Transport, 2009), particularly in rural destinations where it may account for 80–90 per cent of trips in the UK (Dickinson and Dickinson, 2006; Dickinson and Robbins, 2008). In the USA, it is estimated that 82 per cent of all long-distance leisure trips involve personal use vehicles (Bureau of Transportation Statistics, 1995). Sharpley (2009) suggests that car-based tourism is likely to be higher than estimated, due to a lack of detailed monitoring in many countries. Furthermore, if infrastructure construction, car manufacture and disposal are included, car-based tourism has a high environmental burden. In this respect, car-based travel for tourism is likely to become more significant in terms of the potential for carbon savings in the tourism sector. This will require visitors to travel less distance by car and/or use alternative modes.

The above analysis of tourism's contribution to climate change highlights the pressing need to address GHG emissions that arise from transport for tourism. While there are potential emissions savings to be made in the accommodation and activity sectors of tourism, the most substantial opportunities to mitigate the climate change impacts of tourism lie in modifications to the structure of tourism movements from origin to destination (Peeters and Schouten, 2006). Though awareness has grown with regard to this issue, there is currently little in the way of specific policy that addresses tourism and climate change. The next section analyses relevant policy directions.

International and national climate change policy

Based on current mitigation policies and practices, GHG emissions will continue to grow over the next few decades (IPCC, 2007). In light of the projected impacts, a number of international and national policy frameworks have been drawn up to address climate change. There is little policy that is specific to tourism, but there is a growing body of policy that addresses climate change and measures directed at land-based travel. At the same time, the discussion about how policy should be applied to aviation and shipping is important. Currently, the tourism sector has only been indirectly affected by policy decisions, but it is envisaged that future policy will impinge more directly on tourism in due course. Three types of policy approach are likely in order to address GHG emissions: regulatory, market-based (e.g. environmental taxes, emissions charges, subsidies, tradable permits) and voluntary initiatives such as carbon offsetting (Daley and Preston, 2009). However, it will be difficult to select appropriate targets, to delineate measures of integration and to enforce and monitor policies. A combination of policy instruments will be required to afford this (Daley and Preston, 2009). This section summarizes relevant policy directions to date.

The international climate change agreements, to date, are set out in Table 2.1. The most significant international agreement on climate change is the

Table 2.1 *International climate change agreements*

1992	**United Nations Framework Convention on Climate Change** Signed at the United Nations Conference on Environment and Development (UNCED), otherwise known as the Earth Summit, in Rio de Janeiro. The agreement aimed to stabilize GHG emissions in the atmosphere to avoid dangerous climate change.
1997	**Kyoto Protocol – revised United Nations Framework Convention on Climate Change** Established legally-binding GHG emission reduction obligations for developed countries. Aviation was excluded from emissions inventories, but countries were encouraged to account for aviation emissions.
2007	**The Bali Climate Change Conference** Adopted the 'Bali Road Map' that charted the course for further negotiations for a more comprehensive agreement on climate change.
2009	**United Nations Climate Change Conference, Copenhagen** The Copenhagen Accord recognized the need to stabilize GHG emissions so global temperature rise remains below 2°C, agreed the need to cut GHG emissions and established funding to help poorer nations to adapt to climate change.

United Nations Framework Convention on Climate Change, agreed initially at the Earth Summit in Rio de Janeiro in 1992, and revised with the Kyoto Protocol in 1997. The agreement signed in Rio aimed to stabilize GHG in the atmosphere to avoid dangerous climate change, but the commitment to reduce GHG emissions was non-binding. The Kyoto Protocol rectified this and was ratified by over 166 countries, becoming legally binding in 2005. However, the Kyoto Protocol was not ratified by a number of countries, most notably the USA, and negotiations have continued to bind the USA into the process. The Bali Climate Change Conference in December 2007 launched negotiations for a more comprehensive agreement that was to be concluded in December 2009 at the UN Climate Change Conference in Copenhagen. Negotiations at Copenhagen led to the Copenhagen Accord, an agreement that was drawn up in the final hours by leaders from the USA, China, India, Brazil and South Africa. The Accord recognized the need to stabilize GHG emissions so that global temperature rise remains below 2°C. It agreed the need for cuts in emissions, and established that financial assistance would be made available to assist the poorest nations' adaptation to climate change. It is unclear, at the time of writing, whether many states will sign up to the Accord.

At an international level the UNWTO first highlighted the importance of climate change to tourism in 2003, when it convened the first international conference on climate change and tourism in Djerba, Tunisia. Subsequently, a second international conference on climate change and tourism was convened in Davos, Switzerland in 2007. This acknowledged unequivocally that climate change was happening and that the contribution of GHG emissions from the tourism sector was a factor of concern. Among other things, the Davos report recommended action to mitigate the climate change impacts that arise from tourism. Recently, the UNWTO has collaborated with the World Economic

Forum to produce a report 'Travel and Tourism in a Low Carbon Economy', which was their contribution to the Copenhagen process in December 2009. The World Economic Forum (2009) report recommended modal shift from car to mass-transit modes as part of the solution. But it is interesting to note that it did not propose a shift from air travel to other modes. With regard to aviation strategy it recommended a push for the inclusion of aviation in post-Kyoto climate change agreements at an international level.

International legislation and regulation relating to climate change has been gathering pace in recent years. Post-Kyoto, the EU, as a whole, agreed to meet a joint target of an 8 per cent reduction in GHG emissions below 1990 levels by 2012, with greater and lesser targets allocated to different member states to meet the overall reduction. In 2000, the European Commission launched the European Climate Change Programme that resulted in the EU Emissions Trading Scheme (EU ETS), one of the key mechanisms to achieve GHG reduction in the EU. More recently, various EU states have unilaterally set emissions targets based on the aim of stabilizing CO_2 equivalent concentrations in the atmosphere to avoid dangerous climate change; that is, a global average temperature rise not exceeding 2°C above pre-industrial levels. Stabilizing CO_2 equivalent at around 450 parts per million by volume (ppmv) provides a 46 per cent chance of ensuring global mean temperatures do not exceed the 2°C threshold. However, stabilizing a CO_2 equivalent at 550ppmv provides only a 29 per cent chance (Bows et al, 2009b). Current CO_2 levels are 384.78ppmv, as of September 2009 (Tyndall Centre for Climate Change Research, 2009).

In 2007, the European Commission proposed a target of a GHG emission reduction of 60 to 80 per cent by 2050 from a 1990 benchmark (COM, 2007). This target has been adopted in UK legislation (Department for Environment Food and Rural Affairs, 2009). In December 2008, EU leaders agreed a climate change action and renewable energy package. This was a unilateral agreement to reduce GHG emissions by 20 per cent by 2020 compared to 1990 levels, with a commitment to 30 per cent reductions if there is a wider international agreement to reduce GHG emissions (COM, 2009a).

The Kyoto Protocol encouraged countries to account for emissions from international aviation, but these are reported separately to those within national borders (Becken and Hay, 2007), excluded from binding targets and therefore outside of emissions trading.

Air transport is a significant obstacle to the tourism sector's attempts to achieve emissions reductions (Janic, 1999). The principal reason is that aviation is currently excluded from national and international policy on GHG emission reductions. This is for a variety of historical reasons linked to the problem of attributing fuel use, and hence aviation fuel taxation, to particular countries, given the international nature of air travel. Shipping is also excluded for similar reasons (Michaelova and Krause, 2000).

Bows et al (2009b) have analysed the aviation contribution to emissions targets in the context of the EU. The current EU target does not include the emissions generated by either international aviation or shipping, although the EU Commission now considers that these sectors should be included (COM,

2009a). Governments have also 'often without due consideration or recognition, accepted that such targets must include all greenhouse gas-producing sectors' (Bows et al, 2009b, p8), but neglect cumulative emissions and carbon-cycle feedback mechanisms. Unless action is taken, then emissions cumulatively build up in the atmosphere. For example, Bows et al (2009b) calculated that over the four years 2000–04, cumulative aviation emissions amounted to a significant portion of the overall budget in the period from 2000–50, prompting the conclusion that 'we are spending our carbon budgets very rapidly' (Bows et al, 2009b, p12). Based on a cumulative growth argument, the authors show how aviation could exceed the total EU CO_2 budget between 2036 and 2048, based on stabilizing CO_2 equivalent at the lower 450ppmv level. In summary, there is a growing opinion that GHG needs to be stabilized at an even lower level of 350ppmv CO_2 equivalent, to avoid uncertain risks (COM, 2009a).

In setting its priorities for Copenhagen 2009, the EU stated the following: 'To have a reasonable chance of staying below the 2°C threshold, global GHG emissions must be reduced to less than 50 per cent of 1990 levels by 2050' (COM, 2009c, p3). The EU aimed to achieve an international agreement, setting out a 30 per cent reduction by 2020, but this was not achieved. The EU also recommended that shipping and aviation should be brought into the targets, as these are global activities that require global measures (COM, 2009c).

In the UK the Climate Change Act became law on 26 November 2008 (Department for Environment Food and Rural Affairs, 2009). The Act set a legally binding target to reduce GHG emissions for the year 2050 by at least 80 per cent, and to reduce CO_2 emissions by at least 26 per cent by 2020, from a 1990 baseline. In addition:

> The Government will include international aviation and shipping emissions in the Act or explain why not to Parliament by 31 December 2012. (Department for Environment Food and Rural Affairs, 2008)

The Committee on Climate Change, an independent body set up to advise the UK government on setting carbon budgets, reported in December 2009 on the need for constraints on UK aviation growth in order to meet emissions targets. The report suggests a variety of mechanisms to limit aviation growth from 2005 to 2050 to 60 per cent. To set this in context, Becken and Hay (2007) note that if aviation emissions are brought into UK national GHG emissions accounts, aviation would range between 22 per cent, 39 per cent or 67 per cent of the national CO_2 budget in 2050, on assumed annual growth rates of 3, 4 or 5 per cent. Legislation, such as the Climate Change Act, will ultimately have implications for all industries including tourism, whether directly or indirectly through fiscal measures, technological adaptations and energy policy (Department for Environment Food and Rural Affairs, 2008).

Whilst the US government is funding initiatives to reduce GHG emissions through science and technology programmes, and playing a role in current negotiations (US Environmental Protection Agency, 2009), the federal government has yet to set a clear policy that relates to the reduction of emissions through targets. However, individual US states have begun setting GHG emission-reduction targets (Gössling, Hall and Lane, 2008). Australia is in the process of developing an emissions trading scheme, the Carbon Pollution Reduction Scheme, which is planned to include domestic aviation. However, at the time of writing (December 2009), the Australian Senate had rejected the Bill.

Emissions trading

The EU Emissions Trading Scheme (EU ETS), introduced as part of the process of reducing EU emissions in 2005 (see Table 2.2), has significance for travel and tourism at the current time (2009). Under the EU ETS, participating industry sectors are allocated a carbon allowance, depending on their anticipated need. This allowance is capped. A proportion of the allowance is allocated at no cost to companies. Companies are then driven to reduce emissions, in which case they can auction any of their excess free allowance. If they require more emissions permits, these must be purchased. To date this has had limited implications for the tourism industry; however, in December 2006, the EU Commission proposed the inclusion of aviation in the EU ETS. Within the proposal, emissions from all domestic and international flights between EU

Table 2.2 *The EU Emissions Trading Scheme*

Background
Introduced in January 2005 as a mechanism to reduce EU GHG emissions. The scheme arose from Directive 2003/87/EC in 2003. It was the first CO_2 emissions trading scheme in the world and was developed as a mechanism to help EU countries comply with the Kyoto Protocol targets.

The mechanism
Participating industry sectors are allocated a carbon allowance, determined by each member state. The allocation is on the basis of anticipated need. The allowance is capped to stimulate reduction in emissions. A proportion of the allowance is allocated at no cost, while the remainder of emission permits must be purchased at auction. Companies who make emissions cuts are able to trade any excess permits at auction.

Sectors covered
Annex I of the directive specifies industry sectors covered by the ETS. The initial scheme included the main energy-intensive industry sectors that together emit nearly half of Europe's CO_2 emissions. These include energy producers, iron and steel plants, mineral industries, and pulp and paper industries.

Inclusion of aviation
The EU Commission proposed the inclusion of aviation in the scheme in December 2006. The EU Directive 2008/101/EC came into force in February 2009. Emissions from all domestic and international flights between EU airports will be covered from 2011. From 2012 the scheme will expand to include all international flights arriving at or departing from an EU airport.

Aviation permits
Permits will be capped at 97 per cent of the 2004–05 emission levels in 2012 and 95 per cent in 2013. Some 85 per cent of permits will be freely allocated, with the remaining 15 per cent being auctioned.

Source: Duval, 2009; Environment Agency, 2009; Europa, 2009

airports will be covered from 2011, with expansion to all international flights arriving or departing from an EU airport from 2012. This is proposed as a model for wider, global action (Europa, 2009). The number of permits will be capped at 97 per cent of 2004–05 emissions levels, which effectively means an aviation emissions reduction of 3 per cent by 2012. Some 15 per cent of permits will be auctioned, the remaining 85 per cent being allocated freely (Duval, 2009). There are potential challenges to the inclusion of aviation within the EU ETS from the USA and industry. IATA has questioned the legality of the scheme, and the International Civil Aviation Organization, originally tasked with implementing emissions reductions under the Kyoto Protocol, would prefer an alternative strategy to address operating inefficiencies ahead of cap and trade (Duval, 2009), also emphasizing the need for international action (Daley and Preston, 2009). The USA has also threatened legal action on the basis that the scheme contravenes international trade law (Duval, 2009).

Thus, much remains to be seen about the inclusion of aviation within the EU ETS. It has implications for tourism travel, although the impact will not be clear for some time. In the meantime, several studies suggest that the additional costs passed on to passengers, due to purchase of permits, will be limited, and there is likely to be negligible impact on volume of air traffic (Bows et al, 2009a; Gössling, Peeters and Scott, 2008). The scheme is unlikely to threaten the competitive position of many European airlines (Albers et al, 2009). However, the advent of EU ETS has the potential to 'change the transport landscape from cheap and fast (air transport) to slower and more expensive' (Peeters, 2007, p21). If a global aviation emissions trading scheme was to be implemented, with significantly higher costs per ton of CO_2 compared to the EU ETS, then this could have significant implications for global air travel (Gössling, Peeters and Scott, 2008). Bows et al (2009a) suggest carbon prices should be set in the range €100–€300 per tonne, rather than the current €15–€33 per tonne being considered by industry.

Land-based transport

While policy and legislation relating specifically to GHG emissions has been gathering pace, so too has policy relating to land-based transport. For example, the 2001 EU White Paper, *European Transport Policy for 2010: Time to Decide* (COM, 2001), aimed to revitalize the railways as a viable option for long-distance travel (Holden, 2007), and significant improvements have been made to the European rail network in recent years. The EU has also worked with the European automobile industry, making an agreement in 1998 to reduce the average CO_2 emissions of new cars in 2008 by 25 per cent (from a 1995 base); however, overall fuel consumption rose during this period by 8.1 per cent, due to increased car travel (Holden, 2007). Subsequently, EU legislation in 2009 set CO_2 emissions standards for new cars (Regulation (EC) 443/2009). The Commission's review of the 2001 Transport White Paper (COM, 2006) indicates that environmental commitments are an increasing concern and the EU recognizes the need to integrate climate change into transport policy. Transport is recognized as a threat to achieving progress on Kyoto targets, and there is an urgent need to pursue energy efficiency in European transport. These points are reinforced in a 2009 document (COM, 2009b, p11), which highlights that 'in no other sector has the growth rate of greenhouse gas (GHG) emissions been as high as in transport', and there is a need for an inversion of current trends to meet targets. A new EU Transport White Paper is expected in 2010.

In general there is little specific tourism policy that relates to GHG emissions, although it is covered in wider policy on transport and development. However, it is useful to refer to the UK in order to highlight inconsistencies that occur at a national level between UK transport and tourism policy (Robbins and Dickinson, 2007). In the UK, as in many other governmental contexts (Peeters, 2007), transport and tourism policy structures are prepared and delivered by different government departments. While this is not in itself a problem, the respective departmental policies in the UK are to reduce car traffic and to advance tourism growth, much of which is currently car dependent. There is clearly a conflict in policy (Robbins and Dickinson, 2007). Robbins and Dickinson suggest that there is a need to integrate tourism and transport policies so as to facilitate tourism growth and modal shift from cars to other forms of more sustainable transport. This would be appropriate in terms of climatic change mitigation. Since the Climate Change Act, disparity is also apparent between climate change and tourism policy and, perhaps more so, with UK plans to expand airport capacity (Charles et al, 2007).

At an EU level there has been some indication of the direction that tourism policy might take in a communication on sustainable tourism (COM, 2003). A sustainable tourism advisory group was also launched in 2004 (the European Commission Tourism Sustainability Group), which published a report in 2007 highlighting the climate change impacts of tourism. This recommends actions to reduce emissions in the aviation sector and a modal shift from air and car travel towards environmentally friendly forms of transport for tourism (train, coach/bus, water, cycle, foot). While not enshrined in formal policy, this does lay the foundation for the growth of slow travel in the future.

Water-based transport

Another important sector for tourism is shipping. Many tourism trips depend on ferries, and the cruise industry has shown exceptionally strong growth in the past decade (Dowling, 2006). As with aviation, the fuel used for shipping is exempt from taxation and currently is not covered by international regulations such as the Kyoto Protocol or the EU ETS. While there are significant difficulties in accounting for fuel use in this transport sector, there is growing pressure to bring shipping into wider GHG emission accounting systems.

In summary, therefore, tourism has remained largely unaffected by climate change policy and legislation. However, the sector, as represented at an international and governmental level, is increasingly aware of the magnitude of the problem. Policy guidance is slowly being put into place to address the key issues, but as yet there is a considerable gap between policy and delivery at a regional and destination level.

Low-carbon tourism industry strategy

The tourism sector's reaction to climate change has involved two different but related responses: mitigation and adaptation strategies. Mitigation refers to attempts to reduce the impact of tourism on climate change, while adaptation refers to attempts to adapt tourism to climate changes and minimize climate change risks. The tourism sector will also need to make adaptations in response to national mitigation strategies related to GHG emissions, hence the concepts are related. For instance, as a sector totally reliant on transport, national and international mitigation policies related to GHG emissions are likely to increase costs of transport and impact tourism mobility. There are implications for slow travel. For example, it could be argued that slow travel should become a major mitigation response, as part of a cultural change, associated with travel and trip distance reduction.

The Stern Review (2006) suggests GHG emissions can be cut in four ways:

1   reducing demand for emissions-intensive goods and services
2   increased efficiency
3   action on non-energy emissions, such as avoiding deforestation
4   switching to lower-carbon technologies for power, heat and transport.

Within the tourism sector, the World Tourism Organization (2007) identified four major mitigation strategies related to the above:

1   reducing energy use
2   improving energy efficiency
3   sequestering carbon through sinks
4   increasing the use of renewable energy.

Each of these is considered in turn, with a focus on transport for tourism, as is the idea of eco-labelling that cuts across all the above strategies (see Table 2.3 for a summary).

Reducing energy use

Much energy use for transport could be reduced if tourists were to adopt, to a greater degree than hitherto, pro-environmental behaviour. The theory relevant to pro-environmental behaviour is discussed in Chapter 3; however, here a more industry- and policy-led perspective is considered. Eco-efficiency is a tool 'to discover how economic growth can be achieved with the lowest possible level of emissions' (Peeters et al, 2009, p303). Based on an eco-efficiency analysis of tourism, Peeters and Schouten (2006) suggest marketing should focus on sourcing markets closer to destination areas. This involves restructuring destination portfolios (Peeters et al, 2008) and may involve de-marketing, where marketing is discontinued to more distant source markets.

Alternatively, policy mechanisms might increase the cost of travel or develop other barriers that affect behavioural change, including modal shift to low-carbon travel. These types of governmental intervention are not new to tourism. The use of visas, previous limitations on the amount of money a

Table 2.3 *Low-carbon tourism industry strategy*

Strategy	Potential mechanisms	Likely success
Reducing energy use	Promoting pro-environmental behaviour; increasing travel costs; introducing travel barriers; promoting longer stays; promoting nearer markets to reduce travel distance.	Largely unproven to date and some mechanisms likely to be unpopular with industry; however, could bring about significant energy reduction.
Improving energy efficiency	Improved energy efficiency in building design and insulation and introduction of renewable energy schemes.	Small impact due to relatively low contribution of accommodation to tourism emissions.
	Improved fuel efficiency in the transport sector; improved traffic management; increased seat density.	Technology is mature; therefore, limited scope for improvement leading to a marginal contribution.
Sequestering carbon through sinks	Carbon offsetting schemes such as storage of CO_2 in biomass or payment for emission reductions elsewhere.	No attempt to reduce emissions at source; questions about the viability of such schemes.
Increasing the use of renewable energy	Accommodation and activity sectors can generate on site or purchase through a green energy provider.	Good potential for success but small impact due to low contribution by accommodation and activity sectors to emissions relative to transport sector.
	Use of biofuels or other alternative energy sources in the transport sector.	More limited potential for success and significant constraints on development.
Eco-labelling	Predominantly destination-based schemes applicable to accommodation providers and activity sector; increasing carbon labelling of transport options.	Problems due to poor regulation of schemes; uptake is patchy; lack of consumer awareness and interest.

Sources: Becken, 2009; Bows et al, 2009b; Broderick, 2009; Holden, 2007; Peeters and Schouten, 2006; World Tourism Organization, 2007

person can possess on entry or exit to a country and localized tourism taxes have been in operation for decades. One of the most popular approaches is to introduce measures to ensure car use reduction, whilst investment is directed to alternatives.

There have been several studies to evaluate the potential of policy mechanisms to reduce car access while simultaneously increasing investment in alternatives (Banister et al, 2000), with positive results in urban areas (Holding, 2001). However, the tourist experience, in recent decades, has been drawn mainly from small-scale experiments in rural areas. In these cases, the results have not been encouraging (Culinane, 1997). More recent interventions, mainly urban in nature, have achieved very different results, such as the cycle-sharing schemes in France (see Chapter 6 for details) and traffic reduction in cities such as London, Lyon and Paris (Massot et al, 2006; Prud'homme and Bocarejo, 2006); and all point to a way in which the population will respond to alternatives to the car if they are planned and executed at a level that is convenient, are well publicized and do not require a major shift in values and practical response.

A marked benefit would be achieved by encouraging a reduction in air travel in favour of land-based public transport (see Table 4.2, Chapter 4). For example, a policy to invest in a national high-speed rail network in France and Spain has resulted in a considerable reduction of internal air travel (Givoni, 2006). Given its importance to slow travel, low-carbon transport is discussed in an extended section in Chapter 4, as it is one of the core ingredients of slow travel.

Another strategic strand in market behaviour is to encourage an increase in length of stay. However, this needs to be given careful consideration. Studies suggest longer stays spread the travel carbon footprint and improve the eco-efficiency of a holiday (see, for example, Gössling et al, 2005; Peeters et al, 2006; Peeters and Schouten, 2006). The problem is the transport carbon footprint still remains constant, regardless of length of stay, and this is the major energy and emissions output of all holidays. There is, however, a substantial carbon saving if a tourist substitutes three short holidays for one long holiday at a similar distance.

Distance is also another important consideration. Van Goeverden (2007) shows from 1990 to 2001 a 24 per cent growth rate in Dutch travel of 2000–3000km and an 8 per cent growth in travel over 3000km. In this respect, low-cost airlines have opened up air travel to new travellers in many parts of the globe. Introduced in the USA, low-cost aviation has since spread to Europe, Australasia, South East Asia, India, the Gulf states and South America (Nilsson, 2009). An additional point, taken up by Dubois and Ceron (2006b), indicates that the tourism sector continues to promote unsustainable behaviour, as tourists are encouraged to take short duration breaks to more distant destinations. The argument is that this is what the market desires – more shorter holidays, and at longer distances. This is a questionable assumption. The tourism sector continues to portray an imagery that reflects speed, distance and frequency. Peeters (2007, p21) suggests: 'tour operators have to find innovative ways to sell more short- and medium-haul destinations with comparably slow transport modes and preferably a longer length of stay and thus higher revenue per trip.'

The underlying structural issue offers part of the explanation. Mature destinations attempting to survive in a highly competitive market are drawn towards the promotion of short breaks in order to sustain capacity; this mirrors the overall growth-at-all-costs culture. A review of the product life cycle would imply contraction of capacity at destinations during late maturity. It is difficult to rejuvenate or modify products at this stage without substantial investment. However, contraction of capacity enables a destination to be sustained in the longer term, but at a lower capacity. There seems to be a reluctance, for the most part, to move to this type of strategic restructuring for political reasons. Ironically, it is often the case that government support extends a life cycle of a destination during market decline, but is sometimes lacking when new markets are emerging. Slow travel is a good example of this.

A related, but potentially significant, issue is the transport of food and beverages to destinations for tourist consumption. Tourism impact assessment tends to overlook the indirect impacts of tourism activity, which can have a high cumulative effect (Filimonau et al, 2010). Food, for tourist consumption, can have a particularly high carbon footprint in developing economies. This is primarily due to transport costs, when food is sourced at an international level in order to meet the needs of the inbound markets (Filimonau et al, 2010). Tourism businesses tend to have limited awareness, and minimal control, of the environmental issues in their supply chain. There are, of course, a number of initiatives in many countries that focus on the provision of locally sourced foods, but these are unlikely to counterbalance global trends in hospitality. There will be some impact reduction by sourcing local food and products, but in many cases this still remains at a small scale. It is clearly associated with slow food and travel and warrants further research.

Improving energy efficiency

There is evidence to infer that some sectors within tourism (accommodation, transport and activities) are now seeking to improve their energy efficiency. Rising fuel costs have been a key driver, as efficiency can bring considerable cost savings (Becken and Patterson, 2006). In the accommodation sector, energy efficiency has been achieved though building design and improved insulation, together with energy efficiency strategies such as the introduction of renewable energy schemes (Dalton et al, 2008; Önüt and Soner, 2006). However, given the relatively low contribution made by the accommodation sector to tourism emissions as a whole, such a strategy can only make a small, albeit positive, contribution to low-carbon tourism.

On the other hand, improving energy efficiency in the transport sector has far greater potential, given its high share of carbon emissions. Both the aviation and automobile industries have been developing increasingly fuel efficient models. Airlines expect to improve fuel efficiency in some classes of aircraft by 20 to 30 per cent by 2024 (Bows et al, 2009b). Additional gains can be made through more efficient management of air traffic routes, and by increasing seat density. However, given the anticipated increase in demand for flights, any energy efficiency gains are likely to be lost simply because of the predicted growth in air travel. Even with a 'top end' improved technology scenario, passenger growth rates, it is argued, will cancel out technology improvements as aviation is 'technically mature' (Bows et al, 2009b, p21). Most commentators now argue that there is limited scope for further development (Becken and Hay, 2007; Bows et al, 2009b; Chapman, 2007; Peeters, 2007). Bows et al (2009b) note two problems with the 'technology will save us' approach presented by some advocates. Firstly, innovation is risk-laden for individual companies when there may be relatively small gains to be made; and secondly, the rebound effect may absorb savings; that is, people travel more as travel costs reduce due to fuel efficiency (Holden, 2007). While technological gains are possible, there is also a time lag between inception and introduction to a commercial fleet (Chapman, 2007).

In summary, Holden (2007) suggests that we need either massive improvements in energy efficiency or a reduction in distance travelled. Therefore, while improving energy efficiency is an important low-carbon strategy, and one that makes good business sense, it will make only a marginal contribution to a low-carbon tourism scenario of the future.

Sequestering carbon through sinks

One strategy to mitigate GHG emissions is to store CO_2 in biomass, such as forests or other means (WTO, 2007), or to pay for emissions reductions elsewhere (Broderick, 2009). As a result it is possible for industry and consumers to mitigate GHG emissions through various carbon offsetting schemes. This is one of the strategies suggested by the EU (COM, 2003) and offsetting is seen as a solution by many airlines (Peeters, 2007). A plethora of schemes have emerged in recent years linked to tour operators, airlines (see, for example, IATA, 2008a) and independent organizations (see, for example, Climatecare, 2009). Such schemes enable individuals to calculate the carbon footprint of their holiday, or other elements of consumption, and offer the opportunity to offset the emissions through the purchase of equivalent emissions savings elsewhere. Typical schemes include tree planting and energy-saving measures.

There is, however, a considerable degree of scepticism as to the value of carbon offsetting. It may be used as a travel sector approach to reduce emissions by seeking customer compensation when no attempt to reduce fuel use is made (WTO, 2007). There are also issues about the viability of compensation schemes. For example, Boon et al (2007) highlight the lack of availability of land for forestry compensation schemes, and forestry schemes only absorb useful amounts of carbon once trees are fully grown; there is some uncertainty as to the longevity of some schemes (Broderick, 2009). An alternative strategy to afforestation is investment in alternative energy or energy-saving devices in developing countries. Here, there are also ethical criticisms, since offsetting is outsourced to developing countries where the cost is relatively low (Bachram, 2004).

Increasing the use of renewable energy

There is scope in the tourism sector to use renewable energy, such as solar, wind or water power, either by on-site generation or by choosing a green energy provider. Dalton et al (2007), in their analysis of tourism providers in Australia, suggest there is interest in such schemes, subject to practical considerations. There is, however, less scope to use renewable energy in the transport sector, which is currently very reliant on fossil fuels. There has been some attempt to utilize biofuels within aviation (Upham et al, 2009); however, there is still doubt about the contribution this might make (Becken, 2009). There are also questions about the large land-use requirements for biofuels and the impact this might have on food production or carbon release from poorly managed schemes that clear tropical forests (de Fraiture et al, 2008; Upham et al, 2009). Biofuels can have ecological footprints (an analysis that attempts to comprehensively account for a wide range of environmental impacts) as large as, or larger than, conventional fuels, due to the energy input in production and the energy needed for distribution (Holden, 2007).

Attempts to utilize biofuels in cars have been more successful, but many of the above issues on production still apply, especially if the use of biofuels is to become widespread rather than a niche market. Holden (2007) also notes that changing to biofuels might reduce impacts in one area, but introduces new impacts in another environmental category. Upham et al (2009) conclude that there is a potential role for biofuels in aviation, but development must be treated with caution. Overall, there is a better case for using biofuels in power stations where CO_2 can be captured and stored, and it might be best reserved for use in this area (Bows and Anderson, 2007).

Nuclear energy is also considered as a long-term alternative to fossil fuels and is used extensively in some countries. Electricity derived from nuclear energy can be used by train networks. For instance, from 14 November 2007, the day Eurostar began operating from St Pancras International, Eurostar claimed to be carbon neutral, much of their claim being based on the use of electric trains on the French network that relies extensively on nuclear energy as opposed to fossil fuels (see Chapter 5). The remaining carbon footprint has been neutralized, the company argues, by offsetting schemes and the reduced use of energy in all of its processes (Eurostar, 2009). There is a major ethical debate about nuclear energy. While it is carbon neutral, the issues about safe spent fuel disposal remain a matter of concern, as well as issues of terrorism and weaponry (Chapin et al, 2002). It is therefore often considered a poor alternative to renewable energy.

Renewable energy can make a very positive contribution to low-carbon tourism in both the accommodation and activity sectors; however, its contribution to the transport sector is less clear. In a life cycle assessment of alternative fuels for transport, a 'wells to wheels' approach shows only minor CO_2 reductions (Chapman, 2007).

Eco-labelling

Given the implications for destinations that are dependent on air travel, there have been various attempts to highlight the green credentials of destinations and companies through the eco-labelling of tourism products. There has been a rapid increase in eco-labelling schemes in recent years (WTO, 2002). Schemes cover a variety of different strategies, including recycling, energy and water use. In 2002, the WTO identified 104 sustainable tourism-related eco-labels, some being government-regulated and others industry-led. There has also been a move to label products, such as flights, on the basis of their carbon footprint. A number of comparison websites are now available so that consumers can compare the carbon footprints of various options such as transport (see, for example, www.ecopassenger.org).

With growing awareness of climate change within the tourism sector, there has been a move towards achieving 'carbon neutral destination status'

(Gössling, 2009). This is an interesting and innovative development that fits the overall strategic direction of slow travel destinations. Caribsave (2009) is an example of a project with the objective 'to support the transition of the Caribbean region's tourism sector to become the world's first "Carbon Neutral" tourism region'. Gössling (2009) provides a critical discussion of this strategy. Whilst recognizing it as a positive move, Gössling (2009) points to the limitation of a strategy that focuses only on the carbon neutrality within a destination context. He indicates that a comprehensive carbon neutrality scheme needs to include transport to and from the destination as well. To achieve carbon neutral status, destinations will probably include compensation for tourism emissions in another way, perhaps through offsetting schemes.

Given the poor regulation of various labelling schemes (Weaver, 2006) there is doubt about the worth of some schemes. Many schemes also require substantial cost and effort to gain accreditation, and are therefore not particularly useful in a sector dominated by small, medium-sized and micro-enterprises. Once accreditation has been gained, there are also issues related to maintaining accreditation. Many schemes have no ongoing monitoring, so business may lapse into poor practices once accreditation has been gained (Sasidharan et al, 2002). Therefore, while labelling schemes could make a significant contribution to low-carbon tourism, there are many administrative and practical issues still to be resolved.

Low-carbon tourism summary

The strategies summarized in this chapter to reduce the use of energy sources and CO_2 emissions are not likely to balance the climate change impacts of tourism. The above strategies are likely to be driven by international government policy, emissions trading (see Gössling and Upham, 2009) being the first to take effect. In this respect, the adaptation capacity of different actors in tourism is variable (Gössling and Hall, 2006). One fundamental point remains; there will still be a need to address the emissions accruing from transport to destinations.

It should not, however, be assumed that the tourism sector globally will be impacted negatively by mitigation policies. Domestic tourism and tourism that flourishes on near markets will not be heavily impacted in many parts of the world. Given that, in a global context, air travel accounted for just 17 per cent of tourism trips in 2005 (Bows et al, 2009b), most tourism remains feasible without air travel. As Bows et al (2009b, p17) indicate:

> One clear consequence of the introduction of climate change mitigation policies that are strong enough to avoid dangerous climate change, is that air transport will likely become substantially more expensive in the future and may even be less available.

Tourists have good adaptation capacity, as they can shift destination, time of travel and length of stay. The adaptation capacity of tour operators is also good, for similar reasons. However, the adaptation capacity of some destinations may be poor. Bows et al (2009b, p17) suggest where remote destinations are concerned, tour operators should target the high end of the market and 'divert large volumes to more accessible places, with reliable and fast access by more sustainable transport modes and over shorter distances'. Forward-thinking tour operators might anticipate future changes, such as an emissions cap implemented through an emissions trading scheme, by developing low-carbon products, such as slow travel, focused on short- and medium-distance destinations. In this respect, 'the tourism sector is taking a risk, by (apparently) aiming for air transport to become its dominant means of transport' (Bows et al, 2009b, p18). There is a requirement for the development of new tourism products. If tourism is to be sustainable, then it must embrace low-carbon tourism. However, the sustainability of tourism is widely questioned in the literature (Gössling, Peeters and Scott, 2008).

Critique of sustainable tourism

It is perhaps trite to repeat a message delivered so adequately elsewhere (Sharpley, 2009) that there are definitional problems with the concept of sustainable development, but these issues have been persistent and without resolution (Holden, 2007). Sustainable development is characterized by three concepts: safeguarding long-term ecological systems; satisfying basic needs; and promoting inter- and intra-generational equity (Holden, 2007). In translating these to travel more broadly, Holden introduces the idea of a minimum level of mobility. In this scenario, people in developed countries need to travel less as some countries have a high propensity to fly (see, for example, Høyer, 2000), while people in developing countries may need to travel more to achieve equity. Hence, Høyer and Aall (2005) argue that to achieve sustainable mobility, tourism must focus more on domestic visitors and shift radically to rail, buses, walking and cycling. There are also travel inequalities in developed countries. Dubois and Ceron (2006b), in their analysis of French tourism in 2050, suggest leisure travel should be more equitably shared among the French population.

Sustainable development has typically been presented as a tripartite model of environmental, social and economic issues. In tourism, this reflects the impact analysis framework discussed at the start of this chapter. However, Holden (2007) notes that economic growth should not be a goal, but rather it facilitates the three key concepts of sustainable development set out above; that is, it is a means rather than an aim. Economic issues have come to the fore, due to the use of the 'triple bottom line' perspective that was developed to help operationalize the sustainable development concept for business. For this reason the 'triple bottom line' perspective has been widely adopted in tourism. However, the economic emphasis is a somewhat misleading interpretation of sustainable development that mixes business goals with notions of societal welfare. In tourism, this has led to a tendency to emphasize the sustainability of tourism itself, rather than sustainable development achieved through tourism (Sharpley, 2009).

The idea of sustainable tourism has been derived from sustainable development, although most definitions of sustainable tourism reflect a business perspective and include some reference to economic development. A commonly cited definition is that of the World Tourism Organization (2009):

> *sustainable tourism should:*
>
> 1 **Make optimal use of environmental resources** *that constitute a key element in tourism development, maintaining essential ecological processes and helping to conserve natural heritage and biodiversity.*
>
> 2 **Respect the socio-cultural authenticity of host communities,** *conserve their built and living cultural heritage and traditional values, and contribute to inter-cultural understanding and tolerance.*
>
> 3 *Ensure viable, long-term economic operations,* **providing socio-economic benefits to all stakeholders** *that are fairly distributed, including stable employment and income-earning opportunities and social services to host communities, and contributing to poverty alleviation.*

This differs somewhat from the key concepts of sustainable development outlined above. Firstly, there is a strong focus on economic development. Sharpley (2009) points out that the UNWTO ST-EP scheme, with its focus on economic development and absence of environmental concerns, contrasts with sustainable tourism development. Is this an admission by the UNWTO that 'within the context of least developed countries, sustainable tourism development is unachievable' (Sharpley, 2009, p76)? Secondly, the inter- and intra-generational equity is absent. Pearce et al (1996) also observe that while community well-being is a priority consideration, the early emphasis on physical environment and biological aspects persists. This has also been a source of criticism of the concept of sustainable development.

Many authors express doubts about the viability of sustainable tourism. Wheeller (1993) was the first to signal concerns regarding the utility of the concept. His early work has been developed by numerous authors (see, for example, Becken and Simmons, 2002; Roberts and Hall, 2001; Sharpley, 1999; Sharpley, 2009). They argue that it is widely misused as a business concept, with an emphasis on long-term economic sustainability. Furthermore, Sharpley (1999, p93) argues that 'much of the environmental concern surrounding tourism is motivated not by the need to protect the environment *per se*, but to sustain it as the resource upon which tourism depends. In short, the ultimate purpose is to sustain tourism itself.'

Until recently, transport, beyond the immediate destination area, has rarely been considered in studies of sustainable tourism. It has certainly been poorly understood (Hall, cited in Becken, 2002). It is now more widely recognized that transport is a major problem that undermines claims to sustainable tourism (Roberts and Hall, 2001). Where air travel was once almost completely overlooked, recent studies have brought it centre stage and have questioned sustainable tourism set in a global impact context (Becken, 2002; Gössling, Hall and Lane, 2008). This is especially so in discussions of eco-tourism, which may be no more sustainable than mass tourism, particularly given many are car- and air-travel dependent (Wheeller, 1993).

It is imperative to integrate a climate change perspective into the debate, particularly where poverty alleviation is concerned. Given that a redistribution of wealth through tourism requires long-haul transport of western visitors to developing countries, this comes with a significant carbon burden. Nawijn et al (2008) argue that for tourism to raise the income of the poorest 2.7 billion in the world, who live on less than $730 per annum (based on 2002 figures), it would triple the total human contribution to GHG emissions. They therefore caution the promotion of tourism as a poverty alleviation measure if this is at the expense of climate change. They also point out that tourist numbers are likely to decrease to many of the LDCs should temperatures become consistently higher (e.g. in Africa, as temperatures will not be ideal for tourists) and therefore tourism provides a poor development choice in these contexts. According to Nawijn et al (2008) and Bigano et al (2006), a better tourism strategy for many developing countries would be to target local markets of either domestic or existing customers from adjacent countries. In this context slow travel provides a viable alternative for many LDCs, and removes the dependence on international air travel.

Given that climate change will affect developing countries, on the whole, more than developed countries (IPCC, 2007), this further conflicts with the tourism as development strategy that relies on long-haul travel from developed to developing countries. The carbon burden of air travel drives climate change; this in turn will increasingly put more people into poverty. While good quality pro-poor tourism, based on sound principles of sustainable development rather than sustaining tourism, might bring some out of poverty, further research is needed to analyse whether such a positive outcome is negated by the climate change impacts of travel.

Summary

Until relatively recently, tourism impact analysis concentrated on destination-based concerns and generally overlooked the travel to and from the destination area. This has focused on local impacts at the expense of wider global impacts such as climate change. However, climate change is already having a significant impact on many destinations and will have a greater impact in future years. It is therefore essential that a more holistic analysis of tourism impacts is undertaken with a focus on travel.

Travel has undoubtedly changed the way we view the world and has enriched many lives. Yet, on a global scale, international travel is the preserve of the few, and international air travel is enjoyed by only a small fraction (2–3 per cent) of the world's population each year (Gössling, Ceron, Dubois and

Hall, 2009; Simpson et al, 2008). From an equity perspective it has been suggested that travel should be apportioned more equally among the population (Dubois and Ceron, 2006b; Holden, 2007).

Many in the western world see travel as a right that would not be readily given up (Barr et al, 2010; Hares et al, 2010; Shaw and Thomas, 2006). However, if the rest of the world was to engage in comparable levels of international travel, then increased contributions to climate change would be an inevitable consequence. As it stands, the development paths of India and China are likely to result in much increased demand for international travel. This presents severe problems. It is difficult, in ethical terms, for developed nations to impose significant limitations on the GHG emissions of developing countries during climate change negotiations, while their own emissions remain high in the travel sector. There is therefore a need for a very different tourism development path, that is decoupled from high carbon-dependent forms of transport. As it stands, sustainable tourism development appears idealistic and, for some, fundamentally impractical (Sharpley, 2009). On the other hand, we contend that a redefined sustainable tourism model that encapsulates slow travel could provide an appropriate development path for tourism, as it offers an attractive alternative rather than tourism with constraints.

Note

1   There are eight United Nations' Millennium Development Goals to be achieved by 2015: eradicate extreme poverty and hunger; achieve universal primary education; promote gender equality and empower women; reduce child mortality; improve maternal health; combat HIV/aids, malaria and other diseases; ensure environmental sustainability; develop a global partnership for development.

3
Tourism, Transport and Environment: Theoretical Perspectives

There are a number of theoretical developments, important in the field of transport and tourism consumption, that require exploration and provide insights into slow travel. This chapter begins with an analysis of what drives tourist travel, and then explores the modal choice decision-making process. Studies of modal choice are largely rooted in cognitive models assuming a rational choice process. Much work, in the transport field, reviews the potential for widespread behavioural change in order to reduce environmental impacts of travel. Based on cognitive decision-making models, work in this area has identified an attitude–behaviour gap where awareness of environmental problems and positive attitudes towards environmental conservation fail to result in appropriate pro-environmental travel behaviour. This is apparent in all areas of travel, including tourism, where air travel is pervasive even among those who, ironically, have a strong conservation ethic (Barr et al, 2010). The failure to engage in appropriate behaviour is attributed to a number of barriers (Hares et al, 2010). A critique of this apparent attitude–behaviour gap is developed.

The chapter also reviews a number of more recent theoretical developments that offer new insight into travel. These draw on social psychology and the theories of social representations and discourse analysis that offer critiques of the more traditional cognitive psychology approaches. Sociological perspectives are also explored, beginning with social practices theory, which has re-emerged in recent years as a useful analysis framework to understand sustainable consumption (Spaargaren and van Vliet, 2000). A social practice perspective moves away from the realm of an individual consumer to examine the way people collectively engage in particular practices. This highlights the interaction between individual perspectives and societal structures that enable or constrain travel. More recently, the 'new mobilities paradigm' (Urry, 2000) has emerged from the discipline of sociology that explores the interrelationship of both real and virtual travel and social relations. Traditionally, society and transport have been analysed separately. However, their joint analysis sheds new light on both social structure and mobility.

Finally, the chapter explores experiential perspectives of consumption. This analysis focuses not on what motivates travel, but on how it is experienced. This links to work on the relationship between identity and consumption that considers how tourism travel choices are a reflection of identities which individuals wish to project.

The drivers of tourism travel and modal choice decision-making

One driver of leisure travel is the obligation to meet friends, family and others (Stradling and Anable, 2008). At one time, such obligations could be met without the need for travel, given that most social networks were largely proximate. However, with social networks increasingly spread over longer distances (Cwerner, 2009), the obligation to travel in order to maintain important social relationships has increased. This can be linked, in part, to the opportunity to travel (Stradling and Anable, 2008) that has grown through improved infrastructure and reduced travel costs. Given there are a variety of alternatives to travel (such as telephone, email and so on), and that tourism travel, in particular, is desirable but largely unnecessary, another key explanation for travel is 'compulsion to proximity' (Cass et al, 2004, p117), a desire for co-presence that may be an 'obligatory, appropriate or desirable' drive to be with other people or to be in a particular place.

As for leisure travel generally, slow travel may be motivated by obligations, opportunities or inclinations (Stradling and Anable, 2008), or a combination of these. However, slow travellers are choosing a particular way of travelling and have expectations about that travel. This is important to the conceptual basis of slow travel, as it may involve rejection of particular modes of transport. Alternatively, it may be that slow travel has been embraced for a variety of positive opportunities afforded by a given circumstance. The ingredients of slow travel are set out in Chapter 4.

There is a large body of literature on the factors influencing modal choice; it has been studied mainly as a rational choice process (Pooley and Turnbull, 2000). A wide variety of variables have been identified, such as urban form, distance travelled, available infrastructure, relative costs, habitual behaviour, socio-demographic variables, individual attitudes and information provision. Most studies have focused on daily commuting, with a dominance of quantitative methods (Pooley and Turnbull, 2000). However, tourism travel is increasingly gaining attention as its impacts become more significant at both a local and global level (Dickinson et al, 2009; Gössling, 2002).

Travel is usually modelled as a cost to be minimized (Anable and Gatersleben, 2005), both in terms of time and financial outlay. The analysis of travel for tourism is no exception, and research has typically employed rational decision-making frameworks (Dickinson and Robbins, 2008; Guiver, 2007). Studies have focused on economic factors or adopted a spatial or geographic perspective (Prideaux, 2000). In many cases, transport is simply seen as an accessibility tool linking destinations to source markets (Prideaux, 2000). Prideaux (2000, p56) notes:

> *If the ability of tourists to travel to preferred destinations is inhibited by inefficiencies in the transport system such as uncompetitive prices or lengthy journey times, there is a likelihood that they will seek alternative destinations.*

Prideaux argues the time cost may be more important than the monetary cost if the tourist has little time, although both these factors and substitutes are taken into account in travel cost models (Caulkins et al, 1986).

Based on such models, slow travel would be a rational decision in some contexts, where it might represent the most time- or cost-efficient form of travel, or a pragmatic choice due to, for example, a disability or a preference for moderate temperatures found closer to home (Maddison, 2001). However, in many tourism contexts, slow travel would not be seen as a rational decision, as it can take longer and cost more, especially in the current era of low-cost airlines. In terms of a rational decision-making perspective, slow travel could be interpreted as a form of ethical purchasing behaviour (Goodwin and Frances, 2003). This involves applying additional criteria to the typical consumer behaviour perspective; that is, people normally buy the best quality products they can afford, but choose the cheapest if the utility is as good as more expensive options (Harrison et al, 2006). Slow travellers could well be applying additional ethical criteria to take account of the effects their travel behaviour might have on environmental and social concerns, in line with a theory of commitment to society (Fennell, 2006). Slow travel might also be interpreted as an active choice of a particular travel experience, based on a chosen mode, or a preferred mobility style. Slow travellers do not ignore price and time, but are applying additional criteria during decision-making. Peters (2006) refers to this as the construction of a passage for travel (relationship between time and space) where a journey can be made. For some people, the 'slow' element is crucial, as they wish to take time on the journey; it is clearly not perceived as a travel cost but a travel benefit.

Modal choice is also, in many circumstances, linked to structures available in a given society (Randles and Mander, 2009b; Urry, 2007; Urry, 2008). In this respect, studies have examined the importance of habitual behaviour (Ouellette and Wood, 1998). While this may be less important in a tourism context, there is evidence that even irregular tourism travel decisions are to some extent habitual, and people become locked in to high-carbon structures of travel.

Given the importance of reducing various environmental impacts of travel, much work has focused on the potential for behavioural change, particularly from car travel to other forms of transport (see, for example, Anable, 2005; Böhler et al, 2006; Dickinson and Robbins, 2008; Gärling et al, 2000). More recent studies have also explored the behaviour of air travellers and the potential to reduce air travel, given its high contribution to GHG emissions (Hares et al, 2010). Much of the work in this area has drawn on theories that link attitudes and behaviour. For example, the decision to engage in slow travel could be related to an individual's environmental attitudes. The next section takes a critical look at attitude and behaviour research in a travel context.

A critical review of attitude and behaviour research in a travel context

There are a variety of theories of behavioural change that explore individual perspectives, interpersonal and community interactions. Some theories have been developed to examine pro-environmental behaviour in general, whilst others are specific to transport. As with the general studies of modal choice, much of the research analysing travel behaviour and environmental concern is rooted in spatial geography and psychology traditions, which focus on modelling rational behaviour (Dickinson et al, 2010b). Theories relating attitudes and behaviour have facilitated a number of insights into the understanding of mobility choices in relation to environmental values. However, these studies are largely based on mathematical modelling approaches that are overly reliant on quantitative measures and tend to assume that people have consistent values and preferences (Guiver, 2007).

A variety of social psychological studies have explored environmental concern and behaviour (see, for example, Barr et al, 2003; Dietz et al, 1998), many of which attempt to define theoretical links between attitudes and behaviour and to model attitude and behaviour change, although there is no single framework for analysis (Anable et al, 2006; Kollmuss and Agyeman, 2002). Work has been undertaken specific to modal choice (Anable, 2005), but here we will draw, as well, on the wider body of literature on pro-environmental behaviour, including aspects such as recycling and energy use. The link between attitudes and behaviour is far from simple, as evidence points to people holding positive attitudes towards the environment that do not translate into the associated positive behaviour (Barr, 2004; Blake, 1999; Cassidy, 1997; Kollmuss and Agyeman, 2002; Nickerson, 2003). This attitude–behaviour gap presents a considerable challenge with regard to the climate change policy agenda (Anable et al, 2006).

A review of research on pro-environmental behaviour in the context of tourism travel identified several key theories that seek to explain the attitude–behaviour conundrum: Schwartz's norm-activation theory of altruistic behaviour, Ajzen and Fishbein's theory of reasoned action and theory of planned behaviour, social dilemma theory, cognitive dissonance and psychological reactance (Dickinson and Dickinson, 2006).

The theory of reasoned action is based on 'the assumption that human beings are usually rational and make systematic use of the information available to them' (Ajzen and Fishbein, 1980, p5). The precursor to behaviour is 'intention to perform' a behaviour which is a result of the relative strengths of attitude towards the behaviour (personal judgement that performing the behaviour is either good or bad) and subjective norm (social pressure to perform the behaviour). In the theory of reasoned action the specificity of the attitude towards behaviour is very important. Where attitudes are not specific,

the model does not work. For example, it is not about people's general environmental attitudes, but people's specific attitudes towards low-carbon travel
on holiday. The theory of reasoned action highlights the gap between intention and action, the 'value–action gap', where situational control and
psychological variables can determine whether or not values are translated
into behaviour (Barr et al, 2003). This theory has been applied in tourism
studies and studies on attitudes to transport and travel behaviour (e.g.
Anable, 2005; Department for Transport, 2002). There is some suggestion
that the theory does not perform well in relation to pro-environmental
behaviour and that this is therefore different from other behaviours (Gärling
et al, 2003).

Ajzen's (1991) later theory of planned behaviour brings in perceived
behavioural control, and Anable (2005) extends the use of the theory of
planned behaviour by incorporating moral norms and psychological attachment to the car to improve its explanatory power in predicting modal choice.
She argues that it is the combination of 'instrumental, situational and psychological factors' which affects travel choice, and these operate in distinct ways
for distinct groups of people. In a reflection on the theory of planned behaviour, Hares et al (2010) question 'whether climate change is conceptually
linked to tourism at all'. Given their scepticism that climate change is in the
attitudinal set of tourism decisions for most people, they doubt whether much
behavioural change will be apparent in respect to flying.

In relation to perceived behavioural control, Hares et al (2010) found that
flying was considered the only viable option for some tourist destinations, and
that participants were unwilling to modify tourism behaviour by choosing an
alternative destination based on reasons related to reducing climate change.
The lack of personal responsibility displayed by participants in their study is
clearly a barrier to adjusting holiday travel behaviour in favour of lower-
carbon options. A classic example of the attitude–behaviour gap is the
environmentally conscious eco-tourist, keen to support wildlife conservation
efforts yet, through his/her desire to view key species, causing damage through
extended long-haul travel and localized impacts on pristine wildlife destinations (Curtin and Wilkes, 2005; Wall, 1997).

Hares et al (2010) identify three barriers to engaging in lower-carbon
tourism travel behaviour:

1 dismissal of alternative transport modes to air travel – can be seen as a
   structural or psychological barrier
2 reluctance to adapt holidays to mitigate climate change impacts
3 unwillingness to accept personal responsibility for impacts of holidays on
   climate change.

The authors suggest that there is an awareness–attitude gap, rather than an
attitude–behaviour gap. Their analysis of focus groups showed an awareness
of how holiday travel might impact on climate change, but this did not
translate into appropriate pro-environmental attitudes. Therefore, based on
Ajzen's theory of planned behaviour, the attitudes and behaviour were entirely

consistent. By way of explanation, they suggest that the awareness may not be yet strong enough to bring about consistent attitudes, or that the behaviour practice is so powerful that it is influencing attitudes as per cognitive dissonance theory (Festinger, 1957). The authors also refer to a related explanation provided by self-perception theory (Bem, 1967). Self-perception theory suggests people derive attitudes from observations of their own behaviour. Thus, while people are aware of the climate change issues associated with flying, air travel is so embedded in their lifestyle that they are unwilling to consider alternatives (Hares et al, 2010).

It has also been observed that while people seem more readily able to identify with ethical practice in their everyday life (e.g. recycling, walking more, using public transport for work, buying organic), for their one holiday a year they want freedom to do as they please (Barr et al, 2010). One explanation, derived from the social practices literature discussed below, is that the structures to facilitate everyday, green behaviour are better established than those related to tourism travel (Spaargaren, 2004). At the same time, people value the freedom to travel, and do not want to see this freedom disappear (Barr et al, 2010; Becken, 2007; Shaw and Thomas, 2006).

Exploratory research with slow travellers found that while they recognized travel has an impact on climate change, and some were hence adjusting their everyday behaviour, many continued to travel by air and were able to justify this position. Participants used denial strategies and discourses of obligation interlinked with structural travel barriers (predominantly distance). Slow travellers also employed a variety of credibility-enhancing moves, such as criticizing air and car travel, and were willing to discuss negatives of their chosen mode of travel. The latter strategy is a form of stake inoculation, a defence strategy where people acknowledge expected criticisms before they can be made by others (Dickinson et al, 2010b). Such work firmly draws attention to the attitude–behaviour gap and highlights the need for alternative research strategies.

Schwartz's norm-activation theory brings in both individual awareness of the consequences of actions and moral obligation (Dickinson and Dickinson, 2006). Hares et al (2010) found a lack of personal responsibility to adjust holiday travel behaviour in relation to climate change among their participants. Most people are able to make the link between flying and climate change (Barr et al, 2010; Dickinson et al, 2010a), yet it is clear that flying continues and is increasing (Bows et al, 2009b). One potential explanation is that global issues are too remote to activate an obligation to change behaviour, and the consequences for individuals and others are not immediately apparent. Social dilemma theory that focuses on how short-term personal gain tends to win over long-term social gain might provide an explanation here (Cassidy, 1997).

Social dilemma theory is based around the 'tragedy of the commons' reasoning, as explained by Hardin (1968). An individual may gain from acting in self-interest (defecting), and thus causing a small level of environmental damage. However, if all individuals act in self-interest, the individual gain is lost in the long term through considerable environmental damage experienced by all. Car use is a typical social dilemma (Tertoolen et al, 1998). In the short term, each individual benefits from car use rather than using public transport. But in the long term all individuals experience more pollution and environmental damage if all use cars rather than public transport (a cooperation strategy). Tertoolen et al (1998) argue that to cooperate, people must understand the dilemma, and secondly people must believe that others will not defect. There is an element of trustworthiness required. Several studies have found that responsibility for climate change is seen to lie with others, for example, with governments, or businesses and other countries (Lorenzoni et al, 2007; Stoll-Kleemann et al, 2001). Furthermore, the social dilemma can clearly be seen in studies of tourist behaviour where lack of action is justified by the inactivity by others (Anable et al, 2006; Hares et al, 2010; Randles and Mander, 2009a; Shaw and Thomas, 2006).

Given that there is much inconsistency between environmental attitudes and behaviour, many have looked to Festinger's explanation of cognitive dissonance. Cognitive dissonance is defined as inconsistency between attitudes, or between attitudes and behaviour. It creates an unpleasant tension and will motivate individuals to either change behaviour or change attitude (Eiser and van der Pligt, 1988; Tertoolen et al, 1998). Work in the transport field suggests that attitudes are reconfigured to fit behaviour (Golob and Hensher, 1998; Tertoolen et al, 1998). There is also evidence of psychological reactance, where people faced with overwhelming evidence that their behaviour should be changed react by striving to maintain the desired behaviour. Evidence for this has been found in campaigns and structural measures to restrain transport behaviour (Tertoolen et al, 1998).

The above theoretical approaches have all made a useful contribution to the understanding of behavioural decisions; however, they all focus on individual decision-making. They assume people make rational decisions on the basis of the information available, and have stable attitudes (Dickinson and Dickinson, 2006). However, attitudes are complex and interdependent (Cassidy, 1997). Attitudes can also contradict, be context-specific and short-lived (Billig, 1996; Clark et al, 1994; Macnaghten, 1993; Macnaghten, 1995; Macnaghten et al, 1992). The above theories say only a little about social processes and the way society shapes views and behaviour. People frequently contradict themselves, but may be unaware of these contradictions (Billig, 1996; Billig et al, 1988), and express dilemmas rather than fixed views (Dickinson and Dickinson, 2006). For instance, research with a small group of self-identified slow travellers highlighted dilemmas and various rhetorical strategies employed to justify air travel (Dickinson et al, 2010b). Earlier work by Macnaghten (1995) concludes that views on environmental and transport issues are influenced by societal and policy agendas that are often contradictory, paradoxical and highly controversial. This is also the case with air travel.

Thus, there is a body of work that contests or seeks to modify much of the attitude and behaviour literature. These studies all argue that people are likely to hold dilemmas rather than fixed attitudes in relation to transport, tourism and climate change, particularly as it becomes an increasingly contested issue.

Representations and discourses of travel

During the 1970s and 1980s, social psychologists began to question the cognitive approach which underpins much work on attitude and behaviour research. Subsequently, alternative approaches focused on the 'socially constituted nature of environmental problems' (Kurz et al, 2005, p604). Studies began to question the rationality of attitudes as the basis for behaviour.

One of the critiques of attitude behaviour theory stems from social representations theory developed by the French social psychologist Moscovici (1981). Social representations theory proposes that people draw on shared views of the world that are constructed through social interaction, media portrayals and actual experiences. These collective views, known as representations, are shared by group members, although people can be members of multiple groups and may thus be exposed, through social interaction, to different representations in different contexts. People can therefore have access to more than one representation of a phenomenon and draw on the representation most appropriate to a given context.

When faced with something new, such as climate change, people draw on these widely held views to develop their understanding. As Becken (2007, p352) puts it, 'what people know about climate change is strongly influenced by its representation and the discourse that surrounds it'. In this way, ideas about something that is relatively poorly understood can become suffused through society as a representation; however, such representations are predominantly socially constructed, rather than based on concrete experiences. In the case of climate change, the media has had a major role in developing understanding, but reporting can lack accuracy and may misrepresent uncertainty around climate change (Zehr, 2000). In this sense, representations have also been compared to myths (Moscovici, 1981) that circulate in society.

In a transport for tourism context, Dickinson et al (2009) have explored the representations of transport that are diffused in a UK rural tourism destination. They found residents and visitors had limited experience of alternatives to the car, and drew on a socially constructed reality to justify their car use even though alternatives were available. While people were collectively able to embrace public transport as a public good, and suggested they would use it more were improvements made, observation of actual behaviour showed little use of public transport even where reasonably frequent services were available. A representation was found that non-car alternatives must be improved before car use can be managed (i.e. restricted) in any way. This representation helps justify car use even where people recognize there are significant car-related impacts and alternatives available.

This social representations perspective is critical of cognitive attitude–behaviour theory, in that the latter pays little attention to the ways in which people contextualize their behaviour and draw on pervasive arguments to justify their behaviour relevant to the particular context. Thus, far from attitudes being inconsistent with behaviour, social representations theory would suggest that attitudes are far from consistent at all. People draw on diverse representations of the world and access those most relevant to explain their current situation. In this way people may appear to be inconsistent.

A similar critique is also provided from a discourse analysis perspective which is also, perhaps somewhat surprisingly, critical of social representations theory, particularly given that the two perspectives share some similar ideas. The discourse critique of social representations suggests the concept is too vague and pays little attention to power and ideology while representations are too prescriptive, requiring passive acceptance of ideas by social groups (Voelklein and Howarth, 2005). Discourse analysis, on the other hand, focuses on the power of spoken and written language as a functional tool that structures actions in relation to context (Potter and Wetherell, 1987). Discourse is important in the reproduction of ideas in everyday life (Van Dijk, 1997). Discourse can vary across conversational contexts and thus people exhibit apparently different perspectives according to the social context (Willig, 2003).

There has been limited application of discourse analysis in the tourism or transport field, although there is considerable potential to apply this perspective particularly in the contested area of climate change (Dickinson et al, 2010b). For example, Becken (2007) argues the discourse of air travel and climate change has been largely produced by the aviation industry. Gössling and Peeters (2007) identify four major discourses used by airlines that do not concur with the current scientific understanding. Such discourses can therefore be employed by individuals to justify air travel even where individuals may be well aware of the climate change impacts. As Frändberg (2005, p275) suggests, 'particular ways of understanding environmental problems and their solutions are "co-produced" and "co-refused"'. In this respect, discourses are more powerful than the actual sense conveyed by the words, as they can actually construct and perpetuate a social reality. For instance, Frändberg's (2005) discourse analysis of tourism and the environment in the mid-1990s identified four 'story lines' that focus on the benign nature of tourism and exclude the problems caused by transport. In a similar vein, Guiver (2007) shows how bus travel is frequently constructed on the basis of 'worst case scenarios', while car travel is not, highlighting the strategic use of a discourse strategy to generate an unequal status for bus travel.

Qualitative research has revealed that people can experience a level of discomfort when discussing holiday travel and climate change (Dickinson et al, 2010b), and Dickinson et al (2010a) show how people ably employ a variety of discursive strategies to maintain a positive self-presentation. One such discursive strategy is for people to question their power to act. This was achieved through the use of three discourses: politics preventing progress – making reference to limited government activity to address climate change (a finding also consistent with Becken, 2007); scientific scepticism – references to a conflicting basis for the science of climate change; and claiming limited awareness of climate change. A second discursive strategy was to express ambivalence towards appropriate climate change mitigation actions in a holiday context. This was predominantly expressed through exhibiting green credentials in other aspects of life that were felt to offset potential holiday impacts. Thus participants were seen to carefully manage their stake and interest (Willig, 2003), and were able to deny responsibility. Tourism discourses are often carefully phrased to highlight personal and societal benefits, while ignoring negative impacts (Becken, 2007; Gössling and Peeters, 2007), which 'legitimizes tourists' desire to participate in global mobility' (Becken, 2007, p364).

In research on slow travel, people also use rhetoric to criticize modes of transport, both to justify their choice of mode (by explaining a problem with air or car travel), but also, and perhaps more surprisingly, to criticize the slow travel mode used (Dickinson et al, 2010b). In the latter case, Dickinson et al (2010b) interpret this as an attempt to defend self-concept as people raise typical criticisms of their chosen form of transport before such issues can be raised by others. In discourse terms this is known as 'stake inoculation' (Horton-Salway, 2001). Discursive strategies can also be adapted to suit a particular context; for example, Dickinson et al (2010b) show how discourses of travel time and travel cost were varyingly used to justify taking more time in a slow travel context and flying in another. Discourse analysis also provides an avenue through which to explore travel identity that is discussed later in this chapter. While the debate about the value of a discourse or social representations perspective will no doubt continue in social psychology, both perspectives potentially provide useful insight into the tourism, transport and climate change debate.

Tourism practices

Within sociology, a social practices perspective has recently come to the fore as a means to examine consumption (see, for example, Warde, 2005). A social practices perspective departs from the predominantly individual perspective of consumption which assumes that individuals, given a range of travel choices and information on those choices, have the freedom to make appropriate choices. The preceding discussion on travel motivations, for example, has taken so far an individual perspective based on social psychological models that tend to privilege the role of attitudes and values in people's environmental behaviour decisions. However, Southerton et al (2004b) argue that wider forces stimulate consumption and that individuals have little or no alternative to consume if they are to participate in society. They suggest that contrary to the perspective that the consumer is sovereign, consumers are not autonomous individuals but:

> *most consumption is collectively and normatively derived, and conducted routinely in the context of socially differentiated conventions of practice. Strategies for changing patterns of consumption depend ultimately on the transformation of practices. (Southerton et al, 2004b, p33)*

Several recent studies highlight the inertia within the individualized actor/agent perspective (Becken, 2007; Bickerstaff et al, 2008; Randles and

Mander, 2009a), where individuals express positive environmental attitudes which fail to translate into appropriate behaviour. Southerton et al (2004a) question the focus on individuals in environmental policy and consumption approaches:

> *Consumption is embedded in the way that different social groups engage in practices and that practices are almost always shared enterprises that are performed in the (co-) presence of others and therefore subject to collective norms of contextualized engagement. (Southerton et al, 2004b, p34)*

A social practices approach therefore challenges the perspective that individuals have the agency to act independently from society as a whole and its institutionalized structures. Southerton et al (2004a) question the assumption that people will act differently if they understand the impacts of their actions. They argue that such a view fails 'to appreciate the socially situated and socially structured character of consumption' (p5) and that the focus on individual consumers ignores 'the intersection between design, demand and use' (p5). In this perspective, the view that consumers are key to change is challenged (Chappells et al, 2004). Individual responsibility is analysed in conjunction with social structure (Spaargaren, 2004). The approach links the actor-orientated perspective, described above, with the structures available in society. These structures are both physical, in terms of, for example, transport infrastructure, and determined by societal structures and social rules which reproduce particular social practices (Spaargaren and van Vliet, 2000). This is not to say that people have no individual agency to choose at all, but the ability to choose is delineated by the practices available (Warde, 2005).

Examples of physical structures within tourism include both transport infrastructure and the virtual dimensions, such as online booking facilities that shape the choices available. For example, van Goeverden (2009) found that the obligation to make seat reservations reduced the attractiveness of long-distance trains for some market segments. Societal structures can reinforce particular behaviour patterns, and various social rules and resources bind people to particular strategies. For example, there is an institutionalized structure to the working day which has determined time, space and transport infrastructure (Cass et al, 2004). From a tourism perspective, rules about available paid holiday and the convention of this time being taken in one-week blocks, linked in part to school holidays, structures the time available for holidays and tourism infrastructure provision. The increasing availability of fast transport (especially air travel), together with a restricted time frame, has structured holidays on the premise of a quick getaway to a relaxing destination where travel time is minimized and destination time maximized. Other industry structures may also reinforce behaviour. For instance, loyalty schemes such as Air Miles, accumulated by an individual through regular business travel, can be used in leisure time, and generate additional flying (Gössling and Nilsson, 2009). Furthermore, industry structures linked to ownership and control of the tourism sector may limit opportunities for equitable access to

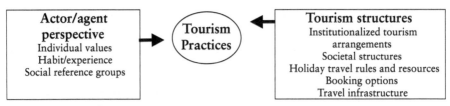

Source: Dickinson et al, 2010a, adapted from Spaargaren and van Vliet, 2000

Figure 3.1 *A tourism social practice perspective*

the benefits of tourism (Sharpley, 2009). Figure 3.1 contextualizes the social practices approach within a tourism context.

Randles and Mander (2009b, p249) use Reckwitz's definition of a practice:

> *A 'practice' [Praktik] is a routinized type of behaviour which consists of several elements, interconnected to one another; forms of bodily activities, forms of mental activities, 'things' and their use, a background knowledge in the form of under- standing, know-how, states of emotion and motivational knowledge. A practice – a way of cooking, of consuming, or working, of investigating, of taking care of oneself or others, etc. – forms so to speak a 'block' whose existence necessarily depends on the existence and specific interconnectedness of these elements, and which cannot be reduced to any of those single elements.*

Within transport and tourism research, studies have examined individual agency and the structures available, but tend to consider these as separate attributes and analyse their relative role in travel decisions. Research rarely focuses on the tourism practices that result from the interaction between the two (Verbeek and Mommaas, 2007). For example, Becken (2007) refers to internal factors (attitudes, values, habits and personal norms) and external fac- tors (regulations, structural incentives or barriers, social factors) that influence behaviour. While Anable and Gatersleben (2005) discuss instrumental (e.g. costs, flexibility, convenience) and affective (e.g. feelings evoked by travelling and sense of control) journey attributes. A social practices approach provides a more integrated perspective as it argues that consumption practices co- evolve through the interaction of people (actors/agents) and the structures available (Randles and Mander, 2009a), and Chappells et al (2004) suggest consumers and providers are involved in co-provision.

Spaargaren (2004) explains how a social practices model differs from atti- tude–behaviour models in several ways. First, a social practices model places actual behaviour practices at the centre, as opposed to individual attitude or norm. Second, it focuses on groups of actors, rather than on specific isolated behavioural items. Third, analyses take place in distinct domains of social life, and explore agency in the context of specific systems of provision. Proponents of a social practices approach suggest that it can provide insights into the ways lifestyles are shaped by socio-technical devices (Spaargaren and van Vliet, 2000).

Within a slow travel context, a social practices approach can help explain why, though people may have a desire to reduce their carbon footprint, they end up choosing high-carbon tourism practices due to the tourism structures available. More enabling structures are required. As Spaargaren (2004, p19) suggests: 'when there is a high level ... of green provisioning, people are more or less brought into a position in which the greening of their corresponding lifestyle segment becomes a feasible option.' For example, it was found that sustainable routines were easier to establish and maintain in a food context in comparison to tourism, as in Europe there are more green options in the food chain compared to the travel industry. However, slow travel could be seen as a route for innovation.

This perspective goes some way to explaining the attitude–behaviour gap. It is also argued that the focus should be on lifestyle, and a green lifestyle is different from an environmental-friendly attitude:

> *Even individuals who state the intention to follow strictly and frequently environmental criteria that form the foundational principles of their lifestyles will act against these intentions certain times and under particular circumstances in some segments of their lifestyle. (Spaargaren, 2004, p18)*

The findings of several recent studies on tourism behaviour and views of climate change are consistent with this view (Dickinson et al, 2010a; Randles and Mander, 2009a). While participants showed awareness of climate change issues, and took action in elements of their life, this failed to translate into appropriate tourism behaviour in respect to travel.

An explanation is provided by Shove (2003), who concludes that there is a need for a systemic review of practices (referred to as ratchets) which lock in behaviour. This has three characteristics:

> *1 Once a practice has shifted to a different ratchet 'notch', then a new configuration of practice – that is a new level of standardized norms comprising conventions of behaviours, knowledge and meaning – and a surrounding sociotechnical infrastructure, is visible. A high level of sociotechnical and institutional lock-in therefore exists.*
>
> *2 This means that there is a high level of historical path dependency.*
>
> *3 The distinctive architecture of institutionalized practice (convention) and their surrounding sociotechnical infrastructures are difficult to reverse. (Randles and Mander, 2009b, p265)*

However, with air travel there is potential to ratchet down as well as up, although currently on a very small scale. Randles and Mander (2009b) identify three elements of flying that have the potential to limit its growth:

- the comfort level of the flying experience
- in part due to the above, there may be upper limits to the number of flights some people are willing to take
- discourses of environmental concern.

However, the authors believe it will be difficult to reverse the trend to fly.

Several studies suggest that individuals feel some aspects of damaging environmental behaviour can be compensated by good behaviour elsewhere (Becken, 2007; Dickinson et al, 2010a; Spaargaren, 2004). However, there is some criticism of this type of compensatory behaviour that Stoll-Kleeman et al (2001) refer to as the 'metaphor of displaced commitment', and Dickinson et al (2010a) question the extent to which tourism behaviours such as flying can be compensated. At the heart of this argument is the question as to whether daily, but relatively low-impact, behaviour such as recycling can compensate for irregular, but high-impact, behaviour such as flying:

> Responsibility seems to differ for the individual as a 'tourist' or a general member of society. The latter seemed to be influenced by norms, while the responsibility as a tourist was mainly discussed in relation to the barriers that limit tourists' behaviour. (Becken, 2007, p356)

Understanding of relative environmental impacts is likely to be poorly developed among consumers and, as Chappells et al (2004, p144) suggest, 'consumer and provider perceptions of what constitutes "sustainable" consumption are highly interpretative, context-dependent and open to negotiation over time'. Consumers also make use of the facilities available. In a European context, recycling facilities are easily accessed by individuals and are even provided on an individual household basis; therefore, this mode of 'green provisioning' is readily available. While slow travel options are also available, in the context of tourism provision, these service options are not so readily accessed or embedded in contemporary tourism practice: 'Whether consumers are able to contribute to the development of more sustainable systems of provision depends on how they are socially situated and on the socio-technical systems to which they are attached' (Chappells et al, 2004, p144). It is therefore difficult to disentangle people from energy-intensive lifestyles (Bickerstaff et al, 2008; Lorenzoni and Pidgeon, 2006).

Social practices research also examines the role of routine behaviour, as many of life's activities are routine. There is some debate about routine behaviour in tourism, given that holidays are not a regular occurrence; however, it has been argued that people do have routines that apply to tourism, such as ways of booking holidays, or particular types of holidays such as car and camping (Verbeek and Mommaas, 2007). Such routine ways of thinking about holidays are hard to change, and this will be a factor when shifting people to slow travel infrastructure. The authors conclude that unsustainable behaviours need to be 'disembedded', and new behaviours embedded in a new tourism context.

In summary, a social practices perspective confronts the 'consumption as choice' perspective; they argue that it is inappropriate. Chappells et al (2004, p148) suggest there is a need to:

- rethink concepts of choice in the context of arguments about the embedded, routine and interconnected basis of social practices, and the ideological construction of 'the consumer' and 'service options';
- take into account the role of social and technical intermediaries and how they reshape contexts for environmental action at different scales of organization;
- appreciate the extent to which infrastructural legacies continue to reinforce or reproduce certain practices and patterns of demand;
- recognize that consumption patterns and practices are dependent on the organization of specific systems of service provision and how they interface with other regimes of everyday life.

To date there has been limited application of a social practices perspective within tourism (see, for example, Verbeek and Mommaas, 2007) or a travel context (see, for example, Randles and Mander, 2009a). The focus has been on household consumption practices, particularly energy and water use, and how this might be reduced. Dickinson et al (2010a) have explored how tourism structures enable and constrain different modes of travel. In general, the existing structures of provision support car use and flying, as modes of tourism access, to a far greater extent than slow travel modes. Physical structures have evolved in conjunction with tourism such that, for many destinations, the obvious choice is to fly. At the same time, rules and expectations have evolved in tourism which overlook slow travel in many contexts. There has also been policy support for aviation. For example, in the UK the Aviation White Paper has supported aviation expansion that arguably undermines environmental interests (Mander and Randles, 2009). It can therefore be difficult for people to both envisage slow travel alternatives and to engage in slow travel should they desire to do so (Dickinson et al, 2010a).

Physical structures in tourism

As passenger transport has improved, it has opened up new tourism opportunities. Indeed, the development of some tourism destinations can be directly linked to improved access (Prideaux, 2000). At the same time, increasingly competitive travel cost structures have enabled people to travel further and faster, through what has been described, perhaps inappropriately, as the democratization of air travel (Nilsson, 2009). Typically, tourism travel has been analysed using the travel cost method; that is, travel distance reduces as costs increase (Clawson and Knetsch, 1966; Prideaux, 2000; Steiner and Bristow, 2000). As low-cost air carriers reduced the cost of travelling long distances, additional demand has been generated (Civil Aviation Authority, 2006; Dennis, 2007). However, long-distance train services between countries have been disappearing, due, in part, to competition from air (van Goeverden, 2007). New air-based markets include weekend breaks to a variety of European destinations, with some indication that people are taking such trips simply because they have the disposable time and the financial outlay is minimal. The cycle of provision, increasing use and the (perceived) reduced costs have helped to embed air travel as a dominant system of provision.

The structures that consumers may engage with in order to take a holiday are also controlled by tour operators, particularly in relation to package holidays. For instance, it can be difficult to book a holiday from the UK to a Mediterranean resort without including air transport. This is due, in part, to the links between tour operators and airlines. Where slow travel options are available, these are generally packaged as a train or coach holiday, rather than as an alternative way to travel to a destination over several days rather than hours. On a small scale, some package alternatives are becoming available. For example, TUI Nordic has developed the Blue Train, a train charter holiday package from Malmö in Sweden to a number of resorts in other parts of Europe (TUI Travel PLC, 2009). Industry structures also link particular modes, such as air travel with car hire. On the other hand, it can be relatively difficult to find information on, or book, train, bus or coach travel in conjunction with a flight. Smith (2008) became exasperated with the structural barriers to booking continental rail trips, and thus set up an advisory service, known as the 'The Man in Seat 61', so that users can seek train travel as an alternative to flights.

Given the rise in independently organized travel via web-based intermediaries, the barriers provided by package options may be less relevant in the future. 'Travel and communication technologies are travel partners', it has been argued by Larsen et al (2006, p124); however, there are many structural problems associated with booking trains. In the UK it is not possible to book more than three months in advance, yet other holidays (including flights) can be booked over a year in advance. It can also be difficult to book train travel where more than one international border is crossed; this usually entails breaking the journey down, for ticketing purposes, into separate trips. Given the likelihood of crossing several borders in Europe, this is a particular problem.

Social rules and expectations in tourism

A variety of social rules and embedded norms also structure expectations and behaviour in tourism. Much of this is interlinked with wider social changes. For example, improving travel infrastructure and reducing travel costs have enabled dispersed social networks to be maintained (Larsen et al, 2006). Similarly, as the time and cost of travel have reduced, people are able to take more short holidays, as opposed to a single two-week holiday per year. This is not universal, and different national vacation structures have particular effects. For instance, the strong work ethic in Japanese society determines that most people are limited to one-week holidays. This has significant implications for travel. Becken (2005) shows how Japanese tourists tend to travel long distances around New Zealand during a week, to take in a variety of iconic destinations.

There is also evidence that many people only conceptualize holiday travel as car- or air-based (Verbeek and Mommaas, 2007). While such people are aware of alternatives, it is not the norm to consider them for holiday travel (Dickinson and Robbins, 2008; Lassen, 2009). Over time, such ideas become pervasive and guide people's actions (Dickinson and Dickinson, 2006), regardless of whether they have experience of slow travel alternatives or their feasibility for a given trip.

Given that a growing proportion of tourism is based on obligations to visit people in particular places (Larsen et al, 2006), this may perpetuate air travel. The World Tourism Organization (2008) categorize 26 per cent of international arrivals as involving visiting friends and relatives, health, religion and other; rather a broad categorization, but one that has showed sustained growth since the 1980s. There are also issues related to the increasingly diverse range of equipment carried by tourists. As part of a general commoditization of leisure time, people increasingly own wetsuits, kayaks, surfboards and so forth, which generally require a car to transport (Dickinson and Dickinson, 2006).

Randles and Manders (2009a) highlight the 'stickiness of practice', as consumers are not free to choose (Spaargaren and van Vliet, 2000). Socially embedded rules of tourism and the travel structures available currently limit slow travel. Dickinson et al (2010a) therefore recommend policy actions to enable structure change and focus industry attention on slow travel provision. To this end, Verbeek and Mommaas (2007) recommend that the holiday practice should become the central unit of analysis.

The sociology of mobility

The notion of mobility as a means of ordering social relations has emerged in recent years (Urry, 2000; 2002; 2007). This perspective, which integrates an analysis of travel patterns with that of social networks, raises questions about the potential to decrease mobility and the development of slow travel that will be explored further. Much social science ignores the movement of people, tending to focus on other economic, social or political factors that shape society. At the same time, the study of transport has largely ignored the social dimensions of travel, and there is 'little understanding of how travel patterns are socially embedded and depend upon complex networks of family life, work and friendship' (Larsen et al, 2006, p3). For instance, in his analysis, Urry (2000, p57) describes the car as:

> the predominant form of 'quasi-private' mobility *which subordinates other 'public' mobilities of walking, cycling, travelling by rail and so on, and reorganises how people negotiate the opportunities for, and constraints upon, work, family life, leisure and pleasure.*

Of significance to the idea of slow travel, many social interactions are dependent on travel, and thus leisure travel is important in shaping social networks and is often a fundamental force in people's lives (Frändberg, 2008). A mobilities perspective therefore opens up a new analytical framework for travel research, which moves transport for tourism beyond a spatial problem that facilitates individualized passage from one place to another. Urry and co-researchers have identified five interdependent mobilities:

1 *Physical travel* of people for work, leisure, family life, pleasure, migration, and escape;
2 *Physical movement* of objects delivered to producers, consumers and retailers;
3 *Imaginative travel* elsewhere through images and memories seen on texts, TV, computer screens and film;
4 *Virtual travel* on the internet;
5 *Communicative travel* through person-to-person messages via letters, postcards, birthday and Christmas cards, telegrams, telephones, faxes, emails, instant messages, videoconferences and 'skyping'. (Larsen et al, 2006, p4)

While physical travel is of most interest here, Urry (2007) argues that this cannot be isolated from the other four mobilities, and these are intrinsically linked in a tourism context. Indeed, Sharpley (2009, p79) asks, 'is it possible or logical to separate tourism from other mobilities?' It is the focus on the multiple ways in which social connections are mediated across distance that is crucial to the study of mobilities (Urry, 2007). For instance, weak ties, maintained by internet communication, may lead to physical travel across the globe. Larsen et al (2006) also suggest it is not helpful to separate business and leisure into exclusive travel categories, as both categories are often mutually linked by social networks.

Movement is socially organized (Urry, 2007). Mobilities research explores how people connect with significant others across the globe in various different forms of travel (Cass et al, 2004). Based on Harvey's (1989; cited by Larsen et al, 2006) concept of 'time space compression', people from western countries are now able to travel quickly, easily and cheaply, resulting in the spread of social networks, and increases in volume and distance of travel, known as time-space distanciation. With families now spread across the globe, some argue, leisure time is increasingly structured to facilitate shorter visits (Cass et al, 2004), to spatially dispersed locations (Larsen et al, 2006), largely dependent on air travel (Urry, 2009). The long weekend has become an important unit of leisure time that can provide sustained, slow-moving quality time with significant others (Larsen et al, 2006). This taking of time with significant others away from home could be important for slow travel if it is reconfigured into the journey context.

In these emergent globalized networks of connectivity, tourism is important because 'travel, visits and hospitality have moved centre-stage to many people's lives' (Larsen et al, 2006, p40). Mobilities research particularly highlights the importance of visiting friends and relatives (VFR), which is a growing trend (National Statistics, 2005; World Tourism Organization, 2008) of what is increasingly viewed as necessary travel, compared to the view of leisure travel as non-essential. In this sense, tourist travel is less 'an escape from home but also a *search* for home(s)' (Larsen et al, 2006, p44) due to the scattering of family and friends. Tourism is also an important contextual setting for social research. As Franklin and Crang (2001, p12) suggest:

> *The excitement of mobilities in these highly mobile times, struc-*
> *tured as they are by the language and practice of tourism, is that*
> *they generate new social relations, new ways of living, new ties*
> *to space, new places, new forms of consumption and leisure and*
> *new aesthetic sensibilities.*

However, in reality there are sections of western societies that have not embraced mobilities, and equally in developing countries mobilities are not as pervasive as discussed in the growing literature on the subject. It is by no means a ubiquitous phenomenon.

Tourism is also an inherently social experience, as it usually involves travel with friends or relatives (Arnould and Price, 1993), and social relations shape consumer experience (Carù and Cova, 2003). Indeed, slow travel provides extended journey times providing opportunities to socialize and bond with family or friends. In the 'search for the authenticity of, and between, themselves ... families are most at home when away from home. Tourists consume places and thereby perform a special kind of togetherness' (Larsen et al, 2006, p45). In this way 'tourism seems to be increasingly about co-present meetings and less about just travelling to see the exotic' (Larsen et al, 2006, p46). Slow travel is part of this re-envisioning of tourism which is more sociable, less exotic and enables engagement with place and with people. Slow travellers seek interactions with friends and relatives and with people encountered en-route (Dickinson et al, 2010b).

Larsen et al (2006) analysed the role played by different modes of transport in people's mobility. The car can become part of people's network capital, 'the capacity to engender and sustain social relations with those people who are not necessarily proximate' (Urry, 2007, p197), as it gives spatial and time flexibility and affords new leisure opportunities and forms of social life (Urry, 2005). As a part of network capital, the freedom to travel has become a much coveted value:

> *... the freedom to move, perpetually a scarce and unequally dis-*
> *tributed commodity, fast becoming the main stratifying factor of*
> *our late-modern or post modern time. (Bauman, 1998; cited by*
> *Letherby and Reynolds, 2009, p205)*

As such, policies to reduce travel will not be viewed positively due to the implications for people's social life, social networks and social capital:

The freedom of the car subjects all of civil society to its power. The shortage of time resulting from the extensive distances that increasingly 'have' to be travelled means that the car remains the only viable means of highly flexibilised mobility. (Urry, 2000, p192)

People have been coerced into new lives of flexibility that can only be maintained by the car, to which society is now 'locked in' (Urry, 2005). In this respect, the ability to access mobility adds to social inequities, as well as contributing to global environmental change (Letherby and Reynolds, 2009): 'Not to drive and not to have a car is to fail to participate fully in western societies' (Urry, 2000, p191). However, trains also offer social benefits, as on the train people 'can sleep, read, talk, eat, text, write, drink or relax after a good dinner or pub visit' (Larsen et al, 2006, p108).

Some forms of transport, such as walking or cycling, are also only possible for those with 'time to spare'. Cass et al (2004, p120) argue that '... in opting for these modes rather than faster alternatives, there is a conscious trade-off between time and the quality of the experience'. Some people have more 'time sovereignty' (Breedveld, 1998; cited in Cass et al, 2004) than others; that is, they have more time flexibility. Therefore, 'differences in the spatial and temporal flexibilities and path-dependencies of individuals, households and transport systems themselves, combined with changing compulsions to proximity, all conspire to structure different social groups' experience of transport infrastructure' (Cass et al, 2004, p123). This is potentially a significant issue for slow travel. In particular, lack of time sovereignty causes problems when using public transport if services are not available at times needed. However, tourists are likely to have a higher degree of flexibility compared to those on utility trips and the time sovereignty to walk, cycle, wait and gaze.

The mobilities paradigm therefore provides a new framework with which to analyse society and movement. The idea of slow travel, with its fundamental focus on people, place, time and distance, is intrinsic to the mobilities analysis. There is clearly much scope for further research to examine different ways of connecting people and organizing social structures which brings together slow travel and the new mobilities paradigm, a subject to which we return in Chapter 10.

The travel experience

In recent years much research in tourism and leisure has moved on from what motivates people to take part in various activities, to a focus on the actual tourism experience. The interest in the tourist experience appears to have been stimulated by the seminal paper by Arnould and Price (1993) on the hedonic experience of white water rafting and, more recently, by the marketing perspective presented by Pine and Gilmore (1999). However, Clawson and Knetsch's (1996) much earlier work, on the outdoor recreation experience, draws attention to different stages of the tourist experience and has been applied extensively in tourism and wider consumer experience literature. Five phases are identified:

- Anticipation of the experience, which includes planning for a trip. Anticipation may be more pleasurable than the actual trip experience.
- Travel to the actual site of the experience, which may be very brief or extended. Clawson and Knetsch recognize that some people may enjoy the travel and suggest that this was more common in the past when people travelled for sheer enjoyment.
- On-site experiences. This is where most experiences research has focused in the tourism literature.
- Travel back. This is 'unlikely to be a duplicate of the travel to the site' (p34). Little is known about the difference between the outward and return trips which could be significant for slow travel.
- Recollection. This may be more positive than the actual experience. Recollection may be the starting point for planning or anticipation of another experience.

There has also been a growing interest in the performance of tourism (Bærenholdt et al, 2004). As Sheller and Urry (2004, p1) explain, places are 'performed', and 'many different mobilities inform tourism, shape the places where tourism is performed, and drive the making and unmaking of tourist destinations'.

While experiential perspectives have emerged in a variety of tourism and leisure contexts, there is little work that examines travel as an experience both during the journey to, or from, the destination and as a part of the destination experience (Lumsdon, 2006; Su and Wall, 2009). In most research, travel is seen as a derived demand (Rhoden and Lumsdon, 2006); however, it is more than that, it is integral to the tourist experience, and, in some instances, it might be the main purpose (Lumsdon, 2006). Several authors allude to a travel experience; for example, Cloke and Perkins (1998) explore the performative desire of adventure tourists to be more than spectators and discuss their participation in the landscape rather than passively travelling through. Such a perspective fits well with slow travellers who are physically engaged with travel, such as cyclists and walkers. One of the few studies to examine the journey to and from the destination is Su and Wall's (2009) analysis of train travellers from China to Tibet. The authors conclude that the train journey was considered an important part of the overall holiday, and, for some people, equally as important as the destination experience.

Pine and Gilmore (1999) report, in their business-focused model of consumer experience, a matrix of experience realms based on two axes, one of which focuses on the environmental relationship. This extends from *absorption*, where the experience simply occupies a person's attention, to *immersion*, where participants become 'physically a part of the experience itself' (p31). Their second axis focuses on level of participation from *passive,* where customers do not directly affect or influence the performance, to *active,* where customers personally affect the performance. Their work uses a theatre metaphor and appears to examine how improved customer experiences can be achieved through various possibilities of customer involvement. Carù and Cova (2003) provide a critique of the consumption experience concept and suggest Pine and Gilmore's perspective strives for every experience to be extraordinary (i.e. it is unrealistic). Drawing on sociology and psychology approaches, they suggest experience implies learning and development. Such a perspective has more relevance to slow travel, where experiences are not staged and where participants may have to invest time organizing trips and are likely to learn from their closer engagement with places. In this respect Carù and Cova note the need for pauses, and slow travel may be a reaction to the perceived need to fill free time with seemingly astonishing experiences. Slow travel might instead provide contemplative time, which Carù and Cova suggest is disappearing in recreation and tourism. Walking, for instance, gives back time to think (Carù and Cova, 2003).

In one of the few studies to explore the tourist transport experience, Rhoden and Lumsdon (2006) have explored the nature of the tourist involvement in the transport experience and have developed a typology of transport-tourist experience (Table 3.1). They make a distinction between 'transport as tourism', where transport is a desired component of the tourist experience, and 'transport for tourism', where transport takes on a more functional role. However, both 'transport as tourism' and 'transport for tourism' are relevant to slow travel. While the former is clearly particularly relevant to the slow travel experience, the latter, 'transport for tourism', also has a role to play and is an area that has been overlooked. In Rhoden and Lumsdon's typology, two groups are relevant: the passive transport tourist; and the active transport tourist. Rhoden and Lumsdon (2006, p9) explain the distinction as follows:

> *Active transport is defined as transport that requires the active involvement of the tourist (e.g., powering a bicycle), whereas passive transport is defined as transport situations in which the tourist has a less involved role (e.g., cruises).*

Experience will be different depending on mode and context of use and will therefore be judged differently by users (Lumsdon, 2006). The socio-psychological benefits of engagement with travel and modes of transport are not well researched. In general, utility networks are adapted to suit tourism and are therefore not designed for the experience sought (Lumsdon, 2006).

Dickinson (2008) has explored the slow travel experience and found there was much positive re-evaluation of the experience during the recollection period, in common with Arnould and Price's (1993) evaluation of white water rafting. She also found evidence of co-creation through the interaction of slow travellers, particularly cyclists, with place.

Salomon and Mokhtarian (1998) discuss the potential for 'excess travel', where, rather than minimizing travel, people choose to travel further than they need to in their everyday lives. They question the axiom that travellers (for both utility and leisure purposes) seek to save travel time. For instance, as

Table 3.1 *Characteristics of involvement of each transport-tourist type*

Transport commodity	Characteristics of tourism involvement	Transport-tourist type
Transport as tourism		
• Urban walking • Hiking/trekking • Mountain biking • Cycling • Kayaking • Undirected car travel • Sailing	• Transport as a desired component of the tourist experience • Transport operated by the tourist • Tourist plans the route • Independent • Freedom of choice at a maximum • Skill competency required • Independent interpretation of environments and cultures	Active transport tourist
• Cruises (sea/river/canal) • Heritage railways • Open top buses • Ballooning • Car trails/tours • Coach tours • City walking tours	• Transport as a desired component of the tourist experience • Transport operated, and route planned, by provider • Transport operated by tourist, but following provider-planned routes/tours • Organized • Environments and cultures interpreted by tour leader	Passive transport tourist
Transport for tourism		
• Flights • Inter-city rail • Scheduled coach • Ferry • Taxi	• Transport to access destinations • Limited freedom of choice • Travel is enjoyed	Positive transport tourist
• Bus • Intra-urban rail • Metro • Car	• Transport to access destinations • Limited freedom of choice • Travel is endured reluctantly	Reluctant transport tourist

Source: Rhoden and Lumsdon, 2006

travel has become faster, people have not saved the time to do other things but have filled this time with more travel. Salomon and Mokhtarian (1998, pp136–7) identify some traits in the population that may lead to excess travel; the following are of interest to slow travel:

- *adventure-seeking*: the quest for novel, exciting, or unusual experiences will in some cases involve travel as part or all of the experience itself, not just as a means to the end ('getting there is half the fun');
- *independence*: the ability to get around on one's own is one common manifestation of this trait;
- *control*: this trait is likely to partially explain travel by car when reasonable transit service is available;

- *status*: travelling a lot, travelling to interesting destinations, and travelling 'in style' (e.g. in a luxury car) can be symbols of a desired socio-economic class or lifestyle;
- *scenery and other amenities*: may lead someone, for example, to take a longer route than necessary to a destination.

In contrast to excess travel and though not focused on travel per se, Csikszentmihalyi, well-known for his work on happiness, has considered the amount of energy consumed during leisure time, and notes that while much energy is consumed, there is no relationship with happiness. He therefore concludes that a 'substantial amount of this energy could be saved without impairing the quality of life, and perhaps actually improving it' (Csikszentmihalyi, 2000, p271). From this it follows that consumption practices could be re-envisioned to involve greater individual engagement, but associated with lower energy and environmental demands. Slow travel is such a re-envisioning.

Travel identities

Identity has become increasingly central to debates on transport choices (Becken, 2007; Dickinson et al, 2010b; Gössling and Nilsson, 2009; Skinner and Rosen, 2007). There is evidence that some people embrace, or reject, the identity associated with particular modes of transport. As with other forms of consumption, people feel judged on the basis of their decision (Warde, 2005). Giddens (1990, pp123–4) describes 'the construction of the self as a *reflexive project*, an elemental part of the reflexivity of modernity; an individual must find her or his identity amid the strategies and opportunities provided by abstract systems'. For instance, for teenagers, public transport is shown to be associated with a low-status identity, while the car is associated with much higher status. Urry (2000, p57) describes the car as 'the major item of *individualized* consumption which provides status to its owner/user through the sign-values with which it is associated (speed, home, safety, sexual desire, career success, freedom, family, masculinity)'. Cyclists are also perceived to have a distinct identity; however, it might be suggested this is far more complex and ambiguous (Skinner and Rosen, 2007). It is thus clear that identity might be projected through travel choices.

Through holiday travel, people are not just choosing a mode of transport; they are also negotiating their personal identity as a tourist. People have their own 'narrative of self-identity' that is their storyline, although this might vary in different spheres of life such as at home or on holiday (Verbeek and Mommaas, 2007, p67). The relationship between tourism mobility and personal identity processes is as yet insufficiently studied. Work in tourism has tended to focus on the potential for personal growth and development of the self (Arnould and Price, 1993). Travel shapes perceptions of self through the experience of other people, cultures or environments, leading to modified traveller identities. At the same time, travellers choose particular forms of travel to affirm who they are (Duffy, 2004; Lassen, 2009). For instance, Ory and Mokhtarian (2005) suggest the style of travel may matter to some people. And, as Britton (1991, p454) suggests:

> *the tourist industry sells 'experiences' ... the value of the travel mode ... lies in the quality and quantity of the experience they promise and symbolise ... the purchase of a life-style; a statement of taste ... a signifier of status.*

Lassen's (2009) study of business travellers shows how international travel enabled participants with families to construct an identity as both cosmopolitan and family person, both 'wings and roots'.

Given the climate change implications of tourism travel, it is of considerable importance to understand how traveller identities emerge, how they shape, and are shaped by, travel patterns and values in society. It is suggested that a new identity is required for people to take meaningful climate change mitigation action (Stoll-Kleemann et al, 2001). As Becken (2007, p364) highlights:

> *tourists' engagement in international air travel goes well beyond individual dimensions of functionality (e.g. relaxation), attitudes and values, but that participation in global travel has a high symbolic meaning and therefore is a fundamental part of an individual's positioning in society. Given the great (perceived) benefit from air travel, it seems unlikely that tourists would voluntarily support mitigation policies that would restrict their ability to travel.*

While slow travel obviously affords opportunities to 'find yourself' through self-development, the interest here lies in how identity is now formed in relation to consumption, and how identity may be a driver to more, or less, consumption:

> *self-identity ... is not something that is just given ... but something that has to be routinely created and sustained in the reflexive activities of the individual ... It is the self as reflexively understood by the person in terms of her or his biography. (Giddens; cited by Southerton et al, 2004b, p35)*

In essence, it is about how we want to be perceived by others:

> *Consumption becomes not simply a choice about goods and services but a choice about a style of life, about who we are and how we wish to be perceived by others in particular social settings. (Southerton et al, 2004b, p36)*

While economic, cultural and social resources impact on what and how people consume, Southerton et al (2004b) also identify normative constraints that relate to an individual's ability to 'fit in' and the importance of an individual's competence in a particular context. In choosing holiday travel, individuals are aware of these normative constraints, and may find it difficult to make choices that do not fit the norm. For example, Dickinson (2008) found slow travellers drew on traditional holiday discourses that describe a variety of personal benefits, known as 'push' factors (see, for example, Crompton, 1979; Dann, 1977; Pizam et al, 1979), and include aspects such as flexibility, freedom, independence, away from constraints of daily life, relaxation, achievement, a story to tell and engagement with people and place. This use of the dominant tourism narrative may be an attempt to normalize the chosen holiday practice. Dickinson et al (2010b) also observed how individuals were able to give a positive spin to quite negative travel experiences, be that as a slow traveller or an air traveller. Thus, people are able to positively reposition their experiences during recollection.

One strand of thinking on identity originates from the perspective of social identity theory (Hogg and Abrams, 1988). However, social identity theory, with its emphasis on 'in' and 'out' groups, may not be particularly applicable to a tourism context. Firstly, such groups do not have time to develop during relatively short duration trips. Secondly, Dickinson et al (2010b) show that individuals move in and out of various tourism travel contexts, embracing air travel in one context and slow travel in another; thus again such groups do not arise. However, there are aspects of social identity theory, such as the positive positioning of self as described by the 'ideological square' that are useful. The ideological square (Oktar, 2001) consists of the following four moves:

1   express/emphasize information that is positive about us
2   express/emphasize information that is negative about them
3   suppress/de-emphasize information that is positive about them
4   suppress/de-emphasize information that is negative about us.

There is, though, an important exception to this positive presentation of experiences, the presentation of problems with public transport, a core element of slow travel. Previous research on transport modes in a UK destination and work on slow travel shows how firmly embedded the idea of problems with public transport is in this context. For example, there is a discourse about late buses and trains, and general discomfort on public transport. There is a norm to engage in a discussion of these problems regardless of direct experience, given that many people rarely use public transport (Dickinson and Dickinson, 2006; Dickinson et al, 2010b; Guiver, 2007).

Several authors in the tourism field have begun to explore how identities are created discursively (Dickinson et al, 2010b; Gössling and Nilsson, 2009). For instance, frequent flyer programmes, which aim to boost airline loyalty, work by influencing individuals' sense of social status and self-esteem by effectively creating a distinction between different groups of air travellers (those entitled to the frequent flyer perks and those not). This perpetuates a view that regular, long-distance travel is associated with social status (Gössling and

Nilsson, 2009). While there are genuine benefits for frequent flyers, such pro-grammes work by articulating positive discourses of flying where, in reality, there is much discomfort involved.

Work with slow travellers suggests people are able to discursively juggle arguments to justify holiday travel choices, even when there are personal con-tradictions such as choosing slow travel for environmental reasons yet flying on the next holiday (Dickinson et al, 2010b). Dickinson et al (2010b) suggest slow travellers use different discursive threads about travel to reinforce a pos-itive self-identity that is context-dependent. In the context of air travel, slow travel can be presented as negative, while in a slow travel context the reverse is true. This contextual rhetoric suggests it will be difficult for policy-makers to articulate clear arguments for reducing air travel. Duffy (2004, p34) dis-cusses how ecotourism shows how 'being thought of as an environmentally aware traveller is an important signifier of social position and a commitment to environmental beliefs'. This is contextualized in the ecotourism environ-ments visited and not in terms of travel to these places.

Work on travel identity in a tourism context is at an early stage. Whether it will make a substantial contribution to the tourism and climate change debate remains to be seen. Many authors currently make reference to identity without fully unpicking what this means or identifying a theoretical frame-work to underpin their comment. Theoretical research needs to be conducted to better understand the role of identity; however, the signs are that this could be a very fruitful line of inquiry to understand travel.

Summary

This overview has attempted to set out key theoretical developments of impor-tance to tourism travel consumption in relation to the way in which tourism is likely to change in future decades. Several theoretical perspectives have shed light and new understanding on, for example, modal choice. The theories applied to pro-environmental behaviour research fall into this category. There are obviously other theories that might be apposite, and we make no claim for this being an extensive review. However, in our opinion, the theoretical per-spectives outlined above provide a starting point for anyone interested in understanding contemporary tourism travel practices in relation to slow travel. The theoretical frameworks have been discussed in a heuristic manner to assist the would be researcher in progressing our knowledge of contemporary tourism.

Other theoretical perspectives, such as the mobilities paradigm, present a new way of thinking about tourism travel. To some extent, mobilities has pro-pelled tourism to the fore of current thinking. Mobilities, as a concept, offers a major opportunity for tourism researchers to engage with issues of move-ment, temporary or permanent, and society. Nevertheless, the world of the mobile is far from ubiquitous, and the interfaces between internet technology and actual travel need far greater attention than afforded by current research. So, as with all theoretical approaches, there is a need for further discussion to refine and move forward to an improved understanding of communication in different cultures and contexts.

The following chapter sets out the ingredients of slow travel. It embraces ideas from many of the theoretical perspectives outlined in this chapter and aims to establish a framework for further analysis. There is considerable scope for further research on tourism, transport and the environment to better understand how the tourism sector can respond to the challenges that lie ahead. Above all, this chapter and the following chapter aim to stimulate debate and focus attention on a critical issue of the future research and reporting of tourism.

4
Slow Travel – the Ingredients

The challenge for tourism in the 21st century is seemingly how to reshape itself so that people can continue to enjoy their leisure time, while, at the same time, the supply sector manages to avoid the worst scenarios of climatic change. One of the contributions of this book is to define slow travel. This will provide a solid foundation on which to build knowledge and to develop theory so as to take low-carbon tourism forward in the coming decades. The ideal scenario would be to develop markets that have low impact and to reduce high-impact tourism. Slow travel has a central role in this process of change.

In Chapter 1 the concept of slow travel was summarized so that the reader could achieve an initial grounding in the topic. It was also noted how we might move to a new tourism system, based on three core principles: reduction of tourism trips, development of low-carbon tourism and enrichment of the tourist experience. This presents something of a challenge for the tourism sector, as previous performance indicates a lack of commitment and a 'business as usual' mentality, regardless of the fine words contained in reams of policy documentation. There are some exceptions, but the hundreds of thousands of small- to medium-sized tourism businesses are decidedly slow to change. It is likely that tourism suppliers will be forced to alter their patterns of trading in light of a diminishing resource base and shifting market conditions, but will this be too late?

There are signs that the market is already changing, perhaps slowly, but nevertheless change is occurring. The pioneers in this diffusion process are gaining some momentum in shaping slow travel. They are publicized in serious newspapers and on numerous web pages (see Table 4.1). These websites illustrate the nature of the discussion. The authors invariably focus on one of three core issues:

• the dilemma of avoiding flights and car use

- the need to address high-carbon emissions (especially how to reduce environmental impact at an individual level)
- the richness of a travel experience that focuses on locality at a destination and, for some, the importance of the journey.

Table 4.1 *Slow travel websites*

Name of organization	*Website address*	*Explanation of slow travel*
Slow Travel	www.slowtrav.com	Focused on holiday accommodation rentals. Interprets slow travel as spending time in the immediate vicinity of rental accommodation: 'Slow down, immerse yourself in the local culture and avoid the fast pace of rushing from one guidebook "must-see" to the next.'
Slow Movement	www.slowmovement.com	Making connections with the place visited: 'One of the defining elements of slow travel is the opportunity to become part of local life and to connect to a place and its people. Slow travel is also about connection to culture.'
Slow Planet	www.slowplanet.com	Slowing the pace of life: 'Slow is not about doing everything at a snail's pace; it's about working, playing and living better by doing everything at the right speed.'
Slow Moves	www.slowmovesblog. blogspot.com/	Taking time on the journey to engage with people and place and avoidance of flights: 'Slowmoves is about enjoying the journey, as well as the destination. Moving away from budget flights and quick getaways to faraway places. And moving towards overnight train journeys, cycle trips and home-stays. Why not start a holiday from when you leave your front door, rather than when you enter your hotel room?'
Slow Travel Europe	www.slowtraveleurope.eu	Taking time on the journey to engage with people and place and avoidance of flights: 'The journey becomes a moment to relax, rather than it being a stressful interlude between home and destination … Slow travellers explore communities along the way, dawdle and pause as the mood takes them and check out spots recommended by the locals. Slow travel is downbeat, eco-friendly and above all fun.'
Slow Canada	www.slowcanada.net	Slowing the pace of life: 'The "SLOW MOVEMENT" is a cultural shift toward slowing down life's pace. It is more than slow food.'
Slow-travel-for-women	www.slow-travel-for-women.com	The richness of the travel experience: 'With our philosophy of Slow Travel for Women, the perceptive and sensitive traveller will be exposed to a "full immersion" of sensations: from the visual, to the audio, to the tactile, the olfative and the gustative. In this way the memories are deeply imbedded into our minds.'

Italy Slow Travel	www.italyslowtravel.com	The richness of the travel experience: 'To travel slowly off the beaten tourist tracks in order to discover new corners of Italy, to intimately experience each region but also to look at the already seen things but from a different point of view, under a new light, without haste.'
Slow Travel Tours	www.slowtraveltours.com	Taking time on the journey to engage with people and place: 'We share a common philosophy about travel. We believe in traveling more slowly and seeing what's around you, immersing yourself in the local landscape, the history and culture, the food and the wine, and the people.'
Hilaya travel	www.hilaya.com	The richness of the travel experience: 'What's unique about our travel services is what we refer to as "Slow Travel, Fine Life" experience – that you are not running around to move from Point A to Point B with a daily checklist to be finished, or take a huge sacrifice for the things you like when you are home (be it your favorite food, wine, music or even a bed sheet) just because you're traveling.'
Go Slow Travel	www.goslowtravel.se	Taking time on the journey: 'Our business idea is to arrange "Slow Trips" that are peaceful, zesty and at the same time learning experiences and impressions that will help to slow down the tempo and brighten your days when you return home.'
Vida Slow (Slow Life)	www.vidaslow.es	Taking time on the journey to engage with people and place: 'Slow travel sugiere degustar lentamente los viajes, ser parte de la vida local y conectarse con los habitantes.' (Slow travel suggests to enjoy slowly the journey, to be part of the local life and connect with the locals.)
Con calma viajes (take it easy travel)	www.concalmaviajes.com	Taking time on the journey to engage with people and place: 'Al viajar lentamente, puedes profundizar mas permaneciendo en un mismo sitio mas tiempo y visitando las cosas que estan mas cerca.' (When you are travelling slow, you can get to know the place deeply staying in the same place for a longer time and visiting places that are nearby.)

Developed by Peter McGrath

The main focus of slow travel web pages, however, is usually the celebration of place and travel as a value to be cherished. Thus, the approach of this eclectic grouping of entrepreneurs and travel writers is not one of reprehension, but encouragement to the traveller to seek fulfilling ways of holidaymaking. They also serve to reduce cognitive dissonance where impacts are apparent (Marshall, 2007). The idea that the level of travel should be reduced to meet the exigencies of climatic change is not currently on the agenda. There is, however, an emerging media and academic discussion which argues that this might be an appropriate way forward. Even in the 1980s, Krippendorf (1984) argued that the tourism system had encouraged an oversupply of provision and that there was a strong case for travelling less. The increasing carbon costs of transporting markets to distant locations has been questioned more recently; there is a case, it is argued, for alternative approaches other than growth in tourism (Hall, 2009).

In order to decouple tourism from its high carbon-dependent path, there is clearly a need to address the way we take holidays and particularly how we travel, since tourism transport is responsible for the major share of tourism emissions (Gössling, 2002). Slow travel has emerged as one potential solution. Given the diversity of interpretations of slow travel expressed in academic and industry literature, and in the media, this chapter sets out to clarify the core ingredients of slow travel. It explores what slow travel is, but also, and just as importantly, what slow travel is not. It begins by explaining the origins of the term and its association with slow food and low-carbon tourism. It then focuses on the elements of slow travel. Some elements are considered essential ingredients, while other aspects of slow travel may only be applicable to some contexts or tourists. This section concludes with an overview of the ingredients and their role in slow travel. The chapter concludes with an exploration of the market for slow travel and how slow travel differs from mainstream tourism.

Origin of the term

Travelling at a slow pace and engaging with places along the way is not new. Prior to the widespread use of cars and air travel, much tourism was slow simply because it relied on modes of transport which, due to limitations of speed, restricted the distance that could be travelled in a day. Travel on foot, by horse, donkey or stagecoach were at one time the only forms of land-based travel, and there is still some limited use of animals as tourism transport. There was also extensive use of navigable rivers and coastlines, and these are the subject of discussion in Chapter 9. Therefore, in one sense, slow travel is revisiting a style of travel romanticized in the Grand Tour, an era when most travel was local, and only the wealthy could afford the time and cost of international journeys (Towner, 2002). However, slow travel in the present day is different for most but not all. There is still a walking world that permeates developing countries, and this is often forgotten (Porter, 2002). There are, however, a multiplicity of destinations that are more readily accessed, and a market that continues to expand, both in the traditional generating countries but equally in the advancing economies of the developing world. In addition, most forms of transport have developed; these facilitate slow as well as fast travel.

An analysis of the references made to slow travel suggests that it fits within a wider discourse of slow being the antithesis of fast (Andrews, 2006; Honoré, 2004). The three core pillars of the slow movement comprise doing things at the right speed, changing attitudes towards time and the use of it, and seeking quality over quantity (Peters, 2006). The philosophy of slow extends to a wide range of aspects, including design, leisure and even sex. Mostly, emphasis is placed on slow as a way of life; as portrayed, for example, by Gayeton (2009) in his description of life in Tuscany. The values presented by the slow movement are clearly discernible in relation to slow food, cities and travel.

Slow travel offers an alternative to air travel and car travel, with travel providing the tourist experience as much as the destination. It is not clear where the term 'slow travel' was first used. One of the earliest attempts to define slow travel was made by Pauline Kenny in 2000, on the slowtravel.com website. This resource encouraged people to consider a different way of taking a holiday, in order to enhance their overall holiday experience. The essence of slow travel, according to Kenny, is about staying in one place and then using the time to explore nearby localities, thus getting to know more about local culture and ways of life (slowtravel.com, 2007). She did not incorporate the idea of the journey to a destination into slow travel. Her argument has remained that travel by rail rather than air, for example, should more properly be referred to as green travel, not to be confused with slow travel which is about enjoying a richer experience at a destination. Another example is Slow Movement (2009), which focuses on connecting to people and place: 'living as opposed to "staying" at your destination'.

However, several other correspondents in the slow travel movement do include the journey to the destination as an integral part of the concept. Slowplanet.com (2009) discusses 'savouring the journey' and travel by train, boat, bicycle or foot, 'reveling in how the landscape, light and people change along the way'. Slow Moves (2009) refers to 'enjoying the journey, as well as the destination. Moving away from budget flights and quick getaways to faraway places. And moving towards overnight train journeys, cycle trips and home-stays.' This has emerged from concern amongst travel writers and several small-scale tourism operators about the major effect of the travel element on climate change (Conrady and Buck, 2008).

It has been said that there are strong ties between slow travel, slow food and Cittáslow. However, the linkages, at one level, appear to be fairly tenuous, in that slow food grew out of interest from townships (in Italy initially) and in particular through the actions of visionary local mayors. The slow food and Cittáslow movements were essentially about binding local residents into social collaboration in relation to their communities. It is interesting to note the findings of the work by Nilsson et al (2007); they reported that many of the proponents of slow cities in Italy expressed a note of caution about tourism development. Thus, slow food emerged as a community initiative for residents. In contrast, the early proponents of slow travel have mainly been small-scale travel companies or travel writers expressing their views principally through the internet, and a growing number of articles in the press and travel media. Gardner (2009) has attempted to galvanize this expression of interest into a manifesto for slow travel that is summarized as follows:

- Slow travel is a state of mind and the idea should start at home by exploring nearby places of interest.
- The mode of travel is important; travellers should travel slow and avoid aircraft. They should enjoy ferries, local buses and slow trains, as 'speed destroys the connection with the landscape' (p13).

- The journey is part of the pleasure.
- Local markets and shops are equally important.
- The slow traveller needs to slow down to enjoy the cityscape.
- It is important to get a feel for languages and dialects.
- The slow traveller should engage with the community at a right level.
- It is good to do as locals do (such as eating times, restaurants, promenading, etc.).
- Make the best of missed connections to seek out the unexpected.
- Look at ways to give back something to the local community.

Cities or regions have not, as yet, emerged as slow travel destinations in quite the same manner as for slow food. Gardner, as with other writers in the movement, takes a consumer perspective and the assumption is that every destination and travel corridor has some potential for the slow traveller. Part of the experience is about 'reinvigorating our habits of perception':

> *I find the process of experiencing a place is essentially phenomenological. The city square was not designed as a place for tourists, but rather as the context for everyday lives. It deserves more than a casual glance – cityscapes are there to be studied and observed in detail. (Gardner, 2009, p13)*

The slow travel perspective, however, is aligned in many respects with the slow food movement. This is not just a matter of nomenclature. The concepts have much in common. Firstly, travel has always involved experiencing local food and beverages (Murray and Graham, 1997; Towner, 1985), and the concept of slow food, with its focus on locally sourced ingredients, traditional recipes and taking time to source, prepare and enjoy food, offers many parallels with slow travel. The slow food movement, inspired by the writer Carlo Petrini (2001), emerged in Italy in the late 1980s and spread across Europe and North America (Hall, 2006). The principal aim of the movement is to encourage the making of good, clean and fair food. There are several underpinning concepts, including the need for biodiversity, animal welfare and the protection of traditional food and beverages. This is set against a background of the homogenization of food production and hospitality on a global scale, as typified by fast food production (Miele and Murdoch, 2002). The slow food movement presents five core benefits that accrue from the adoption of slow food:

- fresh-tasting food made from local varieties
- reduced food miles saving on energy
- gaining local knowledge and control about what we eat
- survival of local recipes and methods
- enhancement of local landscapes.
  (Slow Food, 2009)

These benefits are wider than simply supporting local artisan food and beverage producers. The encouragement of eco-agronomy is diffused with an idea about local communities having more control about what they eat. Leitch (2003) argues that slow food came about at a time when the European Union was seeking to standardize food and hospitality; it represented a counter-balance to:

> a rationalising project which potentially limits the capacity of marginalised rural communities to reproduce themselves as active subjects of history. The Slow Food Movement, with its emphasis on the protection of threatened foods and the diversity of cultural landscapes is, perhaps, one response. (Leitch, 2003, p441)

Slow food also relates to food with ties to local culture and heritage; in many respects it is an approach to maintaining traditional values within each locality (Jones et al, 2003). Food, in this respect, has taken on a symbolic role in relation to the identity of each locality; it is as much a comment about the relevance of place to people's lives (Pietryowski, 2004). Thus, the movement has aptly been described as a 'new kind of civic associationism' (Leitch, 2003, p457).

There have been criticisms of the concept. Chrzan (2004) argues that the term 'slow food' has been used in an indiscriminate manner, and could be the subject of exploitation for commercial gain by companies or destinations. Another criticism is that the slow food movement has sought to focus on the ethics of taste, but that this has the potential drawback of sentimentalizing such regional struggles against global forces (Donati, 2005). Thus, whilst slow food is not political in the sense of partisan politics, the movement represents a counter culture that seeks to protect the 'dignity of the local economy' (Slow Food, 2009). It poses questions indirectly about the late modern societal dimensions of globalization and corporatism in relation to localism and the peculiarities or curiosities of each locality.

Therein lies the main interface with Cittáslow, otherwise known as the slow cities movement. The Cittáslow idea is commonly attributed to Paolo Saturnini, the mayor of Greve-in-Chianti (Italy), getting together with three other mayors to form an association. It was borne out of the success of the slow food movement and engaging similar motives, as explained by one of the four founding mayors, Silvio Barbero:

> It is a logical extension to our opposition to the homogenisation of tastes and traditions ... just as we don't want teenagers the world over consuming Coca-Cola and hamburgers, neither do we want cities to erase or pillage their pasts. If the local butcher is replaced by a jeans shop, or the local farmers' market folds because there is a hypermarket in the next town, towns look sadly similar. (Kennedy, 2000)

The initial group of cities were all in Italy; there are now 100 across the world, although mostly situated in Europe (Miele, 2008). Cittáslow is concerned principally about the quality of life of citizens. Like slow food, Cittáslow is underpinned by a philosophy that emphasizes a slower pace, relaxation, locality and traditional culture (Nilsson et al, 2007). Whilst Cittáslow maintains and supports the ideals of slow food, it is more about creating conditions in which local residents can enjoy a relaxed and socially productive life in their cities. Thus, the original mayors agreed a charter of 50 items to improve the infrastructure and cityscape of their towns and to encourage a social engagement by their citizens (Mayor and Knox, 2006). These included measures to remove traffic from some streets so that the atmosphere is more convivial, and to slow down the pace of life. It also included pledges to oppose unwanted or inappropriate retail development, to encourage local distinctiveness and a unique sense of place. In essence it is very much about action planning, place-making and sociability (Mayer and Knox, 2009).

The 'sense of place' concept is well documented (Gehl, 1996). There is a consensus that it is socially constructed, very often by local people, who walk, sit and visit the buildings of the town. It also includes the spaces in between where social exchange and meetings take place, thus allowing a pleasurable sensory experience (Pink, 2007). Cittáslow is also about creating places, or principally streetscapes that have quality, character and atmosphere (Entrikin, 1991; Jackson, 1994). The term authenticity has also been applied in relation to the genuine nature and atmosphere of the configuration of buildings and streetscapes (Assi, 2000). The imperative is to retain what is good and true about a place and to resist inappropriate 'look-alike' development, for example, intrusive car parks and highways, which will detract from the overall character of a place (Landry and Bianchini, 1995).

Jivén and Larkham (2003) conclude that there is a need for urban designers, architects and planners to take note of the theoretical underpinning of the concept of sense of place in each respective context; they also argue for the need to involve local people in place-making. Knox (2005) builds on the premise that societal norms count for much, and ways of going about life in particular locales are important in the process of the development of the human landscape. There is an equally convincing argument that adherence to these principles in slow cities retains or even re-builds places; in time, the atmosphere and wellbeing becomes an attraction for visitors. This is where some caution has been expressed, as there is a fine line between attracting visitors and visitors overwhelming central zones. However, at least one of the Cittáslow townships, Ludlow in England, publicizes that visitors are to be welcomed as temporary residents.

It is also possible to map the antecedents of slow travel in the academic literature. There are three strands of academic inquiry that have contributed to the emerging discourse on slow travel. The first strand relates to those who have attempted to define the core elements. In France, the idea of 'slow tourism' has emerged principally from the researchers Jean-Paul Ceron and Ghislain Dubois (Ceron and Dubois, 2007; Dubois and Ceron, 2006b), who have drawn on the idea of 'le tourisme lent' used by Matos-Wasem (cited in Ceron and Dubois, 2007). Slow tourism has been used to refer to conventional rail-based tourism and longer stays, and Simpson et al (2008) link 'slow tourism' to slow food as a possible environmental certification option. 'Soft mobility', a second term used by Ceron and Dubois, refers primarily to non-car-based travel around destinations on foot or by cycle. Ceron and Dubois (2007) also embrace the term 'slow travel' with reference to tourist products that are less travel-intensive, using modes such as train, sailing, cruise ships and bus, where the travel is 'pleasant and interesting' (p202) and where the stay is longer.

The second strand relates to a discussion about the nature of tourism and a need for a better tourist experience through different travel behaviour (Müller, 1994). The act of travelling, it is argued, is not fulfilling and cannot compensate for poor quality urban living. The most influential exponent of this was Krippendorf (1984), who argued that the current tourism system does not do much to improve the lot of urban dwellers in late modern society. Many of the approaches suggested by Krippendorf over 25 years ago (such as holidays at home or nearer to home, emphasis on locality and diversity) have been reinvigorated under the umbrella of slow travel.

Thirdly, there has been a growing academic inquiry into transport as a tourist experience (Halsall, 2001). There has also been some discussion about transport as a function of visitor management at the destination. This has been primarily in relation to traffic reduction to improve a destination's attractiveness (Müller, 1999). Lumsdon (2000b), in his discussion of cycle tourism, refers to the appeal of slower forms of travel, and Downward and Lumsdon (2004) recommend that tourist destinations slow down visitors in order to increase visitor spending. Lumsdon (2006) also undertook a study to evaluate the potential of the bus as a way to encourage new forms of tourist travel. The simultaneous experience of transport and tourism with the tourist as co-producer has several parallels with the values written into the travelogues of the great travel writers, such as Newby and Theroux. They provide an enduring representation of slow travel as a way of life. Speakman (2005, p134) summarizes the argument as follows:

> *Contrary to the seductive automobile advertisements, the quality of the experience is not about speed. The real pleasure of travelling on barge or cruise boat along a waterway lies in travelling at a gentle pace through a slowly changing landscape. Walking and cycling are forms of tourism transport that offer so much more than the car in terms of perceiving the environment in far greater detail, and allowing other senses to share in that perception—experience the sounds, the touch, even the taste and smell of the natural world and cultural landscape. In transport for tourism terms, therefore, slow is beautiful.*

In a more utilitarian context, Ory and Mokhtarian (2005) refer to slower, non-motorized modes, 'slow' here being used in the literal sense, while Larsen et al (2006, p103) discuss 'slow moving quality time together' in the context of long weekends away. Other terms include 'slow mobility'.

These three broad strands of academic discussion have not coalesced in any other way than providing a broad base on which to build a more comprehensive approach, referred to here as slow travel as a form of tourism that might develop more strongly in future. In all of the writings there is a growing awareness and description of how the elements are associated with low-carbon travel. Høyer (2000), while not using the term slow travel, suggests sustainable tourism mobility should be based on the low-impact modes of walking, cycling, bus, train and tram.

Acceptance of the term slow travel is also acknowledged in the tourism sector, with Mintel producing a report in 2009 suggesting slow travel represents the 'rediscovery of the pleasure of the journey ... in an era of commoditised air travel' (Mintel, 2009b, p6). However, while Mintel indicates that slow travel has a reduced impact on the environment, the report refers to slow travel as surface travel and includes the private car. Given the discussion in Chapter 2, there is a conflict here discussed later in this chapter.

Slow travel has also been officially defined in Australia's Macquarie Dictionary (2009) as:

> noun 1. *travel conducted at a slow pace to enjoy more fully the places visited and the people met.* 2. *such travel seen as environmentally friendly through its lack of reliance on air transport [modelled on slow food].*

However, as with Mintel, these definitions can encompass car travel, as only air travel is excluded. The media have also embraced slow travel, especially in quality papers such as *Der Spiegel*, *Le Monde*, *The Guardian* and *Observer*, where it is regularly featured in the travel supplement. The media has used slow travel in diverse ways and it has been employed to describe an alternative to air travel, to highlight low-carbon forms of travel, as an antithesis of fast, and associated with slow food.

The ingredients of slow travel

Slow travel encompasses a variety of physical and experiential components. There is likely to be much ongoing debate over what should or should not be classed as slow travel. This book aims to lead and guide these debates and, as much as possible, the aim here is to define slow travel. The answer though is not set in stone; this is an emerging subject, which scholars will address and refine in due course. We have laid out the components in the form of an ingredients list; however, some ingredients may be more important than others, and in some contexts it might be imperative for a particular flavour to come through with a different balance to the ingredients. It is also our thesis that, while we emphasize the importance of the travel component, slow travel refers to the whole holiday or day visit.

There is an important point. It is not about focusing on either travel from origin to destination or at the destination as separate components; both are integral to slow travel. For the most part, previous tourism research has ignored travel, as if arrival at a destination happens by magic; thus much of the tourist experience has been overlooked, as well as the lion's share of environmental impact. Slow travel has emerged as a response to this gap. It is an umbrella term for a 'new tourism', reflecting different motivations and perceptions.

Low-carbon

Low-carbon tourism is an outcome of slow travel. In some cases the desire for low-carbon tourism will also be a driver for slow travel, where consumers or providers are concerned to reduce their holiday carbon footprint. By way of explanation, exploratory research with slow travellers found that only some participants chose slow travel in order to secure environmental benefits (Dickinson et al, 2010b). Guiver, Lumsdon and Morris (2007) also found tourists using buses, but who had a car available, were likely to choose bus travel for personal benefits rather than environmental concerns. Those for whom the environment is considered key have been termed 'hard slow travellers' (Dickinson et al, 2010b). On the other hand, 'soft slow travellers', while seeing environmental benefits as an added bonus, chose slow travel due to a preference for a particular slow travel mode, or sought an experience that slow travel afforded (Dickinson et al, 2010b); that is, for the personal benefits (Guiver, Lumsdon and Morris, 2007). These participants, for example, often took flights for other holidays. Dickinson et al (2010b) describe the distinction between 'hard' and 'soft' slow travel as a 'continuum rather than a marked division'. Ultimately though, whether slow travel is undertaken by 'hard' or 'soft' slow travellers, low-carbon tourism will always be a discernible outcome.

Slow travel comes within the remit of what is increasingly referred to as low-carbon tourism (see, for example, Peeters et al, 2008). This relates to tourism with a low-carbon impact through minimization of GHG emissions. Within the tourism industry, emissions can be attributed by the three main sectors: transport, accommodation and activities. Transport is responsible for by far the greatest emissions (87 per cent), with accommodation second at 9 per cent, and activities 4 per cent (Peeters, 2007). It is therefore evident that in order to achieve low-carbon tourism, transport should be the focus of mitigation measures, and Peeters et al (2008) identify changing transport choices as a key opportunity for the industry. However, to date, most attempts to reduce emissions have been within the accommodation sector, primed as much by rising costs as climate change concerns. There has also been work at a destination level (e.g. carbon neutral destinations, see Chapter 2) and attempts to offset emissions. As the analysis of low-carbon tourism industry strategy in Chapter 2 shows, while there are some positive contributions made by other areas of tourism, low-carbon transport is essential to decarbonize the tourism industry.

Given the importance of climate change, the tourism sector is ethically bound to find ways to reduce its carbon footprint. As Chapter 2 illustrated, not only is tourism failing to reduce its carbon footprint, it is currently expected to increase. Therefore, the contention is that if slow travel is to present a meaningful alternative to current tourism, then low-carbon should be both integral to, and the key outcome of, slow travel.

Current predictions are for tourism consumption to increase as GDP rises in many regions of the world (UNWTO, 2009a). If this increased demand for travel fuels an expanded tourism sector reliant on the aviation and automobile industries, then reduced carbon emissions in other industry sectors will be cancelled out. Even if new tourism demand fails to materialize, the savings made by improved technology and efficiency gains (see Chapter 2) will not reduce the carbon footprint of tourism in line with international policy. Further carbon reduction will have to be met by other industries, and this may not be possible. Therefore, in order to achieve acceptable GHG emissions levels, it is essential that the tourism industry develops a low-carbon strategy. Given that transport is responsible for by far the largest share of tourism's carbon footprint, basic auditing principles indicate that industry actions should be focused on this area. Slow travel is closely associated with moves towards lower-carbon tourism.

Mode of transport

Within our conceptual framework, choice of mode is intrinsically interlinked with the other ingredients of slow travel. An evaluation of the carbon footprint of tourism travel modes indicates there is a continuum from carbon neutral modes such as walking and cycling to carbon intensive modes such as private car and flying (Dickinson et al, 2010b). However, as Table 4.2 indicates, there is a clear divide that separates car and air transport, as the most carbon intensive forms of transport, from rail and coach transport. Air and car travel produce in the region of four times the amount of CO_2 per passenger km compared to rail travel, and up to five times compared to coach travel. Table 4.2 is based on averages and there is obviously some variability, depending on the fuel efficiency of the vehicle and loading factors. Car travel can achieve comparable efficiency to train travel with high loadings, but this is rarely achieved. Given the dominance of car travel, this is discussed in further detail after the ingredients section, along with water-based travel. Water-based travel can make a contribution to slow travel in some areas, although it is ambiguous. Based on the carbon analysis in Table 4.2, walking, cycling, train and coach travel all meet the criteria of low-carbon travel, while car and air travel do not.

There is an inherent link between the mode of transport used to access a destination and the mode of transport used at the destination. If a personal access mode, such as car or cycle, is used, then this is available for use at the destination itself. Of course, many people travel to a destination by one mode and then use another to get around the destination area, such as fly/drive holidays. Modes can be linked by institutionalized industry practices, such as car hire booking facilitated at the time of flight booking.

With respect to slow travel there are some important issues to debate here. If someone flies to a destination but then relies on local public transport, are they a slow traveller? In the destination context, yes, but if their holiday is to meet the low-carbon criteria overall, then the answer is no. There is no doubt

Table 4.2 *Mode-specific CO_2 emission factors for transport*

	kg/passenger km*
Carbon-intensive modes	
Air	
<500km	0.183
500–1000km	0.134
1000–1500km	0.130
1500–2000km	0.121
> 2000km	0.111
Car	0.121
	(0.180v/km)
Less carbon-intensive modes	
Rail	0.033
Coach	0.027
Carbon neutral modes	
Cycle	0
Walk	0

* An average based on various sources (Can Europe, 2008; Eurostar, 2008; National Express, 2008; Peeters et al, 2007)
Source: Adapted from Dickinson et al, 2010a

a benefit, compared to car use, both in reduced carbon footprint and in supporting local public transport networks, but overall the holiday's carbon footprint remains high. Similarly a tourist might take an overnight train from Paris to the Mediterranean and then hire a car. While the carbon footprint is much reduced, were the train a substitute for a flight or car, the car hire and tendency to cover greater distances by car at the destination (Dickinson and Robbins, 2007) would reduce the overall carbon efficiency of such a trip. Such strategies, while recognized as making a contribution to low-carbon travel, represent only a partial approach to slow travel. It is therefore important for slow travel to utilize low-carbon modes for both the travel to and around the destination area.

Exploratory research (Dickinson et al, 2010b) indicates that some tourists have a commitment to certain modes of transport. This was particularly apparent for cycle and train travel, where tourists are often passionate about the mode (Dallen, 2007; Holloway, 2006). These slow travellers are not necessarily concerned about the climate change implications of their travel; indeed, exploratory work showed some took long-haul flights on other occasions, despite being committed to specific slow travel modes. For example, Dickinson et al (2010b) describe a cyclist, with the smallest holiday carbon footprint in the sample, who was sceptical about climate change and flew regularly for other trips. This type of travel has been described by Rhoden and Lumsdon (2006) as 'transport as tourism'.

Engaging with local public transport, such as bus or train, and cycling or walking is likely to result in a greater engagement with the place visited and potential for place- and transport-related experiences, but also more spending in the wider economy beyond the main tourism resorts and attractions. Much though depends on how slow travel is organized. Independent travel is likely to result in more dispersed visitor spending and a diversity of experiences, while organized travel will limit spending opportunities to places on a given itinerary and more staged experiences. Coach tours, for instance, while having a smaller carbon footprint compared to other motorized modes, present somewhat contained opportunities to engage with the places visited. Car travel, on the other hand, allows independent travel to a diversity of places, but there is a much larger carbon footprint and potential for more local impacts such as pollution and congestion. This, however, is a rather limited perspective of coach travel. As the industry has evolved, coach tours now provide opportunities for specialist experiences and, in many cases, access places that tourists, who lack knowledge of the region visited, might never find. Such considerations are important in the overall sustainability of the holiday and can be directly related to the type of experiences sought by tourists. In this respect the choice of mode is intrinsically linked with the other ingredients of slow travel, discussed next.

The travel and destination experience

Within the conceptual framework the distinction between the travel and destination experience is purposely blurred. This is because slow travel encompasses the whole holiday. It is not just about the travel, nor does it exclude the destination-based experience. Within this 'new tourism', and contemporary travel more widely, there is no single destination but multiple destination encounters that involve places, people, modes of transport and co-creation of experience. Travel to a destination includes experiential elements, and destination experiences involve local travel. On this basis, it is not clear why transport has been so overlooked in the tourism literature, given its integral role.

Work on slow travel suggests that engagement with people and place is an important theme for slow travellers (Dickinson et al, 2010b). Slow travellers are involved in the co-creation of experience (Binkhorst and Den Dekker, 2009) through their interaction with people and place. Cyclists, in particular, express a desire for mastery that is well beyond typical tourism spectator roles (Cloke and Perkins, 1998). As a cyclist encountered in the New Forest National Park, UK, described it: 'being in the car is like watching it on TV, cycling is really being there'. The embodied sense of being there, physically coping with the locality and the local transport, and interacting with local people and fellow travellers, form an important discourse and present some of the most memorable stories and nostalgia that can be elaborated post-trip. These stories often relate to more adventurous moments, the overcoming of a variety of obstacles and to shared hardships.

With slow travel there may be a specific destination; however, travel is an integral part of the tourist experience where people enjoy the slow pace of travel (Dickinson et al, 2010b) and enjoy what Larson (2001) describes as the 'travel glance'. For instance, Dickinson et al (2010b) explain how a woman chose a long train ride across France in order to spend time with her teenage children and to take in the scenery. The mode of transport was obviously instrumental, but it was the experience afforded that provided the motivation. In this context, the low-carbon consideration was not a main motivator.

Sociability has recently come to the fore as an important feature of travel (Urry, 2000; 2007) and the social side of travel, such as meeting new people, making friends and being with existing friends, is a feature of slow travel (Dickinson, 2008). Arnould and Price (1993) refer to this as an element of communitas; that is, a sense of group belonging and cooperation. 'Being with family and connecting with others gives a "new perspective on life" and helps people see "what really matters"' (Arnould and Price, 1993, p38). The connection to people can be played out both in relation to encounters with others in destinations and encounters during the course of travel. Such encounters may be with significant others, such as friends or family, or with strangers who may even become friends in the course of a trip.

Drawing on Pine and Gilmore's (1999, p31) matrix of experience realms (Chapter 3), slow travel implies immersion in the environment, where participants become physically a part of the experience itself. However, there is also evidence of absorption, in which the environment is experienced only in passing and holds the participant's attention for a limited period – the travel glance (Larsen, 2001). Pine and Gilmore's ideas on participation also provide a useful framework to analyse slow travel. In slow travel the importance of being involved in the construction of the experience stands out, and this implies a strong active involvement in the creation of slow travel experiences, although it is less clear whether this is a function of independent travel as opposed to slow travel. Pine and Gilmore (1999) suggest this strong involvement enables more influence on the experience. However, people can only influence travel experiences up to a point, and there are occasions where the participation is passive and individuals have little control over the travel situation. This is the case for both slow and non-slow travel and, to some extent, people are always passive and weakly involved in the creation of experiences when travelling due to unexpected events such as bad weather or travel disruption.

Slow travel implies taking time both during travel to and within the destination area. The nature of slow modes of travel provides many opportunities to break the journey at interesting stopping-off places en-route. If desired, such journeys can be extended to allow a longer stopover. Therefore, while slow travel can, undoubtedly, take more time than flying, where longer distances are concerned, the whole trip provides an extended opportunity for tourism encounters beyond the airport lounge. Exploratory work shows that a strong element for slow travellers is the taking of time to recover from hectic life. Carù and Cova (2003) have suggested this is a reaction to extraordinary experiences, and that people do in fact seek out pauses and periods of inactivity: 'Each consumption experience is not necessarily memorable or unforgettable, as the supporters of the economy and experience marketing would like' (Carù and Cova, 2003, p277). Part of the point of any holiday is taking time out of a hurried lifestyle, but this seems to be a special feature for slow travellers. This may be the inevitability of the additional time commitment involved in slow travel. However, slow travel does not have to take longer; indeed, on many shorter trips, slow travel is just as fast as air or car travel, due to good infrastructure and reduced check-in times or congestion.

The spatial structure of slow travel is also important, with its focus on localized engagement with the place visited or the places encountered en-route. Pauline Kenny's early ideas of travel in the vicinity of the accommodation are appropriate here (slowtravel.com, 2007). Slow travel also requires use of local public transport systems that provide an authentic connection with the places visited, as do encounters with local food and food producers. Thus slow travel makes a commitment to locality and slow travellers become more locally embedded, rather than imposing a globalized tourist culture.

Environmental concerns

While research has identified a group of slow travellers for whom environmental considerations are a core motivation, 'hard' slow travellers, there are others for whom the environment, while still a concern, is not the key reason; these are referred to as 'soft' slow travellers (Dickinson et al, 2010b). For those most concerned about the environment, slow travel implies the active choice of low-carbon modes of transport that meet lifestyle objectives. This group is actively choosing to avoid travel by air or car, and this pervades wider life choices beyond tourism. Many 'soft' slow travellers are also very concerned about the environment, but this concern is more evident in their home-based behaviour, such as recycling or conserving energy in the home, rather than in tourism (Dickinson et al, 2010b). This is reflected in other studies that suggest people are more able to articulate environmental concerns based in their home rather than on holiday (Barr et al, 2010; Hares et al, 2010). However, the environmental benefits are welcomed by all slow travellers, though this may not be a key driver.

Linked to environmental concerns about the mode of transport are longer stays and the distance travelled. Some interpretations of slow travel imply a longer stay (slowtravel.com, 2007). Generally, longer stays are viewed positively by the tourism sector, due to greater visitor spend in destinations, although the current trend is for shorter stays. As a result, much destination-based research has focused on extending the length of stay. Given that much of the carbon footprint of tourism accrues from travel, there is an argument for increasing the length of stay to reduce the carbon footprint on a pro-rata per day basis. On the same basis, if fewer but longer holidays are undertaken each year by tourists, the annual individual carbon footprint is much reduced. Hunter and Shaw (2007) suggest there may be a positive benefit in the ecological footprint (an aggregate footprint of the human demands on the natural environment) of a tourist from Florida, USA, flying to Costa Rica, staying three weeks and consuming at the same level as local people, when the substitution effect of not consuming in the USA for those three weeks is taken into account. However, given that it is unlikely that an American would consume at the same level as local Costa Ricans, the prospect of such a benefit is dubious. A number of other authors have begun to include travel to the destination in research on the eco-efficiency of tourism (Gössling et al, 2005; Høyer, 2000; Peeters et al, 2007). These studies include an analysis of the carbon emissions and economic benefits relative to the length of stay.

With slow travel to access a destination, the carbon footprint of a holiday is further reduced. However, there is potential for tourists to engage in carbon-intensive activities at the destination, which might shift the relative impact of the travel element (Filimonau et al, 2010). Current work on the life cycle assessment of tourism argues there may be an optimum length of stay for a holiday where the transport impacts and destination-based impacts are 50:50 (Filimonau et al, 2010).

However, from a slow travel and low-carbon perspective, while such analysis is useful, if travel includes a long-haul flight, and subsequent consumption at the destination is carbon-intensive, there is no benefit of an extended stay. While a tourist might access a destination by slow travel, if subsequent consumption levels result in a high carbon footprint, much of the benefit is lost. For instance, Becken and Simmons (2002) highlight the tendency for tourists to travel considerable distances around New Zealand, as the iconic tourist destinations are spread throughout the country. Tourists might also engage in such high-carbon activities as helicopter rides, and consume at a high level in luxury hotels (Becken, 2002; Becken et al, 2003a). Should tourists travel to the destination by slow travel followed by relatively high-carbon consumption practices, then the 50:50 rule described above may be a useful tool. Therefore, while extending the length of stay is a useful component of slow travel, that can reduce the holiday's carbon footprint on a pro-rata, per day basis, it is crucial for slow travel that the travel component is low-carbon.

There is also the consideration of distance travelled, where there are two issues. First, slow modes of transport pose some limitations on the distance travelled, due to the extended time commitment; and, second, the carbon footprint of any motorized trip increases in relation to distance travelled. Based on modal constraints, it is clear that some forms of transport, particularly walking, significantly limit the distance that can be travelled, unless very extended periods of travel are intended. In the same vein, long-haul travel by coach and train requires more time than flying. While long-haul travel by coach and train is not impossible, with the exception of backpackers and others engaged in an extended period of travel, most tourists would not normally be able to make the required time commitment. This largely limits slow travel to intra-continental travel.

With respect to the second issue, carbon footprint, much analysis has been conducted using an eco-efficiency framework (see Chapter 2). Generally eco-efficiency improves for closer-to-home destinations. For instance, the analysis by Gössling et al (2005) suggests France should attract visitors from Switzerland who travel a short distance and spend extensively, as opposed to visitors from Latin America who travel a long way and spend less. Allied to these low-carbon considerations is the distance travelled to destinations by motorized forms of transport. If someone travels by train or coach over a long distance, there will be a significant carbon footprint (Peeters and Schouten, 2006), even if this footprint is smaller than the corresponding travel by car or air. Likewise, intercontinental travel normally involves travel over water, these days mostly conducted by air. This might be replaced by boat travel, but again there are issues of the carbon footprint (see Chapter 9) and time constraints. Bearing in mind these considerations, slow travel is likely to suit short- to mid-haul, rather than long-haul, travel. It is important, therefore, to note that most international tourism is intra-continental, and there is thus good potential for use of slow travel modes. For example, Table 4.3 illustrates that most international arrivals to the UK and resident departures are European. Table 4.3 also highlights the relative inequality in tourism travel, with considerably more UK resident departures to Asia, Africa, Central and Southern America and the Caribbean than reciprocated visits.

Another consideration is the distance travelled within the destination area. Tourists with a car available within a destination area tend to use it for all trips, and are drawn to attractions beyond their immediate accommodation location (Dickinson and Robbins, 2007). Analysis in a rural area suggests only about one-quarter of these car trips could be undertaken by slow travel modes; however, given many of these trips are unplanned, there is considerable scope for these to be converted to alternative shorter trips that utilize slow travel alternatives (Dickinson and Robbins, 2007), with scope for some to offer a tourist experience in their own right (Rhoden and Lumsdon, 2006). Dickinson and Robbins (2007) recommended a tourist information strategy to highlight local day trips. Such a strategy would increase the potential for slow travel and reduce the distance travelled.

An extension of this spatial discussion is the idea of the 'staycation' (Germann Molz, 2009; Sharma, 2009). Lacho and Kiefer (2008, p23) define staycation as 'stay at home and enjoy what the city has to offer', but the term has been used in various other ways, and staycation can be taken to mean people holidaying at home, close to home or, in the UK context, holidaying in the UK. The term staycation appears to have grown in use during 2008 and 2009, when more North Americans and Europeans opted to holiday at home as a response to increasing oil prices and the global recession. To date there has

Table 4.3 *UK international arrivals and departures by destination*

Origin/destination	International arrivals to the UK		UK resident departures	
	Number (thousands)	%	Number (thousands)	%
EU	23,666	75	54,424	80
North America	3806	12	4629	7
Australasia	1164	4	680	1
Asia	1159	4	3135	5
Middle East	694	2	1115	2
Africa	587	2	2847	4
Central and Southern America	334	1	659	1
Caribbean	71	0.2	947	1

Source: Adapted from the Office for National Statistics, 2009

been little research on this phenomenon. While the staycation removes much of the transport impact of tourism, there is potential to extend other forms of consumption at home, and for much localized car-based travel. Further work is needed to explore this form of consumption.

Issues at the boundary of slow travel

In summary, slow travel is dependent on low-carbon modes of travel, should encourage tourism to destinations closer to home and, once at their destination, tourists should be encouraged to explore the immediate destination area.

The above sets out the ingredients of slow travel; however, there are several issues that remain and require further discussion. Firstly, one major criticism of slow travel is that it takes longer and costs more. Both are widely cited as reasons for car use or air travel but, while they stand up in some contexts, they are generally misconstrued. Secondly, there is the consideration of car travel and water-based travel within the slow travel concept. It is our contention that car travel is excluded from slow travel, and only certain forms of water-based travel included; however, further discussion is required to set out this view. The following section explores these points and addresses the most common critiques.

Distance, time, speed and cost

Slow travel is associated with the reconceptualization of time. Parkins (2004, p363) argues that slow travel is about a 'subversion of the dominance of speed' in our lives. Spending more time adds to the travel experience. However, in both tourism and transport studies, travel is usually modelled as a time and financial cost to be minimized. This is the basic premise of the consumption of recreation, as presented in the travel-cost model (Clawson and Knetsch, 1966; Prideaux, 2000; Steiner and Bristow, 2000). Based on this model, travel distance is related inversely to time and cost. For example, travel time and cost are a significant factor in modal choice over long-distance routes (van Goeverden, 2009).

In recent times, tourism travel distance has grown as travel speeds have increased and travel costs decreased. This was initially through rail development, then road/car development in most countries and finally through the expansion of air travel. Through this process the world has effectively become much smaller, it is argued, and far destinations have become accessible to distant tourist markets, mostly residing in North America and Europe. However, rarely is it questioned whether such a development is positive, or whether there are more desirable alternatives. While travel has opened up opportunities for the wealthy few, even in economically developed nations, relatively high proportions of the population never take international holidays, and it is only a very few who are able to take long-haul flights. In reality, only 2 per cent of the world's population take international flights (Simpson et al, 2008).

Therefore, it is questionable to what extent air travel has been democratized. In fact, the majority of holidays globally are domestic (Sharpley, 2009); even in one of the most developed nations, the USA, more than 94 per cent of holidays are domestic (Bigano et al, 2004). Given this contextualization of tourism, then, the time and cost critique of slow travel is subject to scrutiny, as most tourists do not actually travel far. Most short-haul international slow travel is actually fast relative to air travel (e.g. European inter-city high-speed trains can easily outperform air travel, given significantly reduced check-in times).

There is also the question of the need to travel. Much tourism travel to exotic locations is desired but not necessarily needed. Stradling and Anable (2008) suggest three forces that drive leisure travel decisions: obligations, opportunities and inclinations. While obligations to see friends and family might generate some distant tourism travel (Urry, 2007), much is driven by the opportunity afforded through reduced time and cost, and tourist inclination. This inclination to travel could be redirected to less distant destinations, providing a greater opportunity to engage with slow travel. While a shift of this kind might be negative for some remote destinations relying on distant visitors, many destinations would adjust to markets closer to home.

The criticism of the cost of slow travel is also debatable. The reduced cost of air travel has opened up travel on a global scale to many more people. However, long-haul air travel is, on a global scale, still the preserve of the wealthy few. In a European context (and in other global contexts) the arrival of low-cost airlines has generated additional demand due to falling costs of flights (Civil Aviation Authority, 2006; Dennis, 2007). It is currently the case that flights can cost correspondingly less than rail travel; however, flights are rarely advertised, or sold, at their true cost, additional fees being levied for check-in, luggage and airport taxes. Therefore, it is sometimes difficult for consumers to make accurate cost comparisons. A similar criticism has been made of the real cost of car travel, with high annual running costs hidden on a day-to-day basis (van Goeverden, 2007). At the same time, one of a variety of institutional barriers to slow travel (see Chapter 3) is the difficulty of searching for and booking the cheapest train fares, given the complicated fare systems (van Goeverden, 2007). There is a pervasive discourse that flights are cheap and the alternatives expensive. Such a discourse is a strong behavioural barrier, as many people fail to explore the alternatives to flying, having made the assumption that it is the quickest and cheapest option.

Long-distance train travel can also seem much less competitive than car travel where there is more than one person travelling (Larsen et al, 2006; van Goeverden, 2009), especially as hidden car ownership costs are often excluded. Where a car is available to a household, it reduces train use by between 55 per cent for single travellers and 70 per cent for several people travelling together (van Goeverden, 2009). However, in Europe, the Thalys high-speed train has successfully created a new market, mainly due to shorter travel times and increasing the train's status (van Goeverden, 2007). On long-distance routes, speed is important but frequency is not. However, van Goeverden's analysis (2007) suggests the need to make transfers and seat reservations reduces the train's competitiveness.

Slow travel has much potential as both a climate change mitigation strategy (to reduce the impact of tourism on climate change) and as an adaptation strategy (to help tourism meet increasing obligations to reduce its carbon footprint). However, slow travel is one of many forms of tourism, and while it brings low-carbon benefits, the extent of this depends on whether it is a substitute for less environmentally sensitive travel on holiday or whether slow travel is additional, generated travel. Current tourism predictions are for growth. While it would be positive if much of this growth were accommodated by slow travel, this essentially allows for further tourism consumption, as opposed to the reduced overall consumption that is required to meet climate change obligations. Exploratory research shows that some slow travellers are also air travellers in other contexts, and there is evidence that people are balancing air travel against good environmental behaviour in other spheres of their life (Dickinson et al, 2010a; Randles and Mander, 2009a). Therefore, an annual slow travel holiday might be used as justification for higher consumption elsewhere. Stoll-Kleemann et al (2001) refer to this as the 'metaphor of displaced commitment', and elsewhere it has been described as the rebound effect (Bows et al, 2009b). Such an outcome is not optimal for low-carbon tourism.

Car travel

When exploring the origin of the term 'slow travel', it was apparent that some explanations include car travel (Macquarie Dictionary, 2009; Mintel, 2009b). Some of the features described in this ingredients list readily apply to car travel, such as constraints on distance travelled, stopping off en-route and engagement with places and travel being an integral part of the tourist experience. On the other hand, car travel fails to meet the key criterion of being low-carbon travel. However, as Table 4.2 indicates, given high car loadings and fuel-efficient models, the carbon footprint of car travel is considerably reduced. With five people in a car, especially if it is a fuel-efficient model, then the carbon footprint per passenger km approximates to that of train travel. Therefore, is there a case for including car travel as a slow travel mode? An examination of statistics on car occupancy suggests not. UK figures indicate average car occupancy for holidays/day trips of 2.0, while it is 1.7 for leisure trips generally (National Travel Survey, 2006). In the Netherlands, leisure trip occupancy is 2.2 people (Peeters et al, 2007). In both countries, car occupancy is higher for tourism/leisure trips than commuting, but at these occupancy levels the car is unlikely to achieve comparable carbon footprints to public transport.

At this point it is worth discussing a particular case of car travel, that of hitchhiking. Hitchhiking, once a widely used form of travel for young people, has largely gone out of fashion in developed countries in recent years, due to safety fears of both hitchhikers and car drivers. Hitchhiking was at one point institutionalized in Poland through a very successful voucher system, and in parts of the developing world, with poorly developed private transport systems and stretched public transport, hitchhiking is still a way of life. For instance, on the Caribbean island of Dominica, there is an expectation that car drivers will stop to pick up people waiting at bus stops. Hitchhiking can improve car loadings and reduce the carbon footprint for the car driver;

however, much depends on whether hitchhiking substitutes for an additional car trip, a bus journey, train ride or no trip at all. Hitchhiking also brings additional benefits to both car driver and hitchhiker. The driver passes the time more quickly and stays more alert through conversation, and the hitchhiker, while also gaining social benefits, may access local knowledge and gain an insider's view of the place visited. Ultimately then, hitchhiking on a widespread basis has the potential to improve the carbon footprint of car travel and to open up experiential travel opportunities. However, given contemporary western society's negative view of hitchhiking, it is unlikely that it will play a significant role in slow travel frameworks in the near future without a major institutional change in practice.

While some explanations of slow travel have not explicitly excluded car travel (Mintel, 2009b), we are critical of its inclusion for a variety of reasons. First, as explained above, while cars used for tourism or leisure purposes have higher vehicle loadings, they are rarely full. Second, the 'average' car is not the most fuel-efficient. Increasingly, car manufacturers are producing more fuel-efficient models, but new models take several years to gain a large share of the market. In the meantime, older, less fuel-efficient models dominate. Also, when travelling for a holiday, families will typically take a larger vehicle, if more than one car is available to the household, which again implies that tourism travel by car will fail to achieve high fuel efficiency. Therefore, while on paper, car travel, with high loadings, might appear to be able to achieve a similar CO_2 emission per passenger km to a train, in practice this is very rarely achieved in a tourism scenario.

There are also other factors with car use that might influence the overall carbon footprint of a holiday. Visitors who travel to a destination by cars are inclined to use it more when they are there. Dickinson and Robbins (2007) found that the car was used for 40 per cent of trips less than 1km within a UK rural destination area. Such trips can easily be walked. At the same time, cars generate longer trips within destination areas, compared to other modes (Dickinson and Robbins, 2007). Cars also facilitate detours on the journey to destinations. Such detours could, however, be considered a feature of slow travel. However, as a whole, car travel tends to facilitate unnecessary, additional, longer trips. As such, there is potential for a much greater carbon footprint than might be assumed.

Beyond factors relating to carbon, car-based tourism is widely identified as a problem in destination areas (Andereck et al, 2005; King et al, 1993; Lindberg and Johnson, 1997; Liu et al, 1987; McCool and Martin, 1994; Perdue et al, 1990). It is, for example, responsible for significant congestion on routes to popular tourism regions such as the Alps in central Europe (Dickinson et al, 2004; Shailes et al, 2001). These issues were covered in Chapter 2. It is, however, worth recalling that while cars can facilitate access to relatively remote areas, off the beaten track, there are significant environmental, social and economic consequences.

Taken as a whole, there are therefore three reasons to exclude car use from slow travel. First, car travel is inconsistent with the low-carbon travel scenario that is a fundamental outcome of slow travel. Second, car travel can extend the distance travelled, which is again inconsistent with the low-carbon travel scenario and also with engaging with the immediate destination area. Third, there are a variety of other negative environmental and social impacts of car-based travel.

The camper van also needs to be considered at this point. Camper vans are larger than the average car and generally have comparatively poor fuel consumption. Driven by consumer demand in some quarters, camper van manufacturers have tried to address this, and LPG vehicles are now available that are more efficient. Even so, given the relative size and weight of the vehicles, due to equipment carried, they are much less fuel-efficient than cars relative to the number of people travelling and have a higher carbon footprint per passenger km. Camper vans do, however, provide travel and destination experiences, the travel is at a relatively slow pace, and some members of the camper van community see engagement with the natural environment as a core component and have strong environmental concerns. During exploratory research by Dickinson (2008), several potential participants came forward to discuss their slow travel experiences using a camper van. Therefore, within the camper van community, some consider it as slow travel. However, there is much against the inclusion of camper van tourism within slow travel. First, the same considerations for the car apply to camper van tourism and it is likely to have an even higher carbon footprint. Second, while there are opportunities for travel and destination experiences, camper van travellers can exist in isolation to the place visited. It is possible for people to camp at the roadside, either legally or illegally, depending on the country visited, and to bring food and other essentials from home. Thus camper van travellers may engage little with place and add little to the local economy. As for car travel, due to these considerations, camper van tourism is excluded from slow travel.

Water-based travel

There are several ambiguities surrounding the inclusion of various forms of water-based travel within the conceptual framework of slow travel. A UN report suggests emissions from shipping have been significantly underestimated, and the industry reportedly generates three times more emissions than previously thought, accounting for around 4.5 per cent of emissions globally (Vidal, 2008). High-speed vessels such as hydrofoils, which are often used in tourism, have particularly high emissions. At the other extreme, canoes and yachts, when under sail, are carbon neutral. A more detailed analysis of water-based travel is included in Chapter 9. We conclude that some water-based travel can be aligned with slow travel, although much depends on how it is integrated with other modes of transport. However, cruise shipping has been specifically excluded from slow travel, due to high carbon impacts and low potential for engagement with destinations on the journey.

The market for slow travel

Two recent marketing research studies suggest slow travel is a growth area (Euromonitor International, 2007; Mintel, 2009b), but who are slow travellers and how might they be profiled? It is still early days in the emergence of slow travel as a market. There is a need to better understand this distinct new form of tourism. However, here is an initial exploratory analysis, based on the limited amount of existing data available. Segmentation may well be possible using the following perspectives.

By environmental concern

The level of environmental concern expressed by slow travellers and the continuum from 'hard' to 'soft' slow travel has been discussed earlier. This continuum alludes to dark greens and light greens, and it is obvious that slow travel is attractive to those with environmental concerns and who are keen to minimize their carbon footprint. However, slow travel is not the preserve of this group alone; it also appeals to others. While environmental concern is a core ingredient, and low-carbon tourism a fundamental outcome, this may not be the key motivational driver for some. Thus the concept is applicable much more widely than to individuals with environmental concerns.

By travel mode

Low-carbon travel modes are integral to slow travel, and data are readily available from national and international statistics on mode of transport (see, for example, Table 4.4). There are also studies that have attempted to segment the population on the basis of mobility styles (Anable, 2005; Lanzendorf, 2000). Anable (2005, p70) segmented day-trippers into potential mode switchers using cluster analysis, which identified six groups:

- Malcontented motorists: perceive high level of constraints with public transport despite feeling unhappy with car travel and believing they have a moral responsibility to change behaviour.
- Complacent car addicts: admit use of alternatives is possible, but do not feel any moral imperative or other incentive to alter car use.
- Aspiring environmentalists: have reduced car use for environmental and health reasons, but appreciate practical advantages of car travel and therefore reluctant to give up ownership.
- Diehard drivers: fond of cars and car travel, believe in right to drive cheaply and freely, have negative feelings towards all other modes.

Table 4.4 *UK international arrivals and departures by mode with global comparison for 2008*

Mode	International arrivals to the UK Number (thousands)	%	UK resident departures Number (thousands)	%	Global inbound tourism %
Air	24,024	75	56,041	85	52
Sea	4495	14	8145	12	6
Tunnel/rail	3369	11	4825	7	3
Road					39

Adapted from Office for National Statistics, 2009; and UNWTO, 2009c

- Car-less crusaders: sacrificed car for environmental reasons and have positive evaluation of other modes.
- Reluctant riders: involuntary users of public transport due to health or financial reasons, would prefer car.

Some studies also indicate that air and train travellers are different markets 'which would imply that modal choice precedes destination choice' (van Goeverden, 2007, p116). Exploratory work on slow travel suggests air travellers choose destinations and then work out how to get there, while slow travellers tend to choose their mode and then decide where they go (Dickinson et al, 2010a).

There are also studies that analyse modal choice on the basis of various geographical characteristics. For instance, van Goeverden (2009) found that the larger the origin or destination city (the effect was strongest for destination city), the higher the probability of train use. The effect was also enhanced where people are travelling to the core of an urban area rather than the periphery. On this basis, the market for train use could be profiled on home and destination cities.

By distance

In earlier discussion, slow travel was associated with short- to mid-haul rather than long-haul travel. For instance, Peeters (2007) suggests trains and coaches are viable over distances shorter than 1500–2000km. Slow travel is therefore particularly suited to travel within Europe, North America, South America and South East Asia, but poorly suited to travel from, for example, Europe to South East Asia, even though this is feasible overland by slow travel modes. For most slow travellers, distance is likely to be limited by time and comfort concerns to intra-regional travel up to 2000km. For a few travellers/backpackers, longer inter-continental trips are feasible, such as the OZ bus service from London to Australia, initiated in 2007 (Sethi, 2007). As the concept develops, there are likely to be regions that are keen, or more able, to embrace the idea. In this respect, it is envisaged that slow travel locations might emerge to serve slow travellers, willing to develop the experiential elements of slow travel. Given its allegiance with the slow food movement and its well-developed public transport network, Italy would be an obvious contender. Such a move presupposes a need to investigate further how people engage with localities and make decisions about components of a holiday in order to engage with low-carbon modes of tourism.

By the tourist transport experience

Page (1999, p8) first noted that there was a gap in the research regarding the intrinsic experience that might exist in tourism transport:

> The mode of transport tourists choose can often form an integral part of their journeys and experience, a feature often neglected in the existing research on tourism.

Lumsdon and Page (2004) set out a theoretical continuum of tourism transport where they suggested that some forms of transport have a low intrinsic value as a tourism experience, whereas others have a high intrinsic value. Thus, they indicated that the taxi, urban bus and metro would offer low intrinsic value, and cycling or walking holidays a high intrinsic value. The authors admitted that each and every case would have to be subject to exception; some taxi rides can have high intrinsic value if the driver acts as a guide and the environment is engaging. Nevertheless, the continuum offered a rule of thumb as to the experiential nature of each mode in tourism. Rhoden and Lumsdon's (2006) typology of transport-tourist experience sought to modify this approach. Their co-axial framework of 'transport for tourism' to 'transport as tourism' and 'passive' to 'active' involvement could provide a framework to analyse slow travel in future. Ongoing work by Lumsdon and McGrath in relation to recreational buses (Institute of Transport and Tourism, 2008) indicates that the nature of the transport experience is the destination, and involves both passivity and activity.

By tour operator involvement

Work by Dickinson et al (2010b) suggests independent travel is an important feature of current slow travel. They suggest:

> the slow travel identity describes independent people who are tough, resilient, good at beating the odds and coping with problems. They also seek more novel experiences that involve meeting new people and socialising.

Therefore, slow travellers might be segmented into categories of independent and organized tourism. Plog's model of tourism destination preference, which describes allocentric tourists who are keen to explore new places, might have some application here (Plog, 1974). However, it is evident that the above description might best be described as the specialist market and Dickinson et al (2010b) suggest there is an emerging role for tour operators to control less desirable aspects of slow travel in order to cultivate a participant market segment, where some elements such as overnight accommodation are made more certain. With the exception of coach tours, train tours and guided cycling holidays, much contemporary slow travel is independently organized. While there is a general move to more independent travel arrangements, there is considerable scope to facilitate easier booking of slow travel.

How slow travel differs from mainstream tourism

Our vision of slow travel is a 'new tourism' model driven by different consumer motivations and a business model more focused on integral and extended travel experiences, rather than rapid, and vapid, short duration trips involving increased distances. In order to set out the difference it is necessary to explore current business models and practices and analyse what is really meant by a holiday to contextualize slow travel.

Current business models and practices

As tourism has evolved, at least in a western context, the sector has seen fairly consistent growth (UNWTO, 2009c), although there is no certainty that this growth will continue as predicted. As populations have become wealthier, tourist numbers have grown and tourists have increasingly been able to take holidays more often, and further away, as travel costs have decreased. The result has been a trend for regular short trips at an increasing distance. However, in the context of climate change, the trend is going in the wrong direction (Ceron and Dubois, 2007). Short, regular and longer-distance trips result in greater GHG emissions. Instead, it is argued that we should be moving to longer stays, closer to home, and holidays less often (Ceron and Dubois, 2007).

Travel has also become increasingly easy to organize through web-based intermediaries. This has led to a rise in independently organized travel where travel and accommodation can be booked with ease. Here there is a potential opportunity for slow travel as individuals can more easily select a preferred travel option, whereas previously most holidays were sold as packages. Packages, however, still have an important role to play in the sector and typical resort holiday options are difficult to organize other than through a travel agent intermediary who tend to package holidays together with a flight. It can be difficult to break this pattern. Travel agents offer choice but a commercialized choice, essentially variations of the same thing. Tourism has also created structures that implicitly link destinations with source markets via air travel. It can be difficult to organize an alternative or it can be impossible to separate out components.

Urry (2007, p278), in his discussion of the car, refers to 'locked-in institutional processes', where the car and everyday life have become so interlinked that it can be hard to participate in mainstream social life without a car. In tourism, too, tourists are often locked in to flights, airport transfers, car hire or self drive. While there are other options available, these often require extended decision-making processes to organize and there are societal norms that direct tourists to travel in particular ways. As Randles and Mander (2009a) conclude, it is unlikely that tourists' decision-making will shift to any extent while the industry is locked in to air travel.

In this respect tourism is driven by powerful actors, notably the airline industry, which sets up linkages that are difficult to break. There is a mutual relationship between air travel and tourism to the extent that much air travel growth would not have been possible without tourism (Høyer, 2000). In this way patterns of tourism become institutionalized. It is also to the advantage of the tourism sector if consumers are locked-in to particular patterns. For instance, frequent flyer programmes aim to promote loyalty to a particular airline and habitual behaviour. Not only does this perpetuate air travel, but it may also indirectly result in longer flights as customers use air miles accumulated with a particular airline rather than the airline with the most direct flight (Gössling and Nilsson, 2009). Gössling and Peeters (2007) also show how the aviation industry endeavours to create a positive image of air travel and its environmental performance through careful presentation of science and 'facts'.

Through carefully managed presentation of information the aviation industry may seek to manipulate the public's understanding of climate change impacts so as to reduce potential defection from air travel to other modes.

There is also a continued discussion regarding mass tourism. In many contexts mass tourism may be the most suitable development option (Sharpley, 2009). There are also many examples where mass tourism is much more sustainable than holidays that are marketed as sustainable tourism such as eco-tourism. For instance, traditional UK domestic tourism to holiday centres (e.g. Center Parcs and Butlins) has fewer negative impacts than an eco-tourism trip to the Galapagos Islands (see, for example, Wheeller, 1993). A typical holiday to Butlins would once have been facilitated by rail travel for the vast majority of tourists, and there is considerable scope for slow travel to be reintegrated with some forms of mass tourism.

In order to develop slow travel there is a need for sector engagement to address the structures that currently prevent slow travel options and to create new slow travel options (Dickinson et al, 2010a). This requires destinations to reconsider their source markets and opt for those closer in spatial terms. At the same time, tour operators need to reconsider the tourism transport interface and re-package opportunities to visit near-to-home destinations by slow modes. This may require western society as a whole to reconsider the nature of a holiday.

What is a holiday?

The idea of the holiday has evolved over time. The term originated in the middle ages where many holidays were linked to the church's holy days and fitted into the rhythm of the working countryside, and included wakes, feasts, fairs and markets (Torkildsen, 1999). In this way a holiday was integrated with patterns of work. However, the origins are even older, going back further than the Egyptians, Greeks and Romans, as an idea associated with privilege and the elite. Prior to the Second World War, few in Europe were able to afford holidays away from home. However, since then, a rise in disposable income and paid leave has enabled the majority of the population the opportunity to take holidays away from home on at least some occasions. Subsequently, tourism evolved as a global industry, the concept, in part defined as spending leisure time away from home. Today the idea of a holiday is institutionalized as a trip away from home, often packaged as a week or weekend. However, while tourism implies travel away from home – a holiday can be at home – travel other than very short distances is not inevitable. It is also assumed, in the current era, that travel is positive and desirable, so much so that much status is attached to taking holidays and travelling to particular destinations (Gnoth, 1997). Within a short space of time western society has become accustomed to travel, and it is the norm to take an annual holiday appropriate to your status in society.

Yet this ability to travel is not necessarily a positive thing. Chapter 2 explored both environmental impacts and other less than positive outcomes for host communities. There may also be less personal benefits than people might think. It is possible to substitute the perceived personal benefits of travel with other benefits to be gained by staying at home. Earlier in this chapter, staycation was discussed. This is a contemporary term used to describe the substitution of a holiday for a stay at home or near to home and emerged as a positive discourse during the global recession. The benefits of a holiday can be substituted. By staying at home people save money and can engage with leisure in the locality. While there may not be the 'pull' factors that draw people to tourism destinations, the 'push' factors of tourism (see, for example, Crompton, 1979; Dann, 1977; Pizam, Neumann and Reichel, 1979), such as flexibility, freedom, independence, away from constraints of daily life, relaxation and engagement with people and place, can all be found through holidaying at home. In addition, travel is avoided, with all its financial and personal costs. Travel is not easy. There is much media reporting of delays at airports and congestion on roads. Travel is not always pleasant. Indeed, it is hard to imagine something less desired than being crammed into a confined space of an aircraft, unable to leave for several hours, yet this is how many holidays begin and end. However, tourism is so ingrained in the western psyche that the desire to travel is rarely questioned.

Slow travel does, of course, involve travel and there is no doubt that there are equally likely to be hardships through slow travel just as for air and car travel. However, with slow travel the journey is not just a necessary evil. Travel is part of the experience. To briefly recap, slow travel refers to:

- the whole holiday experience with travel as an integral element
- low-carbon tourism as an outcome
- the use of foot, cycle, train, coach and bus travel, but not air and car travel
- the importance of the locality travelled through and as a destination
- the importance of the experience of travel both to and around the destination
- the importance of taking time
- an expression of environmental concern
- longer stays
- less distance.

At present, slow travel is a niche activity; however, there is much scope for it to develop, and the theory of diffusion of innovation could well be applied in this context at both a market and institutional level (Rogers, 1995). As the imperative of climate change impacts on societies, and the contribution of tourism to the problem becomes more widely recognized, it is likely that more consumers will seek to change their ways. This demand will require modified sectoral structures to pave the way for a new tourism, based on a low-carbon future. The first step will be for upstream behavioural change in the institutions that are currently powerful. Slow travel is likely to emerge as a consequence of changed supply chains and changing consumer patterns of behaviour. These dimensions are explored in Chapter 10.

5
Train Tourism

The term 'train tourism' is used throughout this book to describe the fusion between travelling to a destination by rail and the train *as* the destination. The latter includes railway stations, some grand and reflecting times past, and others no more than a platform alongside the tracks in remote countryside. Railway architecture, features such as tunnels and gradients, systems of operation, as well as the near environs through which the train passes, are integral to the travel experience. There is no clear dividing line between the role of the train as a mover of people over spatial distances and as a provider of a tourist experience for those who perceive it as such. For some, the journey is the thing. For others, the train is at least a pleasant enabler, and at best, an integral part of a holiday which makes it distinctive or partially different from everyday life.

Thus, in a similar manner to the way in which scholars have identified the attraction associated with certain places, slow travellers are drawn to railways in an affective manner (Thrift, 2004). The train, more than other forms of transport, illustrates the importance of the travel experience coupled with potential environmental benefits of low-carbon tourism. The green credentials of the train have been highlighted to good effect by several railway operating companies. However, as Givoni et al (2008) note, whilst trains are, in general, less polluting than the car and aeroplane, the generalization depends on the type of train and the sources used to generate electricity to power the traction. For example, the Austrian train operator OBB calculates that 86 per cent of its energy is from hydropower and the Swiss operator SBB estimates that it uses 40 per cent from nuclear power plants, both of which, it is argued, are low-carbon or carbon-neutral sources.

The scale of the railway network remains extensive in some countries, such as Belgium, the Netherlands or UK, whereas in other countries there are no railways at all, as in Iceland or Yemen. If there is, in the foreseeable future, a major shift of demand from aircraft to trains, it is conceivable that some of these countries will invest in developing a network; others will simply remain at a disadvantage in relation to their neighbours. The length of track is not always a measure of passenger use. For example, the USA network is 150,000 miles (240,000km) in length, but this is predominantly used for freight. Passenger km are a more accurate indicator. By this measure, India, Japan and China are the major railway nations of the world, but, as elsewhere, most of these journeys are for utility rather than tourism. For example, there are 396 billion passenger km travelled in Japan every year. This is closely followed by China, with nearly 364 billion passenger km per annum (International Union of Railways, 2009). Figures for passenger km travelled on railway networks across the world are summarized in Table 5.1.

There are some definitional matters to consider. A train uses fixed tracks; conventional systems operate using locomotives or multiple units and carriages with flanged wheels, although monorail technologies have been adopted in Japan and the USA. There is no firm categorization of trains used for tourism purposes. Given that most trains are provided to serve a multitude of markets and for multi-purposes (commuting, business and leisure travel), it is useful to note some of the more generic differences.

A basic categorization of passenger train services can be made in accordance with their main purpose. Thus, many train services are referred to as metro or underground networks, serving commuters and residents making everyday trips into town. There are also suburban trains which focus on commuter traffic, such as S-bahn trains in Germany, or Japanese commuter trains where assistance is given to cram as many people onto the train as feasible. They cater for large flows of passengers into and out of cities and this might, as with metro systems, include tourists exploring destinations by public transport. A second categorization is the intercity train which travels between the major urban areas of a country, or between neighbouring countries as is common across Europe. Some intercity trains are also overnight services offering sleeping compartments, such as City Night Line in Europe.

Trains can also be defined by distance and speed. Short-distance trains are those which operate between destinations less than 100km apart and would be mainly urban and suburban services, or local trains stopping at all or most stations. Quality and frequency of service are important determinants of demand for this type of service (Asensio, 2000). For the most part they are not designed for the tourist, but are used to gain access to accommodation or

Table 5.1 *Passengers carried on the world's railway networks in 2008*

	Passenger km (millions)
Africa	62,167
Americas	13,974
Asia and Oceania	1,950,936
Europe (including EU25)	659,689
World	2,686,766

Source: Railway Statistics Synopsis, 2008; International Union of Railway, 2009

visitor attractions in some cases. These also include rural trains, which often do have a strong tourist appeal because they offer great scenic and sometimes nostalgic value, including features such as old railway buildings and signage.

In some countries, local or regional partnerships have been formed to develop such lines. In the UK, for example, local community rail partnerships estimate that they increase the footfall of such local railway lines by 7 per cent over a three-year period, of which 26 per cent is estimated to be a shift from car use. Many of the promotional schemes developed by such community partnerships are targeted at staying and day visitors (Transport Regeneration Limited, 2009). However, there are concerns about the viability of some rural routes (Haywood, 2007), due to decreasing passenger numbers and hence insufficient revenue to maintain infrastructure. Loss of rural routes is significant for the future of slow travel; once routes are cut, infrastructure is very costly to reinstate at a later date.

Long-distance trains are those which operate beyond 100km, and are more likely to involve a range of 1000km in accordance with a previous EU study, Dateline. However, long-distance trains can cover more than 1500km, and often the journey time is greater than one day. These trains sometimes convey sleeping cars as well as conventional carriages. They may pass through several countries, although in the USA or Australia they offer, in the main, long-distance travel within the country of origin only. According to van Goeverden (2009), 59 per cent of passengers in long-distance trains in Europe are tourists staying one or more nights at a given destination. The long-distance train is likely to pass through scenic landscapes but stop only at the principal stations serving major populations, where onward connections can be made.

An increasing number of long-distance trains are also high-speed trains which travel at speeds of over 150mph (250km per hour), such as the 'Bullet' trains in Japan (Shinkansen), TGV in France, ICE trains in Germany, AVE trains in Spain, and in North America, the Boston to Washington service. These trains have the capability to reduce travel times and, it is argued, without significantly increasing environmental impacts (Blum, Gerceck and Viegas, 1992). This is subject to some discussion (see below). However, most long-distance trains, such as the Trans-Siberian railway at 9010km or the Indian Pacific between Sydney and Perth in Australia, are not high speed; the latter takes three days to cover the 4340km.

There is also a distinction to be made between scheduled railway services, which offer scenic views and are marketed to the 'walk on' tourist trade, and those designed specifically for tourist markets. The latter tend to be pre-booked and operate, in effect, as charter trains, by tour operators where tickets are sold on the internet or through agencies well in advance of the departure date. For example, there are regular steam-hauled charters on the Darjeeling Himalayan train in India which are sold by specialist travel agents throughout the world. Other categorizations include funicular railways operating between low and high quarters of towns or to nearby hills (such as in Braga, Portugal, Naples in Italy and the Unesco World Heritage site in Valparaiso, Chile) and similarly cog railways in mountainous areas, such as

Pikes Peak in Colorado or the mountain railways of Switzerland. There are also heritage railways such as the Grand Canyon railway in Arizona or the Santa Fe Southern Railways in the USA (Halsall, 1992), which offer services hauled by vintage locomotives and carriages; these appeal to those seeking nostalgia and authenticity. With regard to the Grand Canyon railway, this has been developed with accommodation and attractions so as to offer inclusive packages (Davis and Morais, 2004). The Harz Mountain Railway in Germany, for example, is one of Europe's most popular steam-hauled railways, essentially packaged for a wide tourist market.

The association between railways and tourism dates back to the 1840s in England, and the ensuing decades of the 19th century and early years of the 20th century elsewhere in the world. Railways used iconography to good effect in relation to tourism destinations, and attracted a new breed of travel writers keen to make their way by train. The importance is highlighted by McCauley when preparing a visitor guide to Spain (1949, p156):

> *The frontier is within a few miles of Velez Rubio, a town on a gentle hill, on which most guidebooks are silent because the railway does not run that way, and the guidebook writers find it troublesome to leave trains.*

However, the fortunes of the railways were lost as rapidly as they emerged. By the middle decades of the 20th century (earlier in North America), passenger numbers began to decline in the wake of competition from the private motor car and to a lesser extent from bus and coach companies. The decline of the railway as a form of transport and consequently as a way of travel for the tourist has been more or less relentless in many countries throughout the latter part of the 20th century. This is particularly the case in central and south east Europe during the 1990s (Howkins, 2005).

There is, however, incremental evidence to indicate that a rail revival is happening, not only in Europe, but also in other parts of the world. This is being driven principally by an increasing market, albeit from a small base in some countries, such as in the USA, although the economic recession in 2008 has retarded this trend. The structure and ownership of railways differs from country to country. In the main, there has been a move towards privatization across the world, and especially in Europe, although public sector involvement remains a defining characteristic of many passenger railway systems. This has involved some restructuring, deregulation and partial privatization (Jensen, 1998; Thompson, 2003). There are institutional barriers to market development, such as a lack of adherence to market pricing to compete with air travel on short to medium distances. There have been improvements to information and ticketing systems, but these have been slow to develop (Mintel, 2008b).

The renaissance of the train is also a consequence of investment in new lines, or a renewal of old ones and improvements to some long-distance services (European Commission, 2001). This has been strengthened by the introduction of high-speed trains to more peripheral areas across Europe

(Blum et al, 1992). The obsession of early railway companies to push ahead for faster journey times between cities has now returned. It is a major dimension of railway strategies in order to win back markets from airlines and the private car. However, the use of slower routes and rural branches could suffer from a lack of investment. These routes are equally the province of leisure and tourism travel, if not more so, as they facilitate slow travel to good effect. Therein lies an opportunity for train operators to stimulate demand through targeted marketing activities.

In most parts of the world, railways were built to transport freight; the carriage of passengers was secondary to this main purpose, at least, in the early decades of the 19th century. However, the market for passenger travel soon developed and the railways responded accordingly by the introduction of passenger (or mixed passenger/freight) trains between major cities, firstly in Europe, but then in other parts of the world (Vaughan, 1997). By the 20th century, the railways had improved passenger timetables to offer an extensive range of destinations and introduced long-distance overnight trains in Europe and in North America, where, by the 1920s, there were over 10,000 Pullman sleeping cars in operation. These trains met the needs of the emerging middle classes who were demanding opportunities to travel for leisure purposes as well as business traffic. In some countries trains became accessible to the poor, but conditions of travel, firstly in open wagons and then in very basic carriages, were limited in the extreme (Thrift, 1996). In many developing countries, train travel for the poor still remains uncomfortable at best, and often cramped to the point of serious discomfort.

Nevertheless, the railways of the world have played an important role in destination development. In his seminal work of 1885, *The Alpine Journey*, Simmel argued that the railways stimulated mass tourism in the Alps:

> *Destinations which were previously only accessible by remote walks can now be reached by railways, which are appearing at an ever increasing rate. Railways have been built where gradients are too steep for roads to be constructed, as in Muerren or Wanger Alps. The railway line up the Eiger appears to have been finalized, and the same number of climbers who have scaled the difficult peak can now be brought up in a single day by rail. (Simmel et al, 1997, p219)*

It was not, as some scholars have intimated, a rapid development of mass tourism, but rather an incremental approach. Nor was it simply about transport to a destination; railway companies were proactive in encouraging access from their railheads to town centres using horse carriage, buses, rickshaws and eventually motorized taxis. They also built large-scale hotels, or worked in partnership with other entrepreneurs to provide accommodation near to railway terminals. Elsewhere, smaller hotels and hostels grew up around almost every railway station in the world, as this new form of transport replaced the horse-drawn transport that had operated between town squares and inns across Europe and North America. Railways were also important in the opening-up of frontier destinations for tourism in many countries, including India and across North America.

There are examples of railways seeking to develop tourist markets in a more direct way. In Japan, for example, railway companies helped to develop purpose-built bathing resorts and amusement parks (Ogara, 1998). In Australia, the famous Zig Zag railway in the Blue Mountains of New South Wales attracted thousands of passengers annually who travelled to enjoy the scenery (Lee, 2009). The railway company established a public reserve in the 1880s to preserve the surrounding wilderness in order to seduce a growing tourist trade seeking access to nature; this included a platform for passengers to alight upon, to observe the wildlife. Large tracts of wildlife areas were retained near to Canadian railways for similar reasons. The growth of tourism, for many destinations, was therefore inextricably linked with the arrival of the railway, and they were, in many cases, major partners in early stages of development.

The railway sector was also important in the promotion of events. In the 1840s trains were being hired by emergent tourism businesses, such as American Express and Thomas Cook, to operate excursions to major events, ranging from public executions to the Great Exhibition in London in 1851 (Simmons, 1984). Cook and some of his contemporaries recognized the integral nature of the journey to the customer, and prepared travel guides (known in Cook's case as *The Tourist's Guide*). Thus, in many countries, railways have been closely associated with tourism development, and 170 years later this is still occurring but to a lesser extent. Examples of the new wave are the Beijing to Lhasa railway (Su and Wall, 2009) or the railway links developed between Denmark and Sweden in recent years. However, in many parts of the world, including Europe, the railway network is still shrinking.

Motivation for train travel

Whether tourists choose the train mainly for pro-environmental reasons, or simply to maximize personal enjoyment, these motivational factors are likely to be intertwined with more commonly acknowledged reasons. One of the most important factors is that train travel offers great views across landscapes (Löfgren, 2000). The feeling of vastness is aptly described by the travel writer Theroux (1979, p70) in *The Old Patagonian Express, By Train through the Americas*:

> *I could see for fifty miles or more across the blue-green plain. Because the train kept switching back and forth on the hillside, the view continually altered, from this plain to a range of hills and to fertile valleys with tall feathery trees in columns along the banks of frothing rivers, and occasionally a deep gorge of vertical granite slabs. The trees were eucalyptus, as African as the view, which was an enormity of stone and space.*

Other studies refer to the view from the train as a significant motivational factor. Mintel (2009b), for example, refers to the importance of the view in relation to travel across Europe. Su and Wall (2009) also make reference to this as a key motivation for travel between Beijing and Lhasa in Tibet on the Tibetan railway, which operates at an altitude of over 4000 metres for most of the route. Su and Wall (2009, p650) investigated the 'relative importance of the train journey itself' in relation to the pull factors of the destination of Tibet. Most of the tourists on board were educated Chinese people making a first visit to Tibet. The quantitative survey highlighted the motivational elements. Of importance were natural scenery, followed by an interest in Tibetan culture. A third factor reported in the study related to the opening of the new railway. The most important motivational factor was an opportunity to enjoy the views from the train, and secondly a gradual adaptation to the altitude of the destination.

There are some market indicators which highlight the growing importance of travel mode. Market research undertaken by the South West Tourism Board in the UK indicates, for example, that 10 per cent of their visitors actively choose a 'green holiday', one which includes the use of local trains and buses (Transport Regeneration Limited, 2009). However, environmental factors are often washed out by other core indicators, including travel cost, duration, price, comfort, convenience and avoidance of stress (González-Savignat, 2004; Gutierrez, 2001). These factors feature more strongly in long-distance travel. There is also a balance, as travel can be troublesome and the train is no exception (Boorstin, 1987). For example, *El Trên de las Nubes* provides endless spectacular scenery en route from Salta to the Andean mountains in Argentina, but there are medical risks, associated with altitude sickness, as the train reaches 4200 metres above sea level. In contrast, riding an Amtrak train from Seattle to California across the Cascade Mountains and the Glacier National Park offers comfort and relaxation, as the train makes its way through a succession of outstanding landscapes. Both offer scenic reward, but one is potentially more painful than the other.

The travel experience

Travel by train is embedded in the cultural complexity of many societies (Freeman, 2002; Schivelbusch, 1977). It provides an opportunity to engage with people and surroundings, whilst travelling over medium to long distances (Adler, 1989). There are several elements which characterize the train travel experience of the tourist. The assumption is that the passenger is a co-producer of train travel, and the interactions, mood and environment of the journey are integral parts of the process (Anderson, 2004). Watts (2008, p211) describes this as 'how passengers craft their travel time'. The strands of the travel experience are summarized as follows:

- sharing a journey with others
- using the travel time to enhance the journey (i.e. observation of people and landscapes)
- relaxation and having time for oneself.

Urry (2007) refers to the railways as the most important provider of the public realm in the 19th century. The large open spaces designed by the railway companies soon became places where people could meet in public, in the environs of the railway station, on the platform and on trains. He also refers to the ways in which railways encouraged people to travel together as groups of friends and relatives (or alternatively engaging with strangers who shared the journey). This is referred to as 'sociabilities' and associated with it is an etiquette and performance expected of fellow passengers.

Train travel, however, does not always bring a positive experience. Concerns about travelling, in a confined space, with strangers have been a long-standing barrier to use of public transport, and the literature is replete with the perils of travel (see, for example, Stevenson, 2009; Stradling et al, 2007). Nevertheless, sharing the company of others on the journey and at railway stations is considered to be part of the travel experience. This involves initiation of conversation in some instances. Halsall (2001, p159) comments:

> *Individuals create a particular sense of place through their contributions as actors in the atmosphere and scene inside the train.*

For example, backpackers exchange discourses about their past journeys and shared opinions about destinations and travel modes recently explored. On the other hand, avoidance of encounters, by use of diversionary tactics such as reading or other activities, is also part of the process (Goffman, 1963). For some, the art of slow travel is a solitary existence (Danziger, 1999).

There are also encounters with front-line staff on the railway system, those whose role is to provide information, assurance and to ensure the welfare of passengers. This aims to reduce some of the stress of travel; for example, when a train is late on arrival or delayed en route. Some travel writers argue that the positive–negative tensions which exist when travelling are also important (Dann, 1992; Reynolds and Letherby, 2005).

Urry (1990) refers to the tourist gaze, in which tourists frame views of passing scenery and people on their travels. In the context of railways he comments on the association of movement, and the gaze in the following way:

> *The nineteenth century development of the railway was momentous in the development of the mobilised gaze. From the railway carriage the landscape came to be viewed as a swiftly passing series of framed panorama, a 'panoramic perception' rather than something to be lingered over, sketched or painted or in any way captured. (Urry, 2001, p40)*

Larsen (2001) reconfigures this as the tourist glance, the opportunity to gain snapshots of the places through which the train passes. Foster (2005, p6) comments that train travellers:

... with time on their hands and loosened from themselves, they fell to communing with the evanescent terrain sliding past the window, open to what it told them.

A study undertaken by Lyons et al (2007) in the UK noted that passengers travelling for leisure purposes devoted twice as much time than other passengers to gazing. Travel time is also used for other activities while on the move, such as the time to think (de Botton, 2002; Lyons and Urry, 2005). Just over half of passengers in the same study spent some of their time reading for leisure, and over one-third indicated that they spent a third of their time in this activity.

The train has long been associated with the traveller and, through the words of travel writers, with slow travel. The traveller is engaged in the process of the journey which, in turn, might also lead to a change in the self, as summarized by Galani-Moutafi (2000, p205):

> *It can be argued that the journey has the potential to facilitate a re-setting of boundaries as the traveling self, besides moving from one place to another, may embark in additional journeying practice, having constantly to negotiate between the familiar and the unknown between a here, a there and an elsewhere ...*

There is a market that seeks train travel as a destination in its own right, sometimes as a form of nostalgia and with connotations of romanticism. Dann (1994, p779) draws on our cultural links with the past in noting that 'travel by train is not simply a journey between two points. It is full of symbolism which evokes a glorious, aristocratic and adventurous past.' His work on nostalgia and tourism focuses on travel material designed to promote railways in the early 1990s in several parts of the world. He used content analysis to explore the image and the positioning of messages on the part of the railway companies. He concludes that there are five interrelated themes wrapped around the concept of nostalgia and railways:

1   imperialism, which refers to railway-building and colonialism of previous times
2   class distinction, by elevating oneself to first-class travel for a journey; for example, a trip on the Orient Express
3   travail by rail, which alludes to the effort required to make some train journeys; they are not always enjoyable
4   childhood remembrances of travel and playing trains
5   gazing at passing scenery and townscapes.

His work, however, focused very much on train services designed for affluent tourists, such as the Orient Express in Europe, the Ghan train in Australia (Adelaide to Darwin), or heritage trains which accentuate the luxury of travel for the wealthy in past decades. It is therefore questionable whether this motivation for rail travel, as an exploration of the past, is applicable to the slow traveller using trains not designed specifically for tourism purposes.

Graburn (1983, p6) refers to the functionality of Japanese trains as a way of getting from one destination to another, but comments that there still remains, in Japanese culture, 'a very important emotional attachment to trains and what they represent: separations, journeys, nostalgic yearnings for the far-away, etcetera'. There is also a representation of the past in relation to train terminals and railway structures and architecture alongside the lines, which remain as icons of the past to be absorbed by the contemporary passenger (Urry and Sheller, 2004). This is only one part of the train travel gaze; the casual observation of the proximate environs of the railway corridor is an essential ingredient of slow travel. As the urban environment gives way to country landscapes, the train offers glimpses of the areas through which it passes: industrial wastelands, graffiti and rubbish, railway gardens and tight streetscapes of older neighbourhoods leading eventually to the leafier suburban peripheries. Even in the late evening, the shades of light and darkness bring to the imagination different perceptions of places foregone and those which lie ahead.

In sum, the travel experience is not one of passive consumption; the expectation of the journey is tempered by the dextrous crafting of time in the creation of a temporal and spatial identity (Dann, 1999). The slow traveller is very much the co-producer of the train journey, which is in many respects a performance involving other people, buildings and movement; it is multi-faceted and multi-sensory (see, for example, Watts, 2009).

Environmental issues

There is some debate whether or not fast trains can be included in the overall compass of slow travel. The discussion has focused around the introduction of high-speed trains which, it is argued, belie the principles of slow travel. Travel at speeds of 200km per hour over ground is seen as a contradiction with the overall underpinning philosophy of slowness. On the other hand, most trains still operate in a relatively slow manner and over relatively short distances; these definitely fall into the categorization of slow travel.

The argument for inclusion of high-speed trains is more problematic, as the rationale and design of such services are to reduce the duration of travel time between destinations. Nevertheless, the fundamental elements and perceived benefits of slow travel remain apposite for high-speed trains as to their slower counterparts within the network. They still operate from city termini, replete in heritage, social congregation and accessible to residents and tourists. They pass through landscapes at speeds while still allowing perusal through windows, and which reflect the diversity of each region. This is perhaps one of the main objections; the landscapes and urban features are less discernible at high speeds. The slow traveller, however, shares the journey with others; they still co-produce the journey alongside fellow passengers and service delivery staff on board.

Another more substantive issue is whether or not trains live up to their reputation for having a relatively low environmental impact. This is especially relevant to the overall conceptual framework of slow travel, which encompasses environmental consciousness. At least one author has questioned the extent to which railways are more effective in lowering environmental impacts in relation to the car, given the introduction of new technology in automobile production and use (Smith, 2003). There is also a need to factor in infrastructure (build and maintenance), but such issues appertain to the main forms of motorized transport. The comparison between rail and air travel has also come into increasing focus, although much of the literature has focused on modal substitution in relation to journey times, rather than relative energy use and emissions (Jani , 2003; Lopéz-Pita, 2003). The railway sector has responded by seeking to reduce its energy consumption and carbon emissions, whilst at the same time increasing its load factor. Comparisons with other forms of transport such as air and car travel are favourable if load factors are high. Givoni et al (2008, p79), for example, concluded:

> *HST operation results in lower CO_2 emission levels (Givoni, 2007). Although CO_2 emissions from aircraft operation are sensitive to assumptions about the flight they are at least five times greater than emissions from the HST.*

There is no definitive figure regarding CO_2 emissions generated by all railway services operating in the world. Obviously much depends on the type of engine and fuel used. Gössling, Hall and Weaver (2009) report that rail and bus/coach account for 34 per cent of all tourist trips, and, as a consequence, cause 13 per cent of all CO_2 emissions from the tourism sector. In contrast, trips involving long-haul air transport are 2.7 per cent of all tourist journeys, but account for 17 per cent of emissions. This comparative assessment is a recurring theme in the literature. It is argued that travel by train generates per trip 3–10 times less CO_2 emissions than road transport by private car or by air transport (Mintel, 2008b). For example, in the EU, railways account for about 7 per cent of the market for travel and contribute below 2 per cent of the total transport sector emissions (Community of European Railways and Infrastructure Companies and International Union of Railways, 2008). Train travel in New Zealand has an energy intensity of 1.44 megajoules per passenger km, in contrast to domestic air travel of 2.75 (Becken et al, 2003a).

The speed of trains may also have implications for emissions; both in terms of energy used, but also the capacity to travel further within a given time frame. However, high-speed trains employ new technology, which is increasingly energy efficient and are typically electric; thus their emissions depend on the means of electricity generation. If renewable energy is used, then GHG emissions are low. In France, where a large share of electricity is generated by nuclear power, the TGV has a small carbon footprint. Given that a high percentage of railways are electrified and hence offer potential for renewable energy use, it has been argued that trains will replace short- to medium-distance flights across the world.

A study undertaken by Stettler (2009), regarding the impact of mobility on tourism by the year 2030, reported the findings of a survey of 1608 experts drawn from transport, tourism, technology, society and science backgrounds.

The experts were asked to assess whether certain aspects of travel for tourism purposes would become less or more important in 2030. The author concluded that environmental motivations would be far more important than now, and especially in relation to the use of the train as a replacement for air travel. There will, however, be increasing consumer expectations regarding flexibility of travel, but equally regarding the environmental consequence of each mode. The implication for railways is that they will have to become more integrated with other forms of access at destinations and within the tourism sector to meet the needs of future travellers. The German train company Deutsche Bahn, for example, established a project, Fahrtziel Nature (Destination Nature), to encourage travel by rail and bus, and to walk and cycle, to national parks, nature reserves, and so on in 2001. There are now 18 locations served in this way.

The other dimension to consider is the impact of climatic change and changing weather on railway operation and networks, which is currently limited, across Europe (Koetse and Rietveld, 2009). However, rising sea levels and increasing frequency of extreme weather events have greater potential to disrupt rail transport. For example, flash floods and landslides have damaged railways across many parts of Latin America in recent decades. Given the lack of capital to rebuild railways, these events have effectively jeopardized future development of many lines which remain in disuse. For example, the Tacuarembó to Rivera route in Uruguay, which has potential to attract tourist markets, has not been reinstated since falling into disuse. Similarly, extensive sections of railway in Africa are inoperable as a result of damage inflicted in civil wars or by extreme weather events. These are unlikely to be reopened in the foreseeable future.

The following case study, Tread Lightly, explores the environmental considerations of Eurostar operating high-speed train services from London to Paris and Brussels. This illustrates the carbon efficiency of train travel and the mechanisms being employed by the railway industry to improve efficiency in coming years. Train travel is often synonymous with slow travel, and assuming that railway companies retain or even develop entire networks, and not just high-speed lines, the future looks good.

Case study: Tread Lightly

Whilst the train is considered less environmentally damaging than the car and aeroplane, there are still opportunities to make this form of transport more sustainable (Russell, 2007). This case study aims to illustrate ways in which companies can lessen their environmental impact. It focuses on the train operating company, Eurostar, which operates services from London to Brussels and Paris and to the Alps. These services operate on a frequent daily basis, with the exception of the routes to the Alps and Avignon which are weekly, seasonal services.

In 2006, the company commissioned a study of CO_2 emissions per passenger on Eurostar in comparison to air travel to the cities which it serves. The report undertaken by an environmental consultancy, Paul Watkiss Associates, concluded that air travel accounted for ten times more CO_2 emissions. The findings from the study and other internal discussions led to the launch of the Tread Lightly campaign in April 2007, which was directed principally at staff but also to customers. Over 40 staff have agreed to become environmental champions and there is a small team to drive forward the main tasks associated with the campaign.

The campaign has three main thrusts:

- to cut CO_2 emissions by 25 per cent (this was raised to 35 per cent in November 2007) by the year 2012
- to roll out a ten-point action plan to reduce other environmental impacts
- to offset other carbon emissions.

The results to date show considerable progression of the initiative. In 2009, the company reported that it had achieved a 31 per cent reduction in CO_2 emissions. This is attributable to a number of factors, such as greener sources of energy for traction, and optional train speed regulation to achieve efficiency. This is verified by a report undertaken by an environmental consultancy (Paul Watkiss Associates, 2009). The Watkiss report also confirmed the results of the comparison between air and rail travel between London, Avignon, Bourg St Maurice, Brussels, Marne-La-Vallée-Chessy and Paris. It updated statistical calculations using energy logging train data to provide an accurate measurement. Two calculations were made. The first used average supply mix of electricity (as recommended by the UK government) and the other used supplier mix data (as recommended by the French authorities). Table 5.2 provides a useful comparison; the average mix data indicates six to nine times less impact of emissions in relation to air travel to the same destinations, whereas the supplier mix calculation, which is more realistic, gives a reduced emissions factor of ten.

Table 5.2 *Eurostar: Emissions per passenger journey (single trip)*

Route	2006	*kg of CO_2 per passenger single trip* 2007	2008	2010
		Average Mix Calculation		
London–Paris	6.8	7.0	6.3	6.2
London–Marne La Vallée	6.9	6.8	5.6	5.3
London–Brussels	10.5	10.6	8.4	7.6
London–Avignon	12.9	15.7	8.6	9.2
London–Bourg St Maurice	12.5	11.1	9.3	9.4
		Supplier Mix Calculation		
London–Paris	4.5	4.6	3.3	3.3
London–Marne La Vallée	4.6	4.5	2.9	2.8
London–Brussels	6.6	6.5	4.1	3.9
London–Avignon	11.1	13.1	6.5	6.8
London–Bourg St Maurice	10.8	9.3	7.0	6.9

Source: adapted from Paul Watkiss Associates, 2009

The Ten Point Plan (Eurostar, 2009), which seeks to reduce environmental impact (half-lighting, only ceiling lights rather than window lights, sourcing energy from less carbon-intensive sources, maximizing passenger numbers to reduce their individual footprint), has also been rolled out by the company, but it is too early yet to report impacts. However, the company has changed its procurement policy to source local produce, fair-trade beverages, etc., for on-board consumption and has introduced a reduce, reuse and recycle policy at terminals, depots and offices.

The third strand of the initiative relates to offsetting outstanding carbon emissions relating to the Eurostar operation. The idea is to reduce emissions indirectly through some form of market for carbon credits, thus seeking to make the entire travel journey carbon neutral. Eurostar reports that it has done this by buying carbon credits (through two verified schemes) in selected projects across China and India. The offsetting projects are mainly hydro-electric schemes and wind farms, but also include using waste to power a jute factory in India and a biomass plant. To date, the company has procured 85,000 carbon credits to offset 85,000 tonnes of CO_2 equivalent (Eurostar, 2009).

There is a substantial critique of offsetting in the tourism literature which has rendered this dimension of Tread Lightly more subject to critical appraisal than the other elements (see Broderick, 2009). It is questioned whether offsetting is a suitable mitigation approach, however worthy the projects of investment might be. Two fundamental arguments (among a host of others) are that such schemes do not encourage travel reduction using high-carbon modes, nor do they add pressure to change institutional structures or ways of doing business based on high-carbon intensity. In the case of Eurostar these arguments do not appear valid, given that it is achieving modal shift from air and it has addressed its business with a 'reduction, reuse and recycling' approach in a coherent manner. Thus, it has been endorsed by non-governmental organizations, critical of tourism and transport, as a progressive approach to carbon reduction.

There are a number of lessons to be learnt from this mini-case study, although it is based on limited data. Eurostar has taken a holistic approach to carbon reduction and environmental impact. It has embraced all aspects of the business and has instituted monitoring and customer feedback throughout the scheme to date. Above all else, it has proven the environmental efficiency of high-speed train travel (even though the trains are 17 years old) in relation to air travel.

6
Walking and Tourism

In 1979, the Policy Studies Institute published a book, *Walking is Transport*, in which the authors concluded that there was scant research on the subject. Hence, 'it is not surprising that walking has been poorly represented in transport policy, and that the consequences for those in society whose travel needs are frequently met on foot are not brought to light' (Hillman and Whalley, 1979, p1). Thirty years on, there still remains a dearth of information on walking, either as a form of transport or as a tourism pursuit. Yet, in terms of volume and frequency, walking is by far the most important form of transport in the world, and that also applies to travel at the destination. It also has the lowest environmental footprint. In reality, it is the form of travel that is consistently undervalued by transport and tourism planners in terms of planning, funding and provision. This is certainly the case when compared to providing for the car.

Walking is also the gel that makes so many of the faster modes of travel accessible. This is especially the case in the context of the integration of buses, ferries, trams and trains, but also in relation to accessing attractions and destinations. Walking is defined as a trip, made on foot, that involves physical activity, usually to access places for a wide variety of reasons. These include walking trips to work, education, for personal reasons, shopping or simply just to enjoy recreation. The walking trip can be made alone or with others, and the pace is relatively slow at 3–5km per hour. This makes it the ultimate form of travel for the slow traveller, as it enables close contact with landscapes and streetscapes. It allows proximate contact with people going about their daily business and enables absorption of the atmosphere that pervades each locality.

The history of early human development refers to nomadic survival; it involved walking long distances periodically, and constant sourcing of food for daily subsistence. Humans also became good long-distance runners so as to be able to hunt animals or to flee from danger (Amato, 2004). In subsequent centuries, the development of settlements across the world was usually planned such that the distance to be walked from a dwelling to the centre was of no more than 30 minutes' duration; life revolved around the historic core of each of the ancient cities. It is generally the oldest quarters of towns that the tourist seeks to explore in the 21st century; some of these places are now overwhelmed by the level of visitation at peak times (Marchetti, 1994; Orbaşli, 2000). The exploration of place remains invariably on foot, as these ancient thoroughfares were not designed for motorized transport and most city governments have restricted access accordingly (English Historic Town Forum, 1994). This is the very essence of slow travel; exploring at a pace where sensory perception is attuned to the familiar, and in some cases unfamiliar, sights, sounds and smells.

The literature covering the subject of walking is limited, and in the main there is an adherence to the concept of utility; walking to work, to school or to the shops. These trips are considered to be relatively more important in everyday life, in comparison to walking to recreational areas or for recreation (Cerin et al, 2007). This has been a long-standing rule of thumb in transport planning. Utility trips and time-savings are crucial to the economy; travel for enjoyment is not. In recent years, however, a widened interest in the concept of quality of life has led to a more detailed discussion of the nature of all trips. In many cases even utility trips include elements of escapism or pleasure that have been referred to as excess travel (Mokhtarian and Saloman, 2001). There has also been a renewed interest in the design of open spaces in urban areas where walking can flourish (CABE, 2009). In addition, health has been a major focus of research studies during the past decade. The health factor is currently high on the agenda. This is not surprising, given an alarming rise of cardio-vascular diseases, diabetes type 2, strokes and high levels of obesity, associated with sedentary living across the world population (Guthold et al, 2008; Siegel et al, 1995; World Health Organization, 2004). Interventions to encourage increased levels of physical activity have, at their core, walking for health (Cavill and Bauman, 2004; Lumsdon and Mitchell, 1999).

Walking is ubiquitous, and thus an option for most people, regardless of age, wealth, ethnicity or gender, although there are differences in the amount of walking undertaken if analysed by these variables. For example, women are less likely to walk for recreation on their own, the main reason being related to perceived levels of personal security (Cloke et al, 1996; Foster et al, 2004). Walking, nevertheless, is one of the most effective ways to increase physical activity in order to improve the welfare of the population, but the tourism sector is not heavily engaged in these interventions (Eves et al, 2003). There is, however, something of a renaissance of wellness (mental and physical) as a core motivation for tourist activity:

> the scarce research available suggest that those who avail them-
> selves of the plethora of experiences available appear to be not
> only on a touristic journey of physical movement, but also on a
> journey towards greater self-awareness and contentment. (Smith
> and Kelly, 2006, p1)

What emerges from the walking literature is the enormous potential for health tourism and health interventions, to encourage behavioural change and improved walking environments. There is a synergy with the development of slow travel opportunities at destinations that is illustrated by some destinations, such as the Alpine Pearls project, where walking is featured as a major attraction.

Most recreational walking takes place at the urban destination, however. This is an under-developed topic of analysis; it tends to be overshadowed by the omnipresence in the literature of issues such as vulnerable road users, retail planning and similar topics that revolve around the highway and cars. Some interest exists in destination management with regard to the encouragement of walking at events, attractions and the circulation of pedestrian flows through the retail zones, but it is generally not reported in the literature. There is a major challenge for destinations that have invested in highway networks in order to improve access, seemingly at the expense of walking provision. Given a likely low-carbon future, there will be increasing governmental pressure to encourage walking and cycling for short trips.

The academic discussion in relation to leisure and tourism tends to focus on walking for pleasure in the countryside, sometimes referred to as rambling or hiking (Kay, 1999). Edensor (2000) argues that the tradition of walking for pleasure stems from a period when walking was romanticized by those who walked on their Grand Tour or when partaking in other travels abroad. The romantic notion distinguished walking for pleasure from the walking undertaken by the majority of the population in their everyday lives. A smaller segment of the leisure walking market features trekking or tramping (a term from New Zealand) in remote wilderness areas. Here, walkers cover longer distances per day, follow more demanding schedules and sometimes include rough camping.

The dual purpose of walking, utility and pleasure, is every bit as relevant in contemporary society. Walking out of necessity rather than choice is the stark reality for the vast majority of the population in developing countries. For example, walking barefoot to the fields, with heavy tools and children, is a major daily burden for women in many developing countries (IFAD, 2001). Walking in the urban areas of developing countries (which accounts for between 50 and 90 per cent of all urban trips) is a hazardous pursuit, given the lack of investment in pedestrian areas and the rapid increase of cars in limited highway space (I-ce, 2000). This contrasts greatly with the imagery projected in relation to walking holidays located in developing countries. These holidays are set in the mountains or forests, often associated with access to nature and with walkers accompanied by a guide, native porters, quality garments and a back-up vehicle.

Walking is defined in relation to tourism as a trip made on foot, where the choice of mode is made principally for recreation, relaxation or as a form of geotourism to exploit places where earth-science features can be explored (Pralong, 2007). In some cases, walking is simply a means to physical exertion. It represents a conflation of physical exercise (Roberson and Babic, 2009), social engagement (Kyle and Chirk 2004) and access to different places of interest (Markwell et al, 2004). There is, however, no set formula as to the balance between these elements; for example, walking is sometimes chosen as a solitary rather than gregarious pursuit (Michaels, 2000; Wylie, 2005).

There is another dimension to consider; walking allows access to other forms of transport as part of an overall journey (from originating to receiving destination, or whilst at the destination). This may also include elements of recreation or access, but the main reason would be travel to a destination or places within it; equally a visit to an attraction is to enjoy the appeal of the place, rather than a walk per se. There is a difference, and this, of course, applies to other means of travel. The mix between utility and pleasure is variable and dependent on place and form. Nor would we argue that utility walking is devoid of pleasure; in almost all circumstances it is known to be a release from everyday pressures of work and home (Sallis et al, 2004).

Walking is a key element of a holiday or day excursion in the following circumstances:

- when walking at a destination is to enjoy physical exercise and in some cases is event-related, such as walking for charity or challenge
- when walking is to enjoy the company of society in open spaces; one reference to this is the term 'flânerie'
- when walking is the preferred mode to access historic or scenic landscapes, where the combination of movement associated with the tourist gaze is the motivating reason
- when walking is the main pursuit; it is a form of activity that allows passage at a slow pace through a destination area.

There are other definitional considerations worthy of discussion. In a similar manner to cycle tourism, walking can be categorized as a form of casual or serious leisure, depending on the level of engagement and intensity (Stebbins, 2007). With regard to the latter, the tourist is likely to have in their possession outdoor clothing, maps and guidebooks and other specialist equipment. This form of walking can be subdivided as follows:

- Walking holidays, where the main motive is to walk for most days and for most of the day between accommodation points, either on a linear or circular route. The main purpose of the holiday is to explore a destination on foot.
- Holiday walking, where walking is one of several activities undertaken by the tourist; walking may account for one or two days of a stay.
- Day walking, where the main purpose is to explore a destination area. The main activity of the day visit will be walking, although it might include stops for refreshment, sightseeing or to visit an attraction.

There is also a further subdivision: independent walking and guided walking, which take place in either an urban, rural or mixed context. The walking tourism holiday market includes many long-standing companies, such as Ramblers Worldwide Holidays in the UK, TrekAmerica in USA or Inntravel across Europe, which offer guided walks in many parts of the world. The self-guided market is very important in tourism, and the internet has opened a wide range of opportunities and an associated form of communal branding. For example, Wikiloc (originally focused on Catalunya, in Spain, but now available worldwide) is an open access website where people can submit their favourite trails from anywhere in the world. These can be downloaded by others and followed using global positioning satellites (Wikiloc, 2009). There may be reservations about the way in which the site could encourage high carbon-intensity travel, but equally it also offers local trails for walkers and cyclists. This site also illustrates the importance of maps and the way in which we are using them in different ways than hitherto:

> *The world of maps, the world which we map, is changing as new appreciations of the emotional are represented ... and as new technologies change our interactions with maps through Global Positioning Satellites and Satellite Navigation. (Esbester, 2008, p42)*

Another example of community branding is Car Free Walks (2009), located in the UK. This encourages people to submit instructions to a website that features car-free linear walks using buses or trains. In both cases, the websites reflect the emergence of on-line, non-commercial viral marketing, where a shared consciousness about walking and the environment is emerging. Thus consumers are beginning to determine their own community brands in relation to walking (see Muniz and O'Guinn, 2001).

The scale and scope of walking as part of the tourism realm at destinations is difficult to assess. In the USA, for example, an estimated 35 billion walking trips per annum are made, of which 20 per cent are for recreation and exercise, including those on holiday. There is no recorded subdivision of the data. An additional 3 per cent are primarily trips to walk the dog (Agrawal and Schimek, 2007). This is supported by other data, from which it can be inferred that recreational trips (i.e. local trips made by residents and tourists for pleasure) are likely to account for at least 20 per cent of all walking trips in any given country. In relation to walking tourism (rather than all recreational trips), there are no firm figures, only estimates. In the UK, it is estimated that there are 527 million walking tourism trips, contributing £6 billion to local tourism economies per annum (Christie and Matthews, 2003). However, the collection of data on specific walking routes and the needs of those accessing the countryside are limited (Cope et al, 1999).

There is an apparent paradox. Walking as transport is in decline, as 'society is structured to encourage the motor car and not walking' (Darker et al, 2007, p2172), yet walking for recreation and tourism is, at worst, static, and some studies indicate growth (Lane, 1999). The explanation lies partly in major changes in land-use patterns, and partly in changing values towards mobility. At the same time, walking in western cultures is seen as a release from the hectic pace of life, especially in relation to near-to-home recreation and enjoyment of holidays. Walking, as an essential ingredient of slow travel, is explained in relation to the travel experience.

The experience of walking

Why is walking appropriate for slow travel? In a similar manner to many other forms of leisure and tourism, the extent to which a person engages with walking for pleasure is rooted in cultural preferences and, to an extent, is structurally determined (Stebbins, 2005). The demand for recreational walking is determined, as with other recreational pursuits, principally by tastes and availability of disposable income and time (Curry and Ravenscroft, 2001). There are also constraints that deter people from walking, and Ravenscroft (2004) argues that these are more likely to be at an intrapersonal level (e.g. anxieties about walking or attitudes of reference groups) or interpersonal level (such as not having others to walk with), rather than a lack of physical provision of facilities (Williams, 1995). The motivation for walking focuses on a small number of factors, many of which relate to the wider conceptual framework of the tourist experience (Ryan, 2000; 2002). These might include relaxation or escapism. It might also be the actual movement of walking as a way of enjoying natural environments. Rodaway (1994) suggests that it is through use of the senses that we define a particular place when walking (Rodaway, 1994). Edensor (2000, p84) describes the emotional benefits as follows:

> *The walker is able to resolve transformation by recovering past value, experiencing continuity, embracing change, while acquiring poetic sensibilities.*

At one level, it seems almost banal to say that walking is an integral part of a travel experience. However, the relationship between the tourist and consumption of the destination, according to Solnit (2001, p5), is about walking, 'in which the mind, the body and the world are aligned'. Equally, walking is a form of tourist performance at the destination. The tourist glance is determined at a pace that allows absorption of the sights, sounds and smells of each particular locality. In the context of the urban area, the crucial elements are the open spaces and thoroughfares, where there is time to saunter, to depict a past evoked by the proximate architecture and to assimilate the ways of life (albeit it superficially) in each quarter. Yet, the literature on tourist mobility, including walking trips within destinations, is limited (Haldrup, 2004; McKercher and Lau, 2008).

A few studies have reported the importance of improved streetscapes to the encouragement of walking as transport and for leisure (Cao et al, 2009; Giles-Corti and Donovan, 2002). Millinog and Schechtner (2006) suggest that there are three interrelated elements determining the quality of a walking route: physical (route capacity, protection from inclement weather), psychological (attractiveness of surroundings) and mental (route clues, way-finding and reliable landmarks to guide and assure). The tourist expectation is related to the extent to which these elements are present. Walking allows insights into the contemporary nature of the locality, often referred to as a sense of place. For some researchers, open spaces are an integral part of the tourism product. For example, Orbaşli and Shaw (2004, p93) comments that 'the *spaces in between* and the *links* between key attractions or activity nodes are the unifying elements of urban tourism'.

Most tourists explore urban spaces independently and in small groups of friends or family. Some will do this without any knowledge or interest. They will simply be seeking a walk that yields some feelings about a place. Others will come prepared, using maps, guidebooks and on-street interpretation. In some destinations walking trails have been formalized so that tourists can follow pre-described routes, embellished with interpretation and designed so as to offer a unique experience of the city. Lumsdon and Spence (2004) studied the design of 33 urban trails in the UK and concluded that most were initiated by local government, but that the design rarely took into account the needs of the users, residents or businesses in the vicinity. At many destinations there are also guided tours where guides tell the story of the resort or locality to tourists. Tour guides use their 'ability to manipulate unruly elements of the city into a coherent narrative' (Wynne, 2008, p5). Wynne undertook 78 interviews of tour guides and joined 58 tours to describe the world of the tour guide, concluding that they are important culture carriers who are able to condense history and culture into a palatable form for the tourist.

In terms of Cittáslow, walking is an essential part of the tourist experience. The slow traveller is invited to take time to explore each street, to piece together the history of the place (Markwell et al, 2004). They are also enticed to enjoy the hospitality of those providing locally produced food and beverages, a key point that is promoted by most slow travel blogs on the internet. The concept is expressed by travel writer Amanda Kendle (2008, p1):

> *My experience is always that a place feels, how can I put it, more* exhilarating, *when you see it on foot. There's something about getting around entirely under your own steam, no doubt combined with a healthy dose of exercise-produced endorphins, that leaves a special memory of a trip where you spent a lot of time walking.*

Lumsdon (2004) provides an insight into the way in which destinations and tour operators fail to market their cities as places to explore on foot. He undertook a study of hundreds of images presented in brochures of European and North American cities, using semiotic analysis, and concluded:

> *the collected images presented by the tour operators serve a purpose to define and signal heritage to the market. In terms of David Engwicht, this appears to be a very narrow mapping of a mental landscape ... There's clearly a need for the tourism marketer to re-appraise the heritage appeal, which is essentially static and to seek opportunities to differentiate by depicting*

cities as places of diversity rather than monumental enclaves ...
That means paying more attention to the 'spaces in-between'
where much of the social life takes place for both the visitor and
resident alike. (Lumsdon, 2004, p6)

The 'spaces in-between' are the spaces where walking takes place, where the feel of a place can be ascertained through the range of senses available to us.

There is, however, a different experience reported by those walking in the countryside, where the spatial geography, landscape form, smells and sights contrast with the more compact urban historic core or tourist enclave (Bianchini and Schwengel, 1991). Kay and Moxham (1996) argue that walking, in this context, is a means to complex ends and a range of experiences. Chettri et al (2007), for example, reported a quantitative research exercise with a group of walkers in the Grampian Mountains in Australia to determine the nature, magnitude and characteristics of walkers' experiences in natural landscapes. They concluded that the feelings of the 25 respondents in the study could be distilled into the following four principal components:

- desirable experience such as great views
- impelling experience (i.e. the urge to see, move on, to explore more)
- apprehensive experience reflecting trepidation about the walk
- social interaction experience that reflects divergent feelings, such as being crowded to sense of isolation.

The authors also noted that the experience is about 'knowing, believing and recognising. These processes are cognitive and are based on background knowledge, learning and reasoning capabilities of individuals' (Chettri et al, 2007, p33). Lee and Mouldon (2006) report that those walking for recreation (in contrast to utility walkers) like hills, so as to improve physical activity and to enjoy views, and these factors have also been identified by Anderson (2005) and Roberson and Babic (2009). Several researchers, however, have noted that the experience is not a static, nor a homogenous one, it is a sequential flow of relaxation interspersed with high points of excitement during periods of immersion. This may happen part-way through the walking tour or on a walking route (Borrie and Roggenback, 2001; Hull et al, 1992). In contrast, Den Breejen (2007) reports the findings of a qualitative study on a long-distance trail in Scotland, where the 25 respondents noted a high point towards or at the end of their walk. The level of satisfaction or derived benefit has been referred to by Wallace (1993) as the walking cure, reflecting an improved physical and psychological state as a result of the physical activity, space and time for reflection.

There is a small literature on the segmentation of walkers. Kay and Moxham (1996) divide the market into four segments: walkers who like to saunter on shorter distance walks; ramblers who stride out more; trekkers who walk longer distances at a pace, otherwise known as trail walkers; and back packers who seek challenging and esoteric walks. The English Tourist Board (1999) commissioned qualitative research on profiles of people seeking to take walking holidays. The Board concluded that a person's life cycle had a significant bearing on choice of walking holiday. It noted five segments: young socializers, young leisure adventurers, family actives, leisure explorers and older organized. In each case the market segments were seeking a slightly different experience. For example, young socializers were looking for an active walking experience that brings a sense of achievement, with a preference for a wild and open landscape. The older organized segment also wanted real walks, where they could get their boots dirty, but at the same time were looking for a variety of terrains – scenery remains a key factor. They wanted a challenge, but not the longer, more strenuous walks preferred by young socializers. Similar studies undertaken by tourist authorities in other countries show that there is a differentiation in the market for walking.

Trails

One of the major innovations in walking tourism in recent decades has been the introduction of the themed trail. Lane (1999, p1) argues that the early trails (1930s to 1980) were the product of individuals seeking 'utopian creations designed to allow access across the countryside as a grand political gesture'. They were for hardened walkers seeking a challenge. One of the earliest was the Appalachian Trail in the USA, developed in 1921 by Ben Mackaye to encourage freedom and hope in an industrial society:

> *But only mature industrial societies self-consciously create primitive footpaths of 400 kilometres in length whose sole function is to produce the opportunity to walk the distance of the trail. (Burch, 1979)*

This walking trail, 2175 miles in length, sought to encourage 'primitive' outdoor education. It is still managed by a voluntary organization known as the Appalachian Trail Conservancy (see the mini case study presented later in the chapter).

The second phase of development noted by Lane was the period from 1980 to 2000, when many shorter distance trails were created as tourist or recreational ventures, where casual walking could be encouraged. These trails have been developed by partnerships following an economic rationale and often have associated themes such as the Trail of Tears relating to the story of indigenous Americans, or at a more local level the Dismal Swamp Canal Trail in North Carolina or the Sacramento Trail in California.

There is a rich literature on these younger multi-use trails and how they can be used to good effect by tourists, either walking, cycling or horse riding (Hugo, 1999). A common format has been for a group of stakeholders, usually a combination from the public and voluntary sector, to pioneer a trail, and then subsequently to find ways to manage it (Morrow, 2005). Trails that include urban sections are often designed as multi-use and multi-purpose trails. They are categorized as greenways that include walking or cycling facilities, or both. Lindsey (1999, p145) defines a greenway as:

Linear open spaces along natural or artificial corridors such as riverfronts, streams, ridgelines, abandoned rail-road rights of ways, canals or scenic roads.

The European Greenways Association (Otero, 2001) has already developed an extensive network of greenways across parts of Europe, but especially in Belgium and France (known as Voies Vertes) and Spain (Vias Verdes), where thousands of miles of old railway routes have been converted to traffic-free routes catering for non-motorized journeys. There is also extensive provision of such routes, more commonly referred to as rail trails, across North America and to a lesser extent in Australasia.

However, as discussed by Lane (1999), the term 'trail' has wider connotations, in that it also refers to longer distance routes designed principally for one or more of these groups – walkers, cyclists, horse riders and cross-country skiers in winter months. On the other hand, the term trail is also used to describe the more recent short routes of six to ten miles in length, usually linking urban areas to their rural periphery. In either case, walking trails are attractive to slow travellers who seek more formalized access to the countryside, aided by interpretation and other services, as well as those wishing to seek the challenge of a longer trek such as the less formal trails of Latin America.

There has been a gradual commodification of trails, with a concomitant increase of spatial development of the corridor(s) through which they pass. For example, Murray and Graham (1997) report the changing nature of the market and supply sectors in relation to the old pilgrimage routes to Santiago de Compostela in Spain. As a result there are tensions between those who would have liked the routes to have remained as simple pilgrim ways for those on a spiritual journey, rather than upgraded trails for a greater number of tourists. There is, therefore, a continued tension between those in favour of retaining authenticity of the pilgrimage routes and those who want the economic gain of contemporary tourism development. Similar reports have been made with regard to the Andean Trail to Machu Picchu in Peru. A study undertaken by Kyoto University reported that these ancient Inca ruins (World Heritage Site) are under threat from the continued demand of 300,000 visitors per annum. The concern was that there would be a landslide, given that the western slope is moving downwards by up to 1cm per month (Hadfield, 2001). Subsequently, in 2010, a period of heavy rain triggered landslides in the region, temporarily trapping tourists.

Health and environment

The relationship between walking, health and tourism is a strong one. The pilgrimage was by far the most important walking pursuit prior to the 18th century, and it remains important to this day. Some pilgrimages attract overwhelming numbers of participants, such as the Kumbh Mela Festival in 2001, located on the banks of the River Ganges in India, estimated to have attracted over 30 million people. The walking element of the pilgrimage is still considered to be part of the spiritual experience, requiring a commitment and level of physical energy in order to arrive.

The step-change came in the development of resorts in the 18th and 19th centuries. These places featured walking as a major pursuit; walking was a social pastime, an opportunity to meet and greet others in the social circuit that required grand promenades, parks and other open spaces where society could meet. In some cases, this provision was strongly associated with health. The great spa resorts of Europe such as Bath, Baden Baden, Karlovy Vary and Sofia were all designed to encourage walking along the grand terraces. It was part of the process in the world of preventative and curative treatments.

Today, walking has become less fashionable in everyday life in most developed countries, which is a major issue for those seeking to improve standards of health by encouraging, for example, brisk walking for 30 minutes (Cavill et al, 2006). Nordic walking (fast walking with sticks) has become more fashionable across Europe, Japan and North America as a result of a renewed interest in walking for health (Shove and Pantzar, 2005). However, contemporary incursions into brisk walking are for the minority. In reality, the lack of activity has reached epidemic proportions. In the USA, for example, an analysis of the US Department of Transportation National Household Travel Survey in 2001 highlighted that 84 per cent of citizens reported not making any walking trips in the previous week. The authors concluded that 'most Americans do not walk at all' (2007, p548). It is estimated that 60 per cent of men and 70 per cent of females in the UK are insufficiently physically active to maintain their health (Metz, 2009). Therefore, there is a renewed interest in encouraging walking for utility and leisure, but principally to encourage walking and cycling as an aid to preventative health care (Wang et al, 2004).

Walking tourism generates some environmental impacts. There are conflicts of use and damage to ecological cycles if demand for walking routes is not managed. Bestard and Font (2009) discuss this in relation to forests in Mallorca, suggesting that visitation rates exceed carrying capacity by a factor of between four and eight times the appropriate level. Walking routes or trails have been studied in detail to explore the changes to adjoining vegetation and wildlife. For example, Hill and Pickering (2007) noted that the recreational use of trails does have an impact on proximate native species, some of which are rare, and encourages the spread of non-native weeds. They argue for more ecology-related monitoring studies. The message is reinforced by Hawes et al (2006). They undertook trials to establish how recreational impacts might be monitored in the Tasmanian Wilderness World Heritage Park, arguing that monitoring should be an essential component of trail management. Aiken and Leigh (1986) undertook a survey of walking routes in the rain forests and noted that the problem of erosion and formation of gullies on walking routes occurs at lower elevations, while the problem recedes at higher elevations. In summary, there are minor impacts from recreational use of trails on the ecology of the corridors through which they pass. There is a need for monitoring to ensure that the impacts do not become significant.

The impact of increased demand for trekking expeditions on the ancient spiritual or pilgrimage trails in the Himalayas has been monitored by Kuniyal et al (1998). The main impacts relate to human excrement and litter deposited on or near the trails by users and stall-holders who set up in proximity to the routes. Kuniyal et al (1998) advocate a number of basic measures, such as regulation of traders, education of users and basic waste disposal systems to manage the problem. On a more global scale, while walking is carbon neutral, there are ancillary impacts, just as with any tourist activity. People travel to pursue walking in exotic locations. Tours to remote, but iconic, mountain ranges, such as the Himalayas, can have a high carbon footprint, given that long-haul flights and often local helicopter shuttles are involved. Thus, a holistic assessment of walking within the overall holiday context is required to fully appreciate impacts on a global scale.

Summary

The importance of walking in relation to mass tourism, especially in city destinations, is under-estimated and under-researched (Gehl, 1987). Walking in cities is an integral part of slow travel, and there is much that researchers need to learn about the interface between the tourist and the specificities of urban locations which make them places where the tourist wants to be seen, and places for them to see. Walking is pivotal in the analysis of sense of place or, as Tolley and Walker (2004) conclude, the mental and social topographies of cities:

> In cities for people, there is more to walking than walking: staying, playing, walking, talking, smiling ... we must stop thinking about how fast our feet are moving and start listening to our hearts and studying the faces of our cities to see if they are alive and well. (Tolley and Walker, 2004, p1)

The art of walking as a means of accessing the countryside represents a more fragmented market, in terms of inclination, motivation, strolling and hiking, or by distance, duration and level of energy required (Kay and Moxham, 1996). A route march through the countryside is different to a saunter across landscape, where time is spent to enjoy what the countryside has to offer, to pick the berries, to understand farming and local culture or to experience wilderness. It is this diversity that is so appealing, and in each country there have emerged different rights of access (Hammitt et al, 1992).

Trails, of various forms, have given walking a new tourist focus in recent years. They have attracted attention to a form of travel that is largely underplayed in tourism planning and management. Health and environmental concerns have both brought walking to the attention of policy-makers and have increased interest in walking as a leisure activity. This has been especially the case in relation to urban areas, greenways and localities where access is easy.

Slow travel encompasses all of these dimensions. It is for the person who seeks to walk in the locality from their accommodation, and for those following a linear trail over a mountain range. The psychological dynamics may well be different, but the fundamental principles appertain across the spatial and environmental variations. It is a tourism pursuit that is slower than the normality experienced in everyday life (Morris, 2006).

Case study: The Appalachian Trail

The Appalachian Trail follows the crest of the Appalachian mountains through 14 eastern US states (see Figure 6.1). It is 2175 miles (3500km) in length, with numerous climbs and passing through several forests, a national park, several state parks and nature reserves. The trail was the vision of regional planner Ben Mackaye, who sought to establish a walking route from Springer Mountain, Georgia to Mount Katahdin in central Maine for enjoyment of the great outdoors. The vision was written up with extraordinary clarity in a journal article three years after the First World War, at a time of unrest and economic recession; the author had a vision that the trail would represent far more than a recreational trail. It would help to enhance citizenship, ward against mental illness and unease in the population, and encourage rural settlement (Mackaye, 1921).

By the mid-1920s several progressive individuals and clubs (the most important being the Appalachian Trail Conservancy) gathered to support Mackaye in working towards delineating a route on the ground that could be publicized to encourage use by the near urban populations. Thus, between 1922 and 1937, voluntary groups, the private sector (mainly landowners) and the public sector developed a continuous waymarked route across 2000 miles of wilderness and deep rural areas. Throughout the ensuing decades the voluntary sector and public sector have re-routed the trail to follow a line across

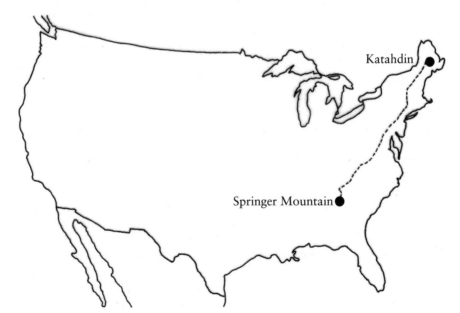

Figure 6.1 *Location of the Appalachian Trail*

protected landscapes, mainly in public ownership. In 1968 it was designated as a National Scenic Trail and is often referred to as the longest national park in the USA.

Trail philosophy

From its inception, the trail has been promoted as a slow travel experience, to facilitate enjoyment of nature and superb landscapes at a walking pace, or, as Bryson (1998) notes, it is approaching the world in a new way; that is, on foot and without comforts for many days. The Comprehensive Plan (Appalachian Trail Conservancy et al, 1981, p2), in defining the trail and its purpose, makes clear the ethos, which survives to this day:

> *The Appalachian Trail is a way, continuous from Katahdin in Maine to Springer Mountain in Georgia, for travel on foot, through the wild scenic, wooded, pastoral and culturally signifi-cant lands of the Appalachian Mountains. It is a means of sojourning among these lands, such that visitors may experience them by their own unaided efforts. In practice, the Trail is usu-ally a simple footpath, purposeful in direction and concept, favouring the heights of land, and located for minimum reliance on construction for protecting the resource. The body of the Trail is protected by the lands it traverses, and its soul is the living stewardship of the volunteers and workers of the Appalachian Trail community.*

The management philosophy set out in the plan refers to the volunteers being the soul of the trail and the management being decentralized, involving local partnerships and stewardship by landowners and local towns. Policy develop-ment, land procurement and resistance to unwarranted development also includes government at various levels, but mainly the National Parks Service and the Forest Service. The dual goals of maintaining a simple footpath with a primitive quality are imbued throughout the documentation.

The walking experience

There is no verifiable overall number of users. However, an extensive survey was undertaken from May to October 1999 involving 1879 useable responses and with a response rate of 66 per cent (Manning et al, 2000). This identified four core user segments, mainly by duration of walking:

- The 'Thru walker', or long-distance walker, seeking to walk the entire length. This segment accounts for 17.8 per cent of all users. The long-distance walker spends an average 167 days on the trail and seeks a rela-tively solitary experience; scenery and photography are more important to them than to other users. The 'Thru walker' will use the primitive shelters or camp as they progress, usually from north to south.
- The 'Section hiker' has a similar motivation to the 'Thru walker', but is only able to complete one section of the trail at a time, perhaps walking

and camping for several days. They account for 14.9 per cent of the entire trail-walking market.

- The 'Overnight user' spends on average two days on the trail, and covers about 13 miles per day. They are motivated by nature, taking in the views and getting some exercise. This group accounts for 31.6 per cent of all users.
- The 'Day user' tends to walk shorter distances and is more willing to stop for picnics, or to admire the views or natural habitats. Average group sizes are two people, although there are larger groupings attributable to this segment.

Most respondents did not experience any major problems on the trail; they expected to share the trail with other users and expected facilities to be simple. There was a general dislike of larger groups walking on the trail and some concern for overall impacts on the environment by users. The association between the walker and the trail reflects the findings of the wide walking literature and stories written on, or based on, the trail (Marshall, 1998). Chase (2003, p6), for example, comments:

> *The seductive quality of such endeavours lies for many people in the elimination of extraneous stimuli. Gone are the honking cars horns, the sticking elevator doors, the demanding bosses. All that's left is the Trail and the necessity of walking it.*

Lessons learned

What is striking about the development of the trail (and throughout its existence) is the way in which the voluntary sector has remained committed to the concept of a simple footpath through beautiful, diverse and protected landscapes. The involvement of the voluntary sector in the management of the trail has been a hallmark of its success that could well be modelled elsewhere to good effect. While users are divided as to the extent to which there should be commercial development associated with the trail, the principles of sustainable development have, to date, been applied so as to conserve what is near and to encourage expenditure in towns and villages just off the route. There also seems to be a very strong and lasting acceptance of the trail as a route of discovery, wellbeing and retreat from the fast pace of everyday life. In an overall appraisal of the trail, Foresta (1987, p78) concluded:

> *From the late 20th century perspective, the trail as an instrument of temporary playful retreat from the pressure of contemporary society seems as reasonable as the juxtaposition of the forested Appalachian ridges with the busy cities of the lowlands, while the concept of the trail as a catalyst for reform seems farfetched.*

Mackaye may not have seen his entire vision unfold, but the Appalachian Trail has certainly become synonymous with slow travel in the walking world.

7
Cycling and Tourism

Cycling achieved remarkable popularity from the 1880s onwards. This followed a decade of rapid technological improvements and increased production. This new form of transport intruded rapidly into the world of walking; cities had been dominated for centuries by the need to travel on foot, and now this was no longer the case. In many respects, cycling had a greater impact on mobility patterns than any other form of transport in the 19th century, because of its wide reach across the population. Fashion changed too, for people began to use the bicycle for recreational outings, mainly from their homes to parks or the near countryside. To a lesser extent it became an accomplished way to explore, including other countries, for those who had the time and resources.

The less well-off seemingly took great advantage of this affordable and revolutionary development for leisure; certainly this was the case in most western countries. It brought about a shift in attitudes and behaviour in relation to recreation (Herlihy, 2004; Sovacool, 2009). The considerable role of the railways in stimulating trips to destinations has been discussed in Chapter 5, but in the late 19th and early 20th centuries the bicycle also played a part in liberating people from their immediate neighbourhoods to visit countryside destinations. The combination of the railway and cycling was a marriage in heaven for those seeking a break away from urban areas to enjoy local resorts. There were even special trains that carried hundreds of cyclists to the countryside until the 1950s, many of them organized by cycling groups. The tradition has not died out altogether. For example, in Switzerland there are special cycle compartments on trains, and in Taiwan special cycle trains were launched by the Taiwanese Railway Administration in 2008 to encourage pollution-free cycling holidays; they are known as environmental protection train services. The extent of their popularity is not yet discernible (China Post, 2008).

The heyday of recreational cycling in most countries occurred in the early decades of the 20th century, prior to the dramatic rise of car ownership. In several parts of the world, cycling clubs were established, one of the most famous being the Clarion Club (founded in the UK in 1895). These clubs organized recreational rides. Many such clubs survive to this day. Thus, there is a strong legacy of recreational cycling that stems from the early decades of cycling, when it flourished both as a pastime and as a form of holiday. In many respects, the early development of cycle tourism has connotations of romanticism, akin to recreational walking in the 18th and 19th centuries. With the advent of the private car and rural bus, however, cycling for pleasure lost its popularity throughout the subsequent decades of the 20th century. Nevertheless, even in the heyday of the package holiday in the mid- to late-1900s, cycle tourism continued to feature in some of the mainstream European brochures. Thus, the tradition of cycling holidays, or cycling on holiday, has endured into the 21st century, with France and Austria leading the market (Mintel, 2003).

In Australasia, Europe and North America, cycle tourism is currently positioned by many authorities as a niche segment, and elsewhere it is presented as a specialist pursuit, such as mountain biking, to be enjoyed at certain locations (see, for example, Dickinson and Robbins, 2009). There are exceptions, however. In some countries, such as Denmark, Germany and the Netherlands, cycling is far more than this and there has been a greater willingness to invest in networks of routes, rather than in singular locations utilizing forestry tracks or old railway lines. In these countries the use of the bicycle when on holiday is more common, and there is also an upward trend. Cycle tourism is increasing in most countries, but only marginally; the pattern varies considerably.

In the context of world transport, however, the bicycle no longer holds the important position that it had 100 years ago. There is a necessary qualification to this generalization. In many of the poorest countries the role of the bicycle (for transport or leisure) has not reached the potential that one might expect. This is simply because of widespread poverty and hence a lack of ownership among populations that would readily use a bicycle to good effect. Nevertheless, in terms of world production of bicycles there has been an increase in recent years. The extent to which bicycles are purchased, principally for utility or specifically for leisure, depends on country or region.

In North America, for example, most bicycles are used for leisure and tourism purposes, with social and leisure cycle trips accounting for 82 per cent of all cycle trips (DeMaio and Gifford, 2004; Pucher and Dijkstra, 2000). In Asia and Africa they are sold invariably to service utility trips. In some countries, such as the UK or Italy, the share of cycle trips (against all other modes) accounts for only 1–2 per cent, whereas in Denmark it is 18 per cent and the Netherlands 27 per cent (Pucher et al, 2008). It is not simply a matter of culture, as is often cited in the wider literature. The level of use relates to land-use planning and investment in cycling routes and facilities including for tourism purposes. Several regional and local governments have invested in the Danube cycleway (Donau-radweg) to good effect in the past 20 years and it is now the most popular tourist cycle route in Europe, attracting over 200,000 cyclists per year in Upper Austria and 150,000 in Lower

Austria (Weinberger, 2009). Many of the towns and villages on the route have expanded their accommodation and hospitality sectors to serve the new market (Bernhofer et al, 2008).

In those countries where low levels of use persist, investment in other forms of transport has tended to make the bicycle a less attractive proposition. In summary, in many developed countries, cycling has been 'engineered' out of people's lives (Saelens et al, 2003). Social processes and perceptions have also marginalized cycling. For example, in the UK, Dickinson and Robbins (2009) suggest cycling is widely seen as being for 'other people', to take place in special locations where there are facilities, such as routes segregated from traffic, and the environment is pleasant. However, to some extent this reflects cycling's significant potential as a form of recreation and tourism.

The use of bicycles in developing countries is very different. In Asia, where the use of the bicycle remains widespread, there is currently a rapid decline in cycle trips. The reason is that car ownership and use is replacing the bicycle for short trips in urban areas. This trend is compounded by government exhortations to modernize, and this has signalled a cultural shift from human-powered transport to automobility where access by the car dominates. In effect, this trend has condemned the bicycle to a much lower position in the transport hierarchy. The future of the bicycle is therefore uncertain, as governments continue to invest heavily in highways and provision for the car. Given the declining market, the role of the bicycle in leisure, and in relation to slow travel, is likely to be limited. This seems to be the case everywhere and especially amongst the nouveau riche, where cultural trends favour long-haul travel to other parts of the world.

There are some definitional issues regarding cycle tourism. Whilst cycle tourism is the generic term to describe the use of the bicycle for travel between places, the actual act of cycling (the movement) is part of the tourist experience. Cycle holidays include touring from place to place or bicycle trips from a single base; cycling is the key motivation for the holiday and is pursued on most if not all days away. Holiday cycling refers to the tourist who seeks to cycle on one or more days while on holiday at a destination. It is not the main pursuit. An early study by Simonsen and Jorgensen (1996) reviewed cycle tourism on the island of Bornholm, Denmark. The authors found that 40 per cent of cycle tourists cycled from a fixed accommodation base, whereas 60 per cent were involved in touring from place to place. This split in the market will vary according to routes, local accommodation providers and user preferences.

The third category included in the definition of cycle tourism is the day cycle trip, a recreational outing from home or a holiday home, where cycling is the main pursuit for all or part of the day. Ritchie (1998) disagrees with this inclusion. He argues that it is more appropriate to define those who stay overnight as cycle tourists and others as day excursionists, and that their motivations and needs are different. There is no evidence to support this from the wider literature. The needs and desires of the cycle tourist do not vary according to day or multiple-day cycling; the core satisfaction factors remain similar (Downward and Lumsdon, 2001). Ritchie also explores whether it is better to define cycle tourism as a continuum, where at one end cycling is a highly specialized, serious leisure activity, and at the other a casual pursuit with lower levels of motivation, commitment and duration. There are some empirical data collected over a number of years in the 1990s to support this approach (Borde Failte, 1998). It may be possible to combine the categorization of duration of stay with level of seriousness and interest.

Sport cycling is a fourth category and tends to be an organized group activity that differs from the wider cycle tourism market in this respect. This is a form of sport tourism (Bull, 2006). Some forms of mountain biking (riding off-road trails) also involves competitor activity within groups, but there are also off-road trail riding and more casual forestry rides that fall within the frameworks of cycle tourism described above.

Cycle tourism is not exclusively a rural tourism phenomenon. The use of the bicycle as part of the city tourism offer is enjoying a renaissance across Europe. This is principally because of the wave of public bicycle-sharing schemes being set up in cities such as Amsterdam, Barcelona, Berlin, Brussels, Copenhagen, Lyon, Oslo, Rennes, Seville, Stockholm and Vienna (Bührmann, 2008). The most extensive scheme is in Paris, which accounted for 27.5 million trips in 2008, although the number of leisure or tourism trips is not known (Midgley, 2009). This followed on from the success achieved in Lyon with the Vélo V network (Borgnat et al, 2009). Paris decided to invest in urban cycling by designing a comprehensive pick-up-drop system, partly funded by the advertising company JCDecaux in return for use of advertising sites. The scheme is known as Velib (Vélo Liberté); it commenced in 2007 with over 20,600 bicycles located at 1450 cycle stations, integrated with other forms of public transport. Designed initially for use by residents, it also has appeal to visitors to the city and is being marketed as a slow travel way of enjoying the destination. Schemes designed for residents are beginning to attract tourist use, especially in saturated destinations such as Barcelona and La Rochelle (Midgley, 2009). There are over a hundred such schemes either in operation or in gestation across the world, including Beijing, Rio de Janeiro, San Francisco and Washington. In addition, there are, in most cities, cycle hire companies who also offer guided tours. For example, in Berlin it is possible to take a self-guided tour following the route of the Berlin Wall that once divided the Eastern Bloc from the West.

The scale and scope of cycle tourism is difficult to determine with any degree of accuracy, for the data on which to make interpretations are not recorded. Most cycle tourism is domestic and focuses on independent travel. Germany is the largest of the European markets, with an estimated spend amounting to 4.5 billion euro, per annum (Trendscope, 2008). However, in some cases destinations attract a high percentage of cycle tourists from neighbouring countries. For example, a high proportion of cycle tourists in Denmark come from Germany (Koucky, 2007). The German market is also important for Austria and Switzerland. Cycle tourism in Europe is closely associated with slow travel, especially in Austria, France and Switzerland, where cycle routes and networks have been developed especially to capture the essence of a destination, such as the Lower Danube or Loire Valley cycle routes. Overall cycle tourism in Europe is estimated to entail 2.8 billion cycle tourism trips (day and staying visitors) and a value of 54 billion euros per annum (European Parliament, 2009). There are estimates for cycle tourism in other parts of the world, but cycling is not usually delineated separately from other categories of recreation or tourism. In the USA the demand for recreational cycling is estimated to have increased from nearly 4 billion outings in 2005 to nearly 4.2 billion in 2008 (Outdoor Industry Foundation, 2009). The increased number of rail trails highlights the growing popularity of cycling for leisure in several US states.

The travel experience

Downward et al (2009) argue that cycle tourism focuses on the transcendental features of the act of cycling in different contexts that condition and define the experience; that is, it connects travel with the features of tourism such as landscape. Ritchie (1998, p580), in a study of cycle tourists in New Zealand, reported that 'cycle tourists travel at a more relaxed and slower pace than other travellers', and that they had a propensity to visit peripheral areas. An analysis of studies undertaken in North America, Australia, Europe and New Zealand indicates that cycle tourists have similar motivations and needs across all countries. Much of the research to support this assertion has focused on trails rather than road cycling or mountain biking, but there are a number of salient motivational factors that apply across cultures. The findings point to a conflation of motivations, such as wanting to relax, to enjoy healthy exercise, and the enjoyment from experiencing nature. Cyclists are co-producers of the experience (Dickinson et al, 2010b). This supports the literature on walking that suggest that positive emotions can be evoked by movement through pleasant landscapes and, as such, cycling is 'travel to enhance human experience' (Schafer et al, 2000, p177).

In the UK, Downward and Lumsdon (2001) noted the importance of constraints such as the perceived lack of safety when cycling on highways; traffic-free routes are rated highly by cycle tourists, especially by those who are less experienced or travelling in family groups. Mintel (2008a) reported reluctance on the part of the population to cycle simply because of the perceived danger of road traffic. With regard to the UK market, it estimated that one in four people perceive this as the major barrier to cycling. A number of preferences have been noted in research studies, such as having a continuous, safe route with pleasant surroundings and with signage to guide the traveller in the right direction (Utiger et al, 2005). On the other hand, some sociological studies acknowledge that a fear of cycling has been socially constructed (Horton, 2007).

There is a paucity of information available regarding aesthetic design of cycle trails. Martins (2009) referred to the work of Sauer (1925), in arguing that the shaping of the landscape is determined by culture rather than the forces of nature. There is therefore, it is argued, a need to direct patrimonial resources to good effect in relation to trail development. The Cicloria scheme in Portugal, for example, seeks to make good use of local materials and architectural designs of the old railway networks to take this idea forward (Mota,

2009). The design of the Vias Verdes (Green Ways) in Spain has incorporated many of the architectural features of the old railway lines, in order to enhance the overall appeal for the cyclist and walker (Aycart, 2004). In the UK, Sustrans, the charity responsible with a wide range of partners for development of the National Cycle Network, has included sculptures and other works of art:

> *Each section of the journey should be considered as a unique 'travelling landscape'. Views can be created, shelters and screens planted, existing structures such as bridges can be enhanced ... everything to make the journey through these public spaces as enjoyable an experience as possible for all those who use them. The journey itself becomes a worthwhile experience.*
> *(Grimshaw, 1998, p7)*

The slow travel experience often involves integration between modes of travel. This dimension of the travel experience, that is, combined modes, is not explored in the literature. In particular, the use of train and bicycle for a slow travel holiday has remained an important part of cycling culture. However, in recent decades, and principally in relation to high-speed and urban trains, the bicycle has also been designed out of railway provision in many countries. The rationale is that loading bicycles onto trains slows down scheduled stops, and that there is no room on board to accommodate them. The picture is very complex, in that each train-operating company in each respective country has a different approach and regulations. In several European countries the carriage of cycles on longer-distance trains has declined because of inconvenience and regulation. In some countries the cycle can still be taken easily on local trains, but in overall terms, despite the EU introducing the Third Railway Package in 2007 to facilitate the carriage of bicycles, train companies are reluctant to encourage cyclists on board in any number. A notable exception is Switzerland, where the Swiss National Railway (SBB) has a policy to cater for cyclists, and demand has increased steadily since 2002. It has also offered an extensive cycle hire scheme at main railway stations that allows linear cycle rides to be made, using the rail journey for the return part of the trip.

Cyclist tours by coach are losing popularity in countries where the market had been, until recently, strong; for example, in the Netherlands. There is no research available on the motivation of cycle coach users. This is also the case with ferries that are used by cyclists on sea routes to the Balearic islands, or between Germany and Denmark.

Rail trails

The concept of developing rail trails originated in the USA, and there are over 950 multi-use trails currently in existence, with many more in gestation (Rail Trails Conservancy, 1998). There are also networks in Canada that use old trackbeds and other off-road facilities to encourage traffic-free cycling, such as the Velo Quebec network. In Europe, rail trails have been developed in several countries, notably in Belgium, the UK and Spain. In the case of Spain, the rail trails, known as Vias Verdes, were developed partly to create an alternative to beach and sun tourism (Otero, 2002). In Australasia, the development of rail trails began in the early 1990s (Bradshaw, 2002), and there are several rural rail trail projects in Australia and New Zealand. There is a continued interest in conversion throughout the USA and Australasia, where freight lines are still being closed.

While most trails are designed to cater for multi-users, they often encourage more cyclists than other types of users; this is principally because of the hard surfaces and easy gradients. Beeton (2003) surveyed three rail trails in the Australian state of Victoria, achieving 454 useable responses and a high response rate of over 45 per cent. Of these, 89 per cent were cyclists. The profile of users was similar to surveys undertaken elsewhere in North America and Europe. The cyclists were mainly male (55 per cent), between 35 and 64 years old, with a large proportion having a higher educational background (46 per cent) and with 50 per cent riding as a couple or in small groups.

In relation to tourism development, most trails have been designed for a wide range of users. Firstly, they are designed principally to encourage local resident use; for example, the Otago Central Rail Trail in New Zealand. In a study of this trail by Blackwell (2002), it was ascertained that the main community benefits were as follows:

- improved wellbeing
- learning about culture and history
- providing an opportunity to be with family and friends
- enhancing social interaction
- giving a sense of pride to local communities.

However, there are limitations regarding the veracity of such general conclusions. This type of study often fails to take into account the structural and intrapersonal constraints of non-users (Curry et al, 2001; Ravenscroft, 2004). They rarely analyse why people do not use a trail. There are, of course, some negative impacts of such trails. These relate principally to access to trails, especially when they encourage substantial visitation by car, as identified by Lumsdon (2000a) in relation to the rail trails of the Peak District National Park in the UK. Furthermore, some writers have asked whether trails are a worthwhile investment of public funds (Crompton, 2001). In response, most hedonic pricing studies of rateable values of properties in the proximity of trails show that businesses benefit and that real estate prices rise:

> The analysis suggests that each foot increase in distance to the trail decreases the sale price of a sample property by $7.05, i.e., being closer to the Little Miami Scenic Trail adds value to single family residential properties. (Kardeniz, 2008, piii)

A wide range of trail-user studies also indicate that direct-user expenditure in local economies offers a major positive impact to places that are not traditional tourism destinations (Tomes and Knock, 2006). There is near consensus in the literature that trails present good lifestyle value in relation to expenditure on their development and maintenance.

Environment and health issues

There has been a considerable increase in the focus on cycling route and trail design to enhance nature and to improve the quality of life, especially improved health, for people. Lumsdon (2000a) argued that cycle tourism meets a number of sustainable development indicators, as identified by the UNEP and the UNWTO (2005) that are listed as follows:

- optimal use of environmental resources
- a respect for the socio-cultural authenticity of host communities
- socio-economic benefits to all stakeholders
- informed partnership of all stakeholders
- continuous monitoring of impacts
- high levels of consumer satisfaction.

However, in reality, such principles are seemingly difficult to implement in developing countries (Mowforth and Munt, 2009; Sharpley, 2009). There is a need to demonstrate that such principles can be translated successfully into practice. The prescription, therefore, is to design cycle routes and networks in accordance with such principles (Hellmund and Smith, 2006). In a study undertaken on behalf of the European Parliament (2009), a case for a European cycle network (EuroVelo) is made. This is discussed in the case study at the end of the chapter.

The main impacts of cycle tourism, as with other forms of slow travel, relate to the journey from the origin to the destination. Cycling is identified by the tourism sector as a low-carbon option (Mintel, 2007), although this depends on several factors. Cycling does increase the intake of oxygen, and hence an increase in CO_2 output from metabolism, but this is a minimal impact (Walsh et al, 2008). More importantly, it depends on the mode used to access cycling facilities. The study for the European Parliament (2009) compared mainstream holidays versus cycling holidays with respect to the German market and in terms of travel and CO_2 emissions. A number of interesting findings were uncovered regarding access to cycle tourism destinations. The share of travel by rail is three times higher for cyclists on holiday than for other holidaymakers; the share of travel by car is 30 per cent lower and air travel is 70 per cent lower. This is corroborated by evidence from Switzerland in relation to access to the Veloland Schweiz network. Over 82 per cent of cycle tourists (day and overnight stays) used a combination of public transport and cycling to access the network.

Further analysis of the German holiday data highlighted that only 7 per cent of cycle tourists travelled by air to their destination. The fly-cycle segment, however, accounted for 40 per cent of all emissions of cycle tourists. In contrast, 28 per cent of cycle tourists travelled by rail for their cycling holiday, and they emitted only 7 per cent of CO_2 emissions. Cycle tourists also tend to travel shorter distances to enjoy their holiday (1146km on average, in comparison to mainstream holidays accounting for a 2417km return trip). The report concluded:

> ... *cycle holidays are considerably more sustainable than main-stream holidays. The key factors are shorter distances travelled between home and destination and a more environmentally-friendly choice of transport mode (less air travel and much more rail travel). (European Parliament, 2009, p46)*

Many impact studies have focused on one route or a small number of routes, but collectively these studies present a generalized picture of the environmental (and social and economic) impacts of cycling. These evaluations have focused on multi-user routes and, for the most part, on economic impacts (Bowker et al, 2006; Institute of Transport and Tourism et al, 2008). In the context of mountain bikes, Cessford (2002) has argued that there are three main impacts: perceptions of physical impacts, safety hazards and cycling in inappropriate natural settings. He undertook a study on the Queen Charlotte Trail in New Zealand and concluded that physical impacts are minimal. Work by Sterl (2008) found few impacts on wildlife when users pass through on a clearly delineated route. Cessford also assessed the tensions between users, in relation to reported accident rates between walkers and cyclists. He concluded that the perception of safety reduction is greater than the reality. User conflict is subjective and studies rarely question the extent to which reported conflicts reflect the users' position rather than the physical reality (Dickinson and Robbins, 2009).

There are a wide range of studies that seek to identify the relationship between the physical environment, cycling and health, but these again refer primarily to trails or open spaces in or near to urban areas (Wendel-Vos et al, 2004). Cycling is recognized as stimulating healthy exercise that in turn helps to reduce cardio-vascular diseases and those associated with obesity. Mintel (2007) suggests that healthy exercise is also an important determinant for cycle tourists, especially those from middle-income groups, seeking cycling holidays. Given the rise in obesity among western populations, cycling provides an opportunity to combine leisure with fitness, and this is an important motivation for many middle-aged or older cyclists.

Summary

There is a natural affinity between cycling and slow travel, and this has worked well in some destinations of the developed world. The core motivations of the slow traveller seeking to cycle are well documented: relaxation, exercise and absorption of the local atmosphere. Nevertheless, cycling remains far less popular than walking for many destinations, and one key factor is the level of traffic which is a deterrent to would-be cycle explorers, although traffic is also a deterrent to walkers as well. One solution would be to invest in more traffic-free routes. Cyclists can also be deterred by terrain unsuited to non-mountain-biking cycling in some destinations.

There is a dilemma in relation to the development of cycle tourism. Those responsible for the design and build of cycle routes and networks are often located in highways departments, and their prime responsibility is to provide for utility transport. In the case of rail trails, canal towpaths and other off-road facilities, the vision is to plan and deliver multi-user routes, but public resources in this sector are limited. Thus, the supply of a sustainable cycle network, designed and brought together by a coordinated group of stakeholders focusing on cycling, is a rarity. One of the most successful examples is Veloland Schweiz, which brought together organizations representing land-owners, sports organizations, the accommodation and public transport sectors, as well as the tourism destinations, in order to design and implement a recreational and tourism cycle network for Switzerland. This is a model that other destinations might seek to follow. It is an enabler of slow travel.

It would be false to suggest that all cycle tourism is always associated with low-carbon travel. As with other forms of holiday-taking, the origin–destination trip is a key element. However, the evidence available from the Dutch and German markets indicates that cycle tourism attracts people who travel shorter distances, have a greater propensity to use a train and who are more likely to adopt pro-environmental behaviour in their travel choice decision. Thus, in meeting the principles of low-carbon and providing a highly valued travel experience, cycle tourism has the potential to facilitate slow travel in developed countries. The following case study of EuroVelo sets out a vision for a sustainable European transport and tourism network.

Case study: EuroVelo

The aim of EuroVelo fits with the overall mission of the European Cyclists' Federation; that is, to ensure that the cycle realizes its fullest potential in achieving sustainable mobility, public wellbeing and economic development through tourism (European Cyclists' Federation, 2009). The aim of this case study is to illustrate the importance of stakeholder commitment to development of networks that can facilitate slow travel.

EuroVelo relates to an overall approach in offering a sustainable transport and tourism network of the highest grade across all countries in Europe. It comprises 12 long-distance cycle routes that cover 66,000km, of which approximately 45,000km are in existence on the ground as continuous sign-posted routes, following best practice guidelines. The network will soon be augmented by another proposed long-distance route, the Iron Curtain Trail, from the Barents Sea to the Black Sea. The latter trail was first pioneered by Michael Cramer (MEP) in the early years of the 21st century and will be incorporated into EuroVelo as it meets the criteria for development. EuroVelo is, therefore, a European cycle route network in the making.

There are currently no exact estimates for levels of demand on the EuroVelo network. Assessment is difficult because the EuroVelo network uses existing routes in countries that are already developed and branded at a national level, such as the D routes in Germany. Hence, these existing routes attract many short-distance utility and tourism trips through the localized branding. The study for the European Parliament (2009) made some estimates of potential demand and revenue using a geographically-based model, and concluded that EuroVelo had the potential to generate 5 billion euros per annum (12.5 million holidaymakers spending 4.4 billion euros, and 33.3 million day trips adding 0.54 billion euros). These values represent gross revenues.

The development of the network has been slow. EuroVelo was first mooted in the 1980s by a small group of visionary advocates who have argued consistently that cyclists need a network of international as well as local, national and regional routes. In the past decade, progress has been made in several countries, through partnership with municipalities and using existing long-distance national routes, to piece together an international network. A substantial amount of work has gone into the development of standardized signage, interpretation and promotion, so as to ensure that the EuroVelo brand is more widely recognized as being quality routes for cycle tourism. The EuroVelo network is now managed by the European Cyclists' Federation (a non-governmental organization), advocating improved facilities to encourage cycling across all countries in Europe. It is working hard to ensure that all routes offer high standards of design, signage and promotion throughout Europe.

The aim of the EuroVelo network is also to encourage interchange between cycling and other modes of transport; principally tram, train, bus and ferry. It is seeking to encourage transport operators to offer seamless interchange and service facilities such as secure cycle parking and cycle hire. The integration refers to:

- physical interchange facilities such as between platforms or access paths to a railway station, such as in the Netherlands and Germany
- fares integration, to encourage a shift between modes such as zonal fares and family fares that include carriage of cycles, as in Switzerland
- information integration between the transport and tourism sectors so that information about use of different modes and the bicycle is easily available from transport operators, tourism offices and accommodation providers, as in Denmark and Italy.

Lessons learned

In conclusion, EuroVelo offers a potential to encourage a Europe-wide network of long-distance cycle routes, principally for tourism but also serving the needs of the communities through which it passes. The lessons to be learnt from the case study are the importance of partnerships between advocates, municipalities and other organizations in order to progress a vision based on the principles of sustainable development. It also illustrates that progress can be slow if policy frameworks are not supportive and hence resources are not committed. Perhaps the most important lesson to note is that emphasized in the report to the European Parliament. This recognized the need for a flagship low-carbon tourism product to provide EU citizens an opportunity to sample a major slow-travel facility. The study concluded that EuroVelo had the potential to:

- enhance domestic tourism and to reduce long-distance tourist travel, thus helping greatly to curb CO_2 emissions
- encourage short-distance cross-border tourism with minimal environmental impact and low level of emissions
- encourage people to use public transport to travel to the cycle destination, resulting in a lower environmental impact than the case of private cars or air transport
- reuse assets such as old railways, forest tracks and canal towpaths
- stimulate economic development in rural areas that are not prime tourist destinations
- bring about a diversification of land-based businesses to provide accommodation, attractions and food and beverage for local consumption
- offer local residents the opportunity to improve their quality of life by taking more physical exercise
- generate near-zero carbon dioxide emissions by users on the route
- offer a form of slow travel which encourages interest in the richness of local gastronomy, heritage and community life across different countries and regions of the EU. (European Parliament, 2009, pp18–19).

The major challenge will be for policy-makers, and those seeking to implement the network, to release sufficient funding to support the delivery and maintenance of the world's first continental slow travel tourism network.

8
Bus and Coach Tourism

Despite being ubiquitous forms of passenger transport at destinations, the role of the bus and coach in the development of tourism is not well researched. The bus and coach have considerable potential to play in developing sustainable tourism mobility, in the form of road trains and open-top buses, as well as scheduled buses, along seafronts and into the centres of destinations. The bus is complemented by the coach, offering transfers, tours and longer-distance services.

The bus is by far the most important form of surface passenger transport in most countries, but the extent to which it is used for leisure purposes is often underestimated by transport and tourism planners. Consider two examples. Firstly, in Berlin, 64 per cent of all trips made by bus are for leisure and shopping purposes (International Association of Passenger Transport, 2009). Secondly, in Sydney, over 30 per cent of trips are for recreation and shopping on a weekday, rising to 78 per cent at weekends (New South Wales Transport, 2002). This pattern of leisure and tourist travel is mirrored in many major cities across the world. The potential of the bus, argues Tyler (2002), is that by its very nature it is inclusive and flexible. It can respond easily to fluctuations of demand between seasons, days of the week, or even at different times during the day, without investment in heavy infrastructure.

The earliest buses ran in England. The first service of any lasting consequence was organized by George Shillibear in London during the late 1820s. The model was set for urban bus growth in industrial cities across the world in the latter part of the 19th and early 20th centuries. London-style horse bus services were copied in North American cities, to be succeeded by motor buses. Provision of regular urban buses then spread to other parts of the world. They were designed mainly for utility, and the supply of bus services, even in postmodern society, reflects this early focus on providing journeys to work or places of education.

The term 'bus' is derived from the Latin word 'omnibus', meaning 'for all', and thus from its inception the bus was perceived as an open access form of transport available for the population of any given city. A bus is a large vehicle designed to carry passengers on a fixed route (sometimes with deviations on passenger request), and operating to a schedule. There are several variations. Minibuses (mainly 16–20 seat vehicles) are often used for scheduled recreational services on roads where larger vehicles cannot operate, and for demand-responsive services which have to be booked in advance. Bus services tend to be sub-categorized into urban and inter-urban, the latter also tending to serve intermediate rural areas.

Coaches are built to a more comfortable specification and are used for tours and transfers (say between airports and hotels). They are also used for scheduled transfers between railway stations, city centres and airports, and on intercity routes, where comfort is required for the longer duration trip. In some parts of the world, such as North America, coaches are referred to as buses, and this may cause some confusion in terminology. In this chapter we maintain the distinction between these two forms of passenger transport.

Coach travel can be divided into three sectors (Cooper et al, 2008). First there are scheduled, regular long-distance routes, such as the Greyhound services in the USA, which have been in existence since 1914. The Greyhound coach network has remained a significant brand in the USA for nearly 100 years. The network serves many rural destinations that do not have nearby railheads or airports, and is thus associated with exploration and slow travel (Walsh, 2000). These long-distance services are typically relatively inexpensive, and passengers trade comfort and time with cost. However, in some countries, for example, Turkey and China, coach travel is relatively fast, and is considered a superior option to train travel.

Second, Cooper et al (2008) identify another category as the coach tour. This is traditionally attractive to an older demographic group, but often attracts people of a higher socio-economic status than scheduled routes. Coach tours are attractive to this segment as they provide a break from driving, offer scenic views and the chance to socialize with others, all key components of slow travel. There has been something of a renaissance in adventure travel by coach for the younger age group, such as the OZ bus travelling overland (mainly) between Europe and Australia, and a new service between Europe and the USA via Alaska. The third sector is hire coaches. These are typically used for destination transfers, but there is also a significant market for private tours. Cooper et al (2008) suggest the size of the coach market is significantly under-appreciated. For example, in 2000 an estimated 860 million passengers used coaches in the USA. Of these, the vast majority (90 per cent) were carried by private hire vehicles.

The travel experience

The discussion in the literature focuses mainly on bus travel, principally in relation to shorter bus trips in urban areas rather than longer intercity routes. There has been more written up regarding the determinants of service quality in relation to customer wants and dislikes (Hensher et al, 2003). Thus, the principal factors which encourage use are, for example, reliability, comfort, safety and frequency. These are well documented in the transport journals and studies (Swanson et al, 1997). Some authors have identified the need to investigate underlying perceptions and attitudes of users; they conclude that a high service quality is essential to encourage new users. Once again, there are few studies which focus on motivations for bus use and leisure travel (Beirão and Sarsfield Cabral, 2007). Thompson and Schofield (2007) report a study of tourist perceptions of public transport at an urban destination. They concluded that public transport is only a minor influence on overall destination satisfaction, but, with regard to the factor 'passenger transport', ease of access was found to be more salient than either safety or efficiency. Several authors (Gronau and Kagermeir, 2007; Lumsdon et al, 2006) comment that the use of integrated ticketing and marketing for leisure travel deliver modal shift from the car to bus travel, but only if there are market segments predisposed to change.

There are, however, articles which point to factors discouraging travel by bus, such as anti-social behaviour leading to negative arousal (disturbance from other passengers), but once again the studies are urban-based and in relation to trips for all purposes (Andreassen, 1995). One study provides some useful insights into motivation for bus travel. The authors asked respondents to describe their ideal bus journey, and used Russell's orthogonal typology with dimensions pleasant/unpleasant and activated/de-activated to summarize the findings (Russell, 1980). They concluded that the desire of the bus user is to be calm and contented amid pleasant surroundings, and hence bus travel falls within the pleasant/deactivated quadrant:

> *The state of mind appears to involve being transported while switched off. It is smooth, tranquil, undisturbed, relaxed, absorbed, engaged with the moment but elsewhere and is pleasurable without being ecstatic. (Stradling et al, 2007, p290)*

There is very limited research on the motivation of the tourist on board a local scheduled bus service or a coach trip. The Institute of Transport and Tourism (2006) undertook a comprehensive study of tourists on board rural bus services at scenic destinations across the UK. The study concluded that tourists seek out such services primarily for sightseeing, and also for access to areas to walk without needing a car (Guiver, Lumsdon, Weston and Ferguson, 2007). The study also noted the importance given to using environmentally-friendly transport. Respondents who had a car available on the day of travel stated that the advantages of using the bus over the car were not having to drive on unfamiliar roads, being able to sightsee from the bus, and avoiding congestion or difficult parking. Research undertaken by the Institute of Transport and Tourism (2008) provides additional insight on travel for tourism purposes using a minibus service. The authors reported that tourists enjoy the company of others when using public transport for recreation, even if there is minimal engagement in relation to their own travel experience. This may take the form of brief small talk, listening in to other people's conversations, or simply 'people watching'. In sum, passengers on board this service enjoyed sharing space; it was part of the travel experience. These results support more general findings from studies in the Harz Mountains and Alpine regions of Europe (Hoenninger, 2003; Holding, 2001).

In the UK, bus use in a tourism context is relatively low and, given the public's lack of experience of bus use outside the main urban areas, they are generally viewed rather negatively in comparison to the car and are not conceptualized as a travel option people can or would want to use (Dickinson and Dickinson, 2006; Dickinson et al, 2009). Bus users comment on late running buses and high costs, and they generally identify more problems than car users while, conversely, car use is justified by problems with buses (Dickinson and Robbins, 2008). This is not confined to the UK. There is a consensus that a combination of improved service levels, reduced fares and reliability (e.g. in beating delays in congestion) are the three main elements which would improve patronage, as noted in European, North American and Australasian studies (Currie and Wallis, 2008). The negative perception of buses has made it more difficult to introduce initiatives in a tourism context. In some instances, initial government funding often is withdrawn within a short period, when low levels of use are reported (Dickinson and Dickinson, 2006), yet evidence suggests tourist initiatives must be built up gradually over several years, and take longer to become established than more utilitarian routes (Breakell, 1999; Holding and Kreutner, 1998).

In an early study of the privately-owned bus network on the island of Malta, Robbins (1996) highlighted that the needs of tourists are different to local residents, yet they share the same network. This finding is supported by Lumsdon (2006), who undertook 51 in-depth interviews of tourism and transport planners responsible for designing bus networks in tourism areas. He concluded that most did not understand or recognize the needs of tourists. They were not willing to change the design of services to meet the needs of tourists over residents, given the resource limitations in providing bus services. In order to achieve a greater modal shift from the car, services need to be designed with the tourist experience in mind, but this does not necessarily conflict with the needs of residents.

The International Association of Public Transport (2003) has argued that bus companies seeking to attract tourists to use scheduled services need to adopt a stronger customer orientation, provide door-to-door service and to adapt existing processes such as providing integral day fares. Furthermore, the Association advocates that companies need to tie in more closely with tourism providers in order to serve events, cultural quarters and to gain synergies wherever possible. In order to develop a service, these factors need to be brought together in a promotional plan. Where tourists have been attracted to scheduled bus services, their numbers have been shown to boost services with relatively low use, especially in rural areas (Charlton, 1998).

Buses can also prove attractive to tourists under special circumstances. City tour bus services have grown considerably over the last two decades, with companies such as 'City Sightseeing' operating in many cities across the world. They offer regular hop-on-hop-off services between visitor attractions at urban destinations. There has also been a growth in park and ride services, which were developed originally to ease congestion at popular destinations such as Niagara Falls in the USA and in historic cities such as Chester and Winchester in the UK (Meek et al, 2009; Wall and McDonald, 2007). There are fewer park and ride services feeding into rural destinations such as the Igel bus in the Bavarian National Park in Germany, where a park and ride service fits into a wider integrated network ideally suited for slow travel (Gronau and Kagermeier, 2007). People are also more willing to use buses to access large-scale events such as the Olympic Games (Hensher and Brewer, 2002). At the Sydney Olympics, use of buses was higher than predicted (Hensher and Brewer, 2002), and such situations can provide an opportunity for people who otherwise would not use buses to engage.

There has been a limited analysis of the coach tour experience; it has been characterized as a passive travel option with fixed itineraries (Becken and Gnoth, 2004; Dean, 1993). Such itineraries, however, might not be very relaxing, as many coach tours attempt to include visits to numerous tourism icons (Baloglu and Shoemaker, 2001). Coach tours are 'frequently assumed to involve the seamless visual consumption of spectacle within an "air-conditioned bubble" that limits sensory and experiential diversity' (Edensor and Holloway, 2008, p487).

However, this might not always be the case. Exploratory research under-taken by Dickinson (2009) suggests that coach tourists are much more actively co-producing the experience; this corroborates findings in relation to the Shropshire Hills Shuttles study (Institute of Transport and Tourism, 2008). This also reinforces, to some extent, previous market indicators that the core market for coaches is becoming more adventurous and thus will have an appeal to younger age groups (Mintel, 2009a). It also depends on the nature of the tour. There is, for example, an increasing backpacker coach travel market, such as Busabout in Europe and Greyhound in the USA, which is targeting the 15–24 age group (Mintel, 2004). There is also the OZ bus from Europe to Australia, which takes 13 weeks to complete, and is positioned as a 'trip of a lifetime' for backpackers. There are also a range of backpacker buses in Australia and New Zealand that have a considerable appeal to younger markets.

The scale and scope

Use of the bus and coach is ubiquitous, and whilst it is difficult to offer a global estimate, the following figures provide an idea of the scale of bus use for everyday travel. The International Association of Public Transport (2009) estimate that 60 billion passenger journeys were made in 2008 in the enlarged European Union (EU27 countries), and the trend reflects a small increase in demand. The Association estimates that 10 per cent of all trips are made for leisure or tourism purposes in relation to rural services; this is supported by evidence from the Tourism on Board study in the UK.

The trends in bus patronage are variable across countries and within countries. For example, in the UK, bus use is increasing, but this is principally because of a substantial growth in use in London, whilst many parts of the country have suffered a slight but continuous decline in recent years. Local bus services (measured in vehicle km) increased by 7 per cent, whereas non-local services declined by 3 per cent in the period 1998/99–2007/08. The pattern is uneven. There are signs that bus and coach travel is reviving in Europe, following several years of decline. In France, for example, demand rose by 12 per cent between 2006 and 2008. In Spain, there has been a major increase in demand for inter-urban coach travel, amounting to a 77 per cent increase in patronage overall in the past two decades. Thus, according to Mintel (2009a), buses and coaches generated 539 billion passenger km in Europe in 2007. The two most often quoted causes of growth are service-level improvements and fare reductions (Currie and Rose, 2008).

There are some data regarding the USA, but there is no sub-division between trips for tourism purposes in relation to other travel purposes. In the USA, bus and coach travel is recorded under the heading 'Bus' in terms of passenger miles. Over a ten-year period between 1998/99 and 2007/08, bus passenger miles declined from 148,608 to 147,905 million. A study undertaken by DePaul University (2007) concluded that the advent of the price-sensitive Megabus network had helped to re-stimulate the market for intercity coaches. Other major US companies such as Apex and Greyhound have invested to build on their existing markets.

Given the dearth of publicly available information regarding the scale and scope of bus operation, there have been calls for more data. This has been the subject of detailed discussion in the supply sector and there is now agreement that statistics regarding bus and coach travel will be collected as part of EUROSTAT in future years (Economic and Social Council, 2009).

Environment

Buses are an eco-efficient form of travel (Gössling et al, 2005). Coaches, in particular, operate on high loadings and therefore have lower carbon emissions than other forms of motorized travel (see Table 4.2, Chapter 4). Most studies which point to the green credentials of bus and coach in low-carbon travel are written up by, or on behalf of, suppliers. For example, in the USA, Nathan Associates (2007) undertook a study for the American Bus Association which estimated that a motor coach achieves 148 passenger miles to the gallon, a figure calculated to be four times more efficient than air or the private car. In the UK, the Confederation of Passenger Transport (2008) cites an example of travel between London and the Lake District, using data from the Department for Environment, Food and Rural Affairs/National Atmospheric Emissions Inventory/Energy Saving Trust. This 300-mile (480km) trip by car (assuming average occupancy) had a carbon footprint of 53kg per person, whereas the coach was only 14kg per person. The Confederation of Passenger Transport estimated, as a comparator, that the coach generates about one-sixth of the emissions per passenger of air travel and one-quarter of emissions from car travel. Becken (2005), however, sounds a note of caution as she argues that mobility and hotel accommodation are integral to coach tourism. In the context of New Zealand, that encourages intensive use of energy (Becken et al, 2003b).

However, the industry estimates are corroborated in several scientific studies which point to the comparative advantage of the bus over car travel, especially the importance of load factor (Romilly, 1998; Solyu, 2007). Raux et al (2005), for example, calculated comparative average CO_2 emissions for different modes in the French transport system. Whilst the plane accounts for 169 grams per person km and the car 111, the bus generated 41 grams and the coach only 24. The bus and coach sector is also exploring lower emissions impact in the design and fuel use of vehicles. Santarelli et al (2003) reported on trials between conventional diesel-fuelled buses and hydrogen fuel cell powered vehicles in Italy, concluding that in the medium term fuel cell powered buses could be utilized in urban transport, although they argued that more investment and innovation were required by government.

Summary

The development of bus services (as with other forms of urban transport) throughout the world has been primarily for utility purposes, with little or no regard for tourists or the potential to develop this market (Manente et al, 2000). Yet many bus services attract tourists on board, because they go to places tourists want to visit. Alternatively, they offer a scenic ride between locations, and this has an intrinsic value in its own right. There is considerable potential to develop the leisure market, but, other than marketing trips to retail centres, most bus companies do little to attract other market segments visiting attractions, historic locations or scenic landscapes.

There are exceptions to this rule where services are designed specifically to cater for the movement of tourists around resorts, and these are predominantly seasonal. In some cases, there is an additional interpretation or a tour guide on board. There are also services designed to encourage sustainable access to natural areas instead of taking a car, and these are very attractive to the slow traveller. Several initiatives in the USA, such as bus access to national parks, are attracting slow travellers to nature destinations (Turnbull, 2000).

The coach is a very low-carbon form of tourism when carrying a high-occupancy load. This is a form of tourism often overlooked in the academic literature, and one that potentially has a higher share by mode than is typically recognized. Scheduled inter-urban coaches and explorer tours are two types that fall within the slow traveller's approach to holidaymaking.

The wide range of services, which has been referred to as the bus and coach sector in this chapter, could be a more important part of the sustainable travel solution in future, as argued by Currie and Rose (2008, p10):

> *Changing circumstances, such as climate change, peak oil and technology may add to the list of potential drivers for future public transport demand growth.*

Case study: the Shropshire Hills Shuttle, UK

The Shropshire Hills Area of Outstanding Natural Beauty (AONB) is located in the English West Midlands (see Figure 8.1). It covers 804 square km of sparsely populated landscape, featuring hill country, rolling farmland and wooded river valleys. The AONB (2009) has a management plan which sets out its aims and objectives, which can be summarized as follows:

- Value, conserve and enhance (conserving habitats and heritage).
- Encourage a thriving countryside (land management and sustainable communities).
- Shift to low-carbon (mitigation of climate change).
- Adapting to the future: working alongside nature (landscape scale conservation; social and economic adaptation).
- Helping people connect with the AONB (awareness, enjoyment and adaptation).

Within this context, it seeks to maintain opportunities for residents and visitors to minimize travel, and to seek alternatives to the car to explore the landscape, villages and towns of the area. The approach is very much about slow travel.

Figure 8.1 *Location of the Shropshire Hills AONB, UK*

The Shropshire Hills Shuttle is a seasonal minibus service from two small railhead towns of Church Stretton and Craven Arms into a very rural part of the AONB. The minibus service was originally developed in the mid-1990s by the National Trust, at their property Carding Mill Valley near to Church Stretton. In order to respond to the pressure of car-borne traffic accessing the hills, the Trust decided to employ a local bus operator to run a shuttle bus up a narrow road, the Burway, to the Long Mynd hill ridge. In 2001, administration of the shuttle was transferred to TESS (Transport for Everyone in South Shropshire), a community transport organization. It expanded the Shropshire Hills Shuttles network with government funding. However, in 2004 funding was reduced, and together with continued support from the National Trust, Natural England and Shropshire County Council, three shuttles have been retained: Long Mynd, Stiperstones and Secret Hills Shuttles, offering an hourly service on weekend days.

In 2008, the AONB agreed to manage the Shropshire Hills Shuttle (with the existing partners) in order to stabilize funding support and to coordinate marketing of the service, linking up to plan and implement the operation and marketing of the bus. The Institute of Transport and Tourism (2008) undertook surveys on the service in 2005/06 and 2008. The findings indicated that there are three main types of user, of approximately equal proportions:

- local people on visits to the shops, to meet friends or for a meal
- sightseers – visitors to the area who use the shuttle to see local attractions and landscapes
- walkers, who use the bus to undertake linear walks.

The shuttle travel experience

The researchers reported that users like the service not only for the scenery, but also because it is a social travel experience. Being in such a confined space in the minibus means that passengers and drivers readily engage in conversation on the route and it is a relaxing experience. The report found that the drivers were pivotal to the success of the service. The researchers concluded that there was a form of community branding being established. People even came to visit the area at weekends so that they could ride one of the shuttles as part of the tourist experience. They had built a sense of loyalty and effective feeling for the shuttles, whether they lived nearby or came from far away. Pubs and cafes on the route welcome the business from the shuttles and recommend it to their wider customer base. The study also noted 69 per cent of users in 2008 had a car available on the day of travel, indicating that the service is contributing to the low-carbon strategy of the AONB.

Demand for the shuttles has increased during the past five years (see Table 8.1), including a 19 per cent increase between 2008 and 2009.

Lessons learned

Recreation and tourism services can succeed if they are well planned and designed so as to meet the aspirations of visitors and residents. Success criteria

Table 8.1 *Shropshire Hills Shuttle passenger numbers*

| | | | Passenger numbers | | | |
	2004	2005	2006	2007	2008	2009
Long Mynd Shuttle	1858	1451	2834	3787	3185	6192*
Stiperstones Shuttle	984	941	2139	2572	2069	
Secret Hills Shuttle	424	801	1166	1608	1582	1931
Total	3266	3193	6139	7867	6836	8123

*Data for Long Mynd and Stiperstones Shuttles combined in 2009
Source: The Shropshire Hills AONB, 2009

include frequency (hourly on the two main routes), driver interaction with passengers, and driving that facilitates passenger comfort. Services can be designed to encourage engagement between residents and tourists, and at the same time be integrated with the aspirations of local attractions and places of interest. A final lesson to be learnt is the importance of partnership in terms of financial support (as the service does not break even), commitment and skills. The service is not described as a 'slow travel' product, yet is an ideal example of this form of travel experience as it meanders through quiet lanes so passengers can enjoy superb countryside in a relaxed way and without recourse to a car.

9
Water-Based Travel

As with other forms of travel, much water-based travel first developed for utility purposes, primarily trade, before emerging as forms of travel for tourism. Various different types of craft were developed to cross stretches of river, lake and sea, with water courses being the highways of the past. Tourists, like other travellers, used ferries and made use of major trade routes along European rivers, across the Atlantic and further afield to Africa, Asia and Australasia. Exploration of rivers was an essential part of the romantic period of the Grand Tour. In turn, travel across oceans became more appealing as sailing ships developed. However, early sea voyages were fraught with hazards and primarily undertaken by wealthy travellers intent on exploring new continents, partly on business and partly for adventure. Over time, voyages became safer as ship designs improved and in some cases vessels designed primarily with the tourist in mind were developed.

In the early days of tourism development the steamship played an important role. Steamships plied the main navigable rivers of the world and opened up remote areas to trade and explorers. The Mississippi steamers are perhaps the most famous and their designs soon reflected the need to provide some comforts over basic transportation. New Orleans became an important port and destination through the perseverance of the Charles Morgan Line (Irion and Ball, 2001). Ocean-going steamer ships were also important in stimulating international travel, especially amongst the wealthy seeking adventure. Others, however, had to travel long journeys in far less salubrious conditions on board vessels that were not fitted out to high standards. The first decade of the 20th century saw companies such as the Cunard Steamship Company and the Peninsula & Oriental Steamship Company develop regular services between continents (Bhatia, 2002). The transatlantic routes were the most popular, but passenger liners sailed between many ports of the world, through to the 1960s, when air travel finally superseded travel by sea.

Contemporary water-based transport in tourism takes a variety of different forms encompassing very large craft such as cruise ships and ferries of over 70,000 tonnes, capable of carrying over 2000 passengers, as well as small individual craft such as kayaks. It can be divided into sea travel (ferries and ocean-going cruises), routes along inland waterways, and small craft such as urban ferries and taxis and individual pleasure craft. In the tourism literature, water-based tourism usually refers to water sports activities undertaken at a destination (see, for example, Kokkranikal et al, 2003). This includes small pleasure craft such as kayaks and dinghies, which may be motorized, non-motorized or human-powered. Many of these craft are not normally used for travel, and there is some ambiguity about the inclusion of small pleasure craft within the slow travel concept.

Nevertheless, small pleasure craft, such as kayaks, yachts and motor cruisers, can facilitate travel, albeit often within a relatively small radius of the destination. For example, tourists might go on a whale-watching trip for a day, or hire a canoe for an afternoon on a lake. Such trips, while involving movement, essentially return to the same base within a few hours and may or may not include visiting a different destination (such as an island, in the case of whale-watching, or a settlement further down the lake, in the case of canoe hire). Whilst predominantly destination-based activities, small pleasure craft do embrace many of the core ingredients of slow travel: movement at a slow pace, low-carbon impact and experiential opportunities. They also offer the potential for longer trips. Small boat excursions can also double up as ferries, often performing an important function for isolated communities, and provide opportunities for tourists to travel on routes that are not otherwise available. This is, for example, the case in many parts of the world, such as the Gulf Island ferries in British Columbia, or the ferries in the Western Isles of Scotland. The distinction between a water-based activity and water-based travel can be blurred, and in some cases is not particularly helpful. However, that said, from a slow travel perspective, some forms of water-based travel, such as hourly canoe hire, provide almost no opportunity for actual travel and should be excluded from this analysis as essentially destination-based activities.

Cruising is another ambiguous category, which Cooper et al (2008, p417) describe as a 'holiday product as much as a mode of transport'. Cruises also take different forms, from large ocean-going vessels to small river cruisers and opportunities provided by cargo ships. From a slow travel perspective there is much doubt about the inclusion of cruise ships, due to environmental concerns and limited place encounters, which we discuss in more detail below. Ferries, on the other hand, provide essential links, especially for island communities. For instance, Greece is very dependent on ferries from the mainland to the islands and between islands, with Piraeus port handling 13 million passengers per year (Cooper et al, 2008). Ferries are therefore a component of slow travel.

Slow travel therefore encompasses both destination-based tourism products, to some extent, and also wider forms of water-based transport that are involved in, and facilitate, tourism. Destinations in Europe such as Bruges and Venice are noted for their water transport; it is an integral part of the visitor

Table 9.1 *Typology of water-based travel and compatibility with slow travel*

Typology		Slow travel compatibility
Ferries	• Urban water taxi/ferry • River crossings • Linking coastal and island communities • International sea crossings	Predominantly compatible and considered essential components of some trips; more ambiguity surrounds car ferries since they facilitate driving holidays
Cruises	• Large ocean-going cruise vessels • Cruises on cargo ships • Inland waterway cruises • Inshore coastal vessels	Not compatible with slow travel Compatible with slow travel Predominantly compatible with slow travel, although high-speed vessels excluded
Small pleasure craft	• Canoes/kayaks • Yachts • Speed boats	Compatible with slow travel Not compatible with slow travel

experience. Revitalized waterfronts also utilize small-scale ferries to good effect, and provide great vistas for visiting ships. For example, Boston in the USA and Buenos Aires have stimulated major interest in waterfront development, and this is occurring in some developing countries such as Zanzibar's Stone Town in Africa (Hoyle, 2002). There is no typology of water-based travel; however, for the purpose of this book it has been divided into three broad areas: ferries, cruises and small pleasure craft (see Table 9.1). These broad categories can be further subdivided by size or type of craft involved. The following section explores the slow travel experience offered.

The water-based travel experience

Travel across water is relatively time-consuming and thus provides a platform for travel-based experiences. All forms of water-based travel have in common an engagement with water, whether this is the ocean, a lake or a small river. Given the importance of water to human survival, it is a landscape feature that evokes a strong response. Recall, for instance, the family trip to the seaside and the first glimpse of the sea. Inland waterways also add drama to the landscape of a journey, and are often significant markers en route, especially where the grand rivers of the world are crossed by dramatic bridges (e.g. the suspension bridge across the River Humber in the UK, or the Golden Gate Bridge, San Francisco).

At a more intimate level, Arnould and Price's (1993) seminal paper explores the extraordinary hedonic experiences of tourists on a white water rafting trip of several days. They found that the participants did not recall any negative attributes, such as freezing in wet clothes, but that participants' deep sense of achievement 'leads to emphatic positive re-evaluation of all the negatives that might otherwise dominate evaluation of the experience' (p26). The adventure shared with family, old and newly-formed friends leads to stories that develop the self with three strong themes: communion with nature; communitas – a sense of belonging to a group; and personal growth and renewal of self – a rediscovered sense of self, acquisition of new skills and mastery. Similar experiences are common to other forms of active water-based travel such as sailing, canoeing and kayaking. On the other hand, larger vessels provide more passive forms of involvement, with boat travel providing memorable encounters with wildlife, with deep experiences emerging during reflective moments of travel (Curtin, 2009a; 2009b).

Ferries

In many tourism contexts ferries are unavoidable. For instance, prior to the Channel Tunnel, aside from air travel, the only way to leave the UK was by ferry. Despite initial concerns about competition from the Channel Tunnel, a large number of ferries still operate from the UK to France and Belgium. For many island communities, ferries are still the main option to leave the island.

The range of ferries is very diverse. At the smallest scale there are vessels operated by one man which might link a community split by a river, carrying less than ten passengers. These small ferries perform a very useful tourism function as they minimize distances travelled overland. For instance, walkers on the South West Coast Path in the UK can make use of a number of small ferries which dramatically reduce the distance that would need to be walked to circumnavigate estuaries, such as the River Fowey in Cornwall. At the same time, such ferries provide interesting views from the river and a memorable experience. The same is true of many small vehicle ferries, such as the ferry across the Gironde from Royan to Pointe de Grave in France. In an urban context, ferries have remained important in many historic ports, such as in Hong Kong, China and between New York and islands on the River Hudson.

At the other end of the scale are huge car ferries with the capacity to move several hundred vehicles between counties. Within Europe there are major routes across the English Channel, Baltic Sea and Mediterranean, while in Asia there are many high-speed ferries between Sumatra and Malaysia/Singapore. There are, of course, a wide range of intermediate-sized ferries performing a range of functions, many being essential for day-to-day travel in both developed and developing countries. While certain types of ferry have a relatively high carbon footprint, especially the fast hydrofoils, ferries are a necessary component of slow travel in a number of contexts where water-based travel is inevitable.

Sea crossings provide intensely memorable arrivals and departures. Passengers can be absorbed by views of the harbour and all the activities surrounding a departure. Then there is the immediate experience of leaving the port as the land recedes gradually into the distance. People wave from both ship and land and there is a shared excitement and anticipation of the voyage. While at the other end, the approaching land can be gazed upon in expectation. Passengers can relax on board, take meals, sleep and form plans for the journey ahead. Depending on the length of voyage, there may be entertainment. All in all, ferries are an essential and memorable component of slow travel. Lambert et al (2006, p483) comment:

*While recognising the diversity of images of the sea even within
the Western culture, it is possible to highlight certain recurring
themes in the imaginative geography of the oceans. The first,
and perhaps the most pervasive vision, is the sheer vastness of
the sea.*

Cruises

Large-scale ocean-going vessels

Cruises are a well-established form of tourism that provide the opportunity to
visit multiple destinations within a region, while the accommodation comes
too. This avoids complex transport and accommodation bookings and the
need to unpack and repack luggage on a regular basis. A cruise ship is a 'floating hotel' (Dowling, 2006). The UK and North America are the two main
source markets for cruise passengers, while the Caribbean is the leading destination (Peisley, 2008). The industry has seen significant growth in recent
years of as much as 15 per cent per annum (Dowling, 2006). In 2007 there
were 740 ships providing 102,000 beds and accommodating 16.4 million passengers worldwide (Peisley, 2008). Cruise ships vary in size, from under
10,000 tonnes and 200 passengers to over 70,000 tonnes and over 2000 passengers (Chin, 2008; Dowling, 2006), with the largest vessels now able to
accommodate over 3500 passengers (Dowling, 2006). The average capacity of
new ships in 2006 was double that of 2000 (Peisley, 2008). Cruising has
grown in recent years as it has become more affordable (Chin, 2008). Given
that the speed of vessels is relatively slow compared to air travel, purely in literal terms cruising might be considered slow travel. However, there is doubt
that it meets the criteria of slow travel, notably the low-carbon criterion (discussed in more detail below). There is also doubt about the experiential
aspects. While there is plenty of scope for socializing with other passengers
and crew, the interaction with places visited is much more limited in scope as
excursions are often organized by the cruise company and can be somewhat
staged. Indeed, Dowling (2006, p8) suggests 'ships are now destinations in
themselves and ports of call, in many cases, have become secondary', while the
on-board experience is carefully managed (Sheridan and Teal, 2006).

Also, in the context of sustainable tourism, Chin (2008, p8) highlights the
highly unregulated nature of cruise operations, due to the 'inherently border-
less environment' of the open seas. The industry has been criticized for, among
other things, economic leakage, tax avoidance and lack of regulation through
flying flags of convenience and poor labour regulations (long hours and poor
pay) (Chin, 2008; Dowling, 2006). The ocean cruise industry has been
excluded from slow travel predominantly due to potentially high carbon
impacts and low potential for engagement with destinations on the journey.

Small-scale river, lake and inshore coastal vessels

Aside from the ocean-going cruise sector and major river cruises, there is a
smaller-scale cruise sector that tends to focus on relatively short excursions of

up to one day. However, there is potential for this sector to be integrated with other forms of transport to form individual trip chains on a larger journey. The small-scale cruise sector operates on the sea, rivers and lakes. In many contexts, trips are seasonal and can be weather-dependent. Cruises may also be integrated with ferry operations, and many ferry operators sell underutilized space as day cruises. For example, Brittany Ferries offer day excursions on selected sailings from the UK to the Channel Islands and France. In Norway, there are many such cruises up fjords that also have the potential to develop as opportunities for slow travel. There is some ambiguity with this sector with respect to its utility as a form of travel, as opposed to a destination-based experience; however, as with ferries, there is scope for smaller-scale cruises to play a role in slow travel.

In many countries of the world there exist extensive canal and river networks. Since the demise of freight transport on many smaller canal networks (freight travel is still strong on larger rivers in Europe, the Americas and Asia), this has opened up opportunities for the tourism sector to develop barge and cruise holidays. Within Europe there are 16,000km of navigable waterways and these are popular in Belgium, France, Germany, the Netherlands and the UK (Erfurt-Cooper, 2009). River travel is also popular in Asia, such as the Yangtze River in China (Arlt and Feng, 2009). German river cruises increased by 168 per cent between 1996 and 2003 (Erfurt-Cooper, 2009). Reiter (cited in Erfurt-Cooper, 2009, p103) suggests: 'river cruising allows participants to "halve the speed and double your perception and awareness"'. This implies good experiential opportunities to engage with the landscape en route. Tourists on canal barge holidays travel at a particularly slow pace, often little faster than walking. This significantly limits both the distance that can be travelled and the resultant carbon footprint. On this basis, barge holidays encapsulate the elements of slow travel.

Commercial shipping

A final category of cruising is linked to commercial shipping. While most people associate cruise holidays with the cruise liner, designed specifically with tourists in mind, it is possible to take a cruise on board a cargo vessel, and even to travel around the world. Travelling on a cargo vessel is different to a typical cruise. While the cabins are of a high standard, there is much less in the way of recreation facilities on board, and travellers are advised to bring books and so on to while away the time, as there are no scheduled activities. Facilities also vary, with some providing swimming pools, a gym, lounge, books and films (Johnson, 2007). Cargo vessels will visit ports not typically on a tourist's itinerary, and this provides opportunities for authentic insights into the countries visited. There are also itineraries available to almost any destination in the world (Johnson, 2007).

A number of travel agents specialize in cruises on cargo vessels (see, for example, freightercruises.com or cruisepeople.co.uk). For instance, Freighter World Cruises was established in 1975. Their figures suggest freighter cruises have increased in popularity since this time, as more cabin space has become available through technological changes requiring smaller crews (Freighter

World Cruises Inc, 2009). Available cruises range from two-week trips in a localized area to four-month voyages around the world. Over 35 shipping lines are involved, operating more than 55 different itineraries for around 1200 clients per year. While customers have the opportunity to link cruises with a return flight, most opt for a round voyage and thus avoid the carbon footprint of a flight. Passenger numbers are usually limited to 12 or less; any more and the vessel must carry a doctor. Passengers must therefore certify their good health, and there are upper and lower age limits (Maris Freighter Cruises, 2009).

Passengers can join part of a cruise to make a transatlantic crossing, for example, or book a full itinerary; however, most trips involve a fair commitment to time and some flexibility (Johnson, 2007). This is the main drawback, as these cruises are on working ships running to a freight schedule and subject to last-minute changes (Maris Freighter Cruises, 2009). This can leave less time to visit ports, which may be far from tourist attractions (Johnson, 2007). Freighter travellers can also integrate their trips with land-based travel, as a passenger describes:

> *In Tahiti we had three days shore leave, so we walked through Papeete the first day, took a bus around the island the next, and the ferry to Moorea the third. When we reached Melbourne we jumped ship, took the train to Sydney, and spent two delightful days there before the ship caught up with us. (Maris Freighter Cruises, 2009)*

Costs tend to be less than traditional passenger cruises (Johnson, 2007): Kahler (2009) estimates up to a third or half the cost, but prices are rising. On the whole, cargo cruises would seem best suited to independent travellers who are flexible and able to organize their own trips (Johnson, 2007; Maris Freighter Cruises, 2009).

Freighter cruises provide excellent opportunities to engage with passengers, crew, places visited and the wildlife encountered en route. For instance, Johnson (2007) describes watching dolphins, whales and sea birds, and a passenger describes an encounter with people from the Pitcairn Islands:

> *In the afternoon of March 2nd we saw Pitcairn Island coming up ... We had a number of people come aboard on the rope ladder to sell wares, like T-shirts, small carvings, booklets, stamps, etc. They also traded fruit for soft drinks and meat. (Maris Freighter Cruises, 2009)*

It is also possible for the more adventurous traveller to negotiate passage directly with ships on a one-off basis. For example, within the Caribbean, such a strategy is used by local people to make voyages between the islands of Dominica and Montserrat, which are not connected by a direct flight. This strategy of using commercial shipping might be considered carbon neutral, as the ship is making the journey anyway with or without passengers. For example, the *Observer* writer, Ed Gillespie (2008), used a banana boat from Costa Rica to the UK to complete his journey round the world without flying.

There are clearly capacity limits to the use of commercial shipping, and young children may be prohibited for safety reasons. A significant limitation is also the availability of commercial shipping routes. Sailings can also be irregular, and the time commitment can be prolonged as sailings are subject to freight deliveries and there may be unanticipated stops at ports en route for several days. To this end, travel by commercial shipping is only an option for those with significant time available and commitment to avoidance of flights.

Small pleasure craft

Small pleasure craft include canoes/kayaks and yachts. These are generally covered by literature on water sports. UK data compiled by Mintel (2006) on water sports suggests they attract a broad spectrum of participants, but the core market is aged 20 to 45. The data suggests growth, as 60–75 per cent of participants are beginners, and there is increasing family participation. Statistics on UK residents undertaking water sports in Scotland suggests the market is slightly more male than female, and dominated by more affluent socio-economic groups. Overall, 6–7 per cent of adults are involved in some form of leisure boating in the UK (Mintel, 2006).

Canoe/kayak tours

Given its relative ease of access for beginners, canoeing/kayaking is the most popular water sport in the UK (Mintel, 2006), with an estimated 2 million people taking part each year (Mintel, 2008c). There is a distinction between kayaks and canoes. Kayaks use a double paddle, while canoes use a single paddle, and canoeing usually takes place on flat water. Both canoes and kayaks can be used to undertake tours; however, sea touring by kayak is only for the more experienced (Mintel, 2008d), while even families with young children can canoe on flat water rivers and lakes. Sea kayaking originated from the Inuit people, who use it as a form of travel around the Arctic Sea and Greenland (Jennings, 2003). Given that most participants are beginners (Mintel, 2006), sea kayak tours are a niche market, although this affords an excellent slow travel opportunity to travel along a section of coastline or between islands. In recent years the technology for making canoes/kayaks has improved, with the production of plastic models, which are cheaper and more robust, enabling the industry to expand (Mintel, 2008d). Canoeing and kayaking are generally self-organized by individuals or through clubs, with canoes owned or hired. It is also possible to attend training courses or join organized tours. While canoeing and kayaking are mentioned in articles on tourism and climate change, this is only in the context of activities potentially impacted by climate change through, for example, longer seasons or increased flooding.

As an active form of water-based travel, canoeing/kayaking can provide an intense experience, especially where trips are made to remote areas and there is much individual effort involved (Kane and Zink, 2004). Such trips play a significant role in identity formation for participants, who share experiences with other kayakers and use the trips to project image and status to peers (Duffy, 2004). Kane and Zink (2004) highlight the extensive telling of stories within an organized kayaking trip in New Zealand, which reinforces group membership and acceptance.

Yacht tours

Sailing is a sector of considerable size, although growth is currently slow (Mintel, 2008d). It is dominated by men and higher socio-economic groups (Mintel, 2008d). The sector is very diverse, and as for canoeing/kayaking, it is predominantly seen as a destination-based water sport activity. Sailing does, however, have potential as a form of slow travel as, aside from the use of onboard motors to negotiate difficult conditions and harbour entrances, it is a low-carbon activity. The Caribbean is most popular for charters (here there are significant climate change implications of travel from the USA and Europe), and the Mediterranean is the most popular cruising location (Jennings, 2003). Jennings (2003) identifies three cruise market segments: those who circumnavigate a region; fly-cruisers; and those on longer global trips. There are also lifestyle sailors (Macbeth, 2000), who opt to spend months or years at sea. As with canoeing and kayaking, participants co-produce the experience with their yachts and the environment visited. Travelling in this way can be unpredictable and extreme if bad weather is encountered. As most people travel as couples, families or small friendship groups, it is a sociable experience and one which strengthens bonds through adventure.

Environmental issues

Water-based travel is not without environmental problems, and there are well-recorded localized impacts on ecosystems, water quality, noise and air pollution (see, for example, Warnken and Byrnes, 2004). Table 9.2 sets out the main environmental impacts of water-based travel. The extent to which water-based travel is low-carbon is open to debate, which is set to continue as there is currently little data available on boats or ships (Lamers and Amelung, 2007) with which to make accurate comparisons to aircraft and cars. Canoeing and kayaking are seen as relatively benign activities. However, Gössling (2002) notes that infrastructure (accommodation, transport, etc.) is needed to access locations for canoeing/kayaking, and therefore there is an impact. To canoe, you generally need to transport canoes; therefore, in the majority of situations, the activity is dependent on motorized vehicles. In recent years, the rise in canoe ownership in the UK, due to the availability of cheaper models, has contributed to the increasing quantity of activity-related luggage carried on holiday. Transporting a canoe inevitably leads to car use, and is part of an increasingly consumptive approach to leisure, where large quantities of equipment are required. Kayaking in remote areas may also lead to high carbon footprints. For instance, in New Zealand, heli-kayaking is available, where access to remote white water rivers is achieved by helicopter (Kane and Zink, 2004).

Table 9.2 *Environmental impacts of water-based travel*

Localized environmental impacts

Ecological disturbance
Vessels of all sizes cause disturbance to ecological habitat. Even small personal craft such as canoes can cause wildlife disturbance, especially as they are able to access small and relatively remote rivers and creeks. Ecological damage is recorded in both inland and coastal environments and results from direct physical destruction of habitat, wave damage and more generalized disturbance of wildlife. Various legal instruments protect wetland habitats and can impose restrictions on boat access and speeds, sometimes on a seasonal basis.

Water quality
Water-based travel can affect water quality due to disturbance of sediment, disposal of waste water and spillage of fuel or exhaust waste. Impacts can be particularly acute in relatively contained water bodies such as lakes and canals.

Noise pollution
As with any motorized vehicle, boats can cause noise pollution. High-speed vessels, including small personal craft such as jet skis, are often subject to speed restrictions and zonation to avoid disturbance to other recreation activities.

Air pollution
As well as GHG emissions, ships produce NO_x and SO_2 that are increasingly subject to regulation.

Global environmental impacts

GHG emissions
Motorized vessels rely on fossil fuels and consequently produce GHG emissions.

Sailing, like canoeing, is seen as a relatively benign activity; however, the same infrastructure requirements apply. Sailing is also an activity pursued by relatively high socio-economic groups who are associated with high-carbon lifestyles (Gössling and Nilsson, 2009). While there is no data on travel mode used to sailing destinations, within a domestic tourism context, travel is likely to be predominantly car-based, while international contexts will be predominantly accessed by air. Indeed, sailing tours are sold as packages with a flight to destinations such as the Mediterranean and Caribbean. Therefore, sailing is predominantly a destination-based water sports activity with a relatively high carbon footprint, due to the dependence on air and car travel to access facilities.

A very small proportion of the sailing community, however, are more committed to sailing as a lifestyle choice. These people can spend months or even years away from home, and Macbeth (2000) estimates that there are, at any one time, anything from 500 to 2000 long-term cruising sailors pursuing a 'utopian vision' of unfettered travel somewhere in the world. Such people's pursuit of lifestyle travel by yacht results in a relatively low carbon footprint, compared to other long-term travellers who rely on flights to a much greater extent. It is also possible for yacht owners and crew to use sailing as low-carbon transport to access destinations. For instance, holidays across the North Sea between the Netherlands, Denmark and UK are popular with yacht owners. Such opportunities for low-carbon travel are likely to remain limited to higher socio-economic groups. At the present time, the potential for sailing to provide a low-carbon alternative is limited, and much sailing depends on high-carbon infrastructure.

Kayaks, canoes and yachts are increasingly an integral element of affluent lifestyles for many. Thus, while the activity itself may be carbon neutral, it is associated with high-carbon lifestyles and may be integrated with other forms of carbon-intensive travel. This presents a problem for the categorization of these activities as slow travel, and much depends on their integration with appropriate forms of land-based travel.

With respect to motorized vessels, in general, a review of the literature on marine tourism and cruise shipping shows that, to date, little attention has been paid to climate change impacts of passenger vessels. Barges and narrow boats predominantly rely on motorized propulsion; therefore, there is a carbon footprint. However, given the slow speed of travel and relatively low mileage, the carbon footprint is likely to be comparatively low. Barge travel can also integrate with cycling (Erfurt-Cooper, 2009), resulting in a low-carbon holiday.

Shipping, including passenger vessels, is currently excluded from the Kyoto Protocol (Holmgren et al, 2006). The GHG emissions that arise from shipping are predominantly due to CO_2 (99 per cent) (Holmgren et al, 2006). NO_x and SO_2, which are the subject of emerging emissions control agreements (NERA Consulting, 2005), have a net negative effect on radiative forcing but cause other, significant air-quality problems (Holmgren et al, 2006). While it is recognized that international shipping has important impacts on climate change (Corbett and Farrell, 2002; Corbett and Koehler, 2003), few studies have attempted to quantify the climate change impacts of shipping, and fewer still have focused on passenger ships.

Estimates of the contribution of shipping to GHG emissions vary. Chapman (2007) estimated that shipping as a whole accounted for up to 7 per cent of global GHG emissions in 2000, while Eyring and Corbett (2007) estimate a contribution of 2.7 per cent to all anthropogenic CO_2 emissions in 2000. The variability in these studies is partly due to different accounting systems; however, the different figures also reflect considerable uncertainty in quantifying shipping emissions. Globally, Eyring and Corbett (2007) suggest CO_2 emissions from shipping are of the same order as for aviation. In Europe the total CO_2 from shipping exceeds that of aviation, and on this basis there have been calls to include shipping in the EU ETS (Davies, 2006). Emissions from shipping, as a whole, are increasing, and CO_2 emissions from shipping could double by 2050 from their present levels. However, it is worth noting that shipping is generally considered an environmentally sound form of transport with regards to emissions per unit transported (Pisani, 2002).

Based on the limited material available, the following can be concluded about motorized passenger vessels. Speed is important in the marketing of high-speed ferries and cruise ships. Faster vessels emit more GHG per passenger km (pkm) than slower vessels (based on estimates by Psaraftis and Kontov, 2009). Thus, high-speed, hydrofoil ferries will emit more GHG per pkm than slower ferries of a similar capacity. Size is also important, but is more complex for passenger vessels compared to freight. In a freight context, small vessels emit more GHG per tonne-km than large vessels (Psaraftis and Kontov,

2009), but this pattern is likely to be different for certain passenger vessels. For instance, cruise ships, while large, transport a high volume of infrastructure per passenger, compared to a small, non-vehicle, passenger ferry.

The most recent cruise vessels incorporate a diversity of leisure facilities, such as ice rinks, swimming pools and rock climbing walls, which match the facilities in resorts (Dowling, 2006). Considerable energy is required to move and maintain these floating resorts. Indeed, Peisley (2008) reports that rising fuel costs are an increasingly large proportion of operating costs for a cruise ship. On the basis of the wide diversity of passenger ships and movement patterns, Psaraftis and Kontov (2009) suggest that, without access to detailed data on fuel consumption and travel patterns, it is impossible to calculate ship emissions with any accuracy. A similar conclusion was drawn by Lamers and Amelung (2007) in their study of Antarctic tourism. However, despite the paucity of data available, some estimates suggest that for freight, the carbon footprint measured in tonnes per km is substantially less for shipping than for air freight (Maersk Line, cited in Psaraftis and Kontov, 2009). Whether this analysis applies to passenger vessels will be highly context-dependent.

In 2005, overall estimates for ocean-going cruise shipping put emissions at 34Mt CO_2 (million metric tonnes of CO_2), less than 5 per cent of the global shipping emissions (World Economic Forum, 2009). While passenger ships (cruise and ferries) make up a small proportion of the global shipping fleet (about 6 per cent) (Sweeting and Wayne, 2006), given the high growth rate in the sector, emissions are estimated to rise by 3.6 per cent per year, to reach 98Mt CO_2 by 2035 (World Economic Forum, 2009).

The limited data on passenger vessels tends to suggest a fairly large carbon footprint per pkm for motorized vessels, but given the lack of data on a passenger km basis it is difficult to make comparisons with other modes. For instance, one of the few studies to examine the GHG emissions from cruise shipping focuses on trips to the Antarctic (Lamers and Amelung, 2007), which, given its remote location, involves a relatively long-haul cruise. Lamers and Amelung (2007) calculate that in the 2004/05 season, cruise tourism to Antarctica produced the equivalent of 5.39 tonnes of CO_2 per passenger, although this varied considerably relative to ship size and passenger numbers carried. The relative scale of these emissions can be seen if compared to the average annual CO_2 emissions per person in the EU-25, which equates to nine tonnes (in 2005) (Lamers and Amelung, 2007). Therefore, on the basis of carbon footprint, cruise shipping is excluded from slow travel.

At the other end of the scale, a study of Australian tour boat operators that focused on small- to medium-sized tourist boats (Brynes and Warnken, 2006) found that a typical boat trip averaged 61kg CO_2-equivalent if diesel-fuelled, or 27kg CO_2-equivalent if petrol-fuelled, per person. Brynes and Warnken concluded that marine-based recreation is responsible for a large quantity of GHG emissions. While this equated to only 0.1 per cent of GHG emissions in Australia, it was identified as a growth area through such activities as whale-watching and diving, and one with a fast-growing GHG output. Becken and Simmons (2002) lend support to this view in their analysis of tourist activities, which showed that jet boat operators were high energy users and that boat cruises consumed most energy per tourist after air trips. These figures provide some indication that small motorized boats should be excluded from slow travel, as they do not meet the low-carbon criteria.

Ferries might also be considered a relatively high carbon option; however, in many contexts there is no alternative, especially for island communities such as those in Canada, Greece or Scotland. Here ferries are an essential element of everyday life, as well as providing tourism access. Ferries have the potential for integration with other forms of slow travel. In Dorset, the Dorset Belle ferry company sells tickets that integrate a ferry excursion from Bournemouth to Swanage, with an open-top bus ride on the journey back. On the other hand, ferry travel is integrated with car use in Europe and North America, facilitating long-distance driving holidays that have high carbon footprints. Because of this there will ultimately always be some ambiguity about the inclusion of water-based travel within slow travel.

Summary

While the majority of water-based travel takes place at a slow pace, in comparison to land-based travel, this is only one of the defining features of slow travel. Water-based travel also provides an integral and distinct travel experience. On the other hand, some forms, notably cruise ships, provide rather limited and staged opportunities to engage with people and places en route, and the shared social experience is carefully managed. Cruise ship passengers have little authentic contact with the localities visited, in many respects the destination being the ship itself. There are also environmental considerations. While some forms of water-based travel involve human physical propulsion (e.g. canoes) or rely on renewable energy such as the wind (e.g. yachts), motorized boats and ships have a carbon footprint and localized ecosystem impacts have been attributed to most forms of water craft. Thus, there is considerable debate about the inclusion of water-based travel within slow travel.

While experiential elements play a part, perhaps the most significant issue at stake is the carbon footprint of forms of water-based travel. It is our contention that cruise shipping is excluded from slow travel. While accurate figures on the carbon efficiency of cruise ships are not currently available, there is enough evidence from the few isolated studies to suggest that cruise ships have a relatively high carbon footprint. This is largely due to their considerable size; as floating resorts, customers have come to expect a range of tourist activities on board. Transporting this bulky infrastructure across the ocean is not an energy-efficient way to travel. There are also concerns about the carbon footprint of smaller motorized vessels within the pleasure boat sector. There is certainly some doubt about the carbon efficiency of this form of travel. Until further evidence is made available, we have included smaller motorized pleasure craft within slow travel. Perhaps this will be a wake-up call to this sector. Investment will need to focus on energy-efficient vessels that might even operate at lower speeds.

The sector in general also needs to consider how it is integrated with other forms of travel. The canoe/kayak sector, for instance, could readily meet the requirements of low-carbon tourism, but only if it avoids much of its dependence on motorized travel to access sites and transport canoes. It is important that industry takes a holistic view. The following case studies provide examples of low-carbon water-based travel. Both provide excellent examples of transport as tourism.

Case study: canoe/kayak tours

Canoe tours on the Gudenå River, Denmark

In the Silkeborg region of Denmark, canoe tours of up to five days can be undertaken along the Gudenå River, from Tørring to Silkeborg (see Figure 9.1). These can be arranged as a package with accommodation at campsites, inns or hotels, with participants paddling up to 18km per day (Silkeborg Turistbureau, 2009). Tourist canoeing on the Gudenå River began in 1935, with canoe rental companies emerging in 1949. There are approximately 14 registered companies which rent canoes, spread fairly evenly along the river. Canoe rental companies also provide a compulsory permit which permits access on the river.

There is extensive cooperation between the canoe tour operators and local accommodation providers, with tourists making overnight stays at campsites along the river (an additional camping permit is required), in local bed and breakfast establishments or in hotels. The municipalities (Favrskov,

Figure 9.1 *Location of the section of the Gudenå River, Denmark, where canoe trips take place*

Juelsminde, Silkeborg, Viborg, Horsens, Skanderborg and Randers) through which the river flows all list canoeing as a major tourist attraction and the river in general is a rich tourism resource, providing opportunities for fishing, hiking, cycling and cultural interest that might be linked to a canoe tour.

The overall carbon footprint of such a holiday would depend on how the tour endpoints are accessed; obviously, the canoe travel itself is carbon neutral. There is no data available on mode of transport used to access canoe tours, but car parking is well publicized by canoe rental establishments. It can be generally assumed that the modal split is likely to reflect Danish tourism more widely and be dominated by the car. Transport from the end of trips back to the start is provided by bus.

As well as the carbon footprint caused by car access, there are localized environmental impacts to the river ecosystem due to disturbance. During the 1970s and 1980s canoeing on the river became so popular that it was necessary to reduce the number of canoes, in the interest of nature and wildlife. A total ban was contemplated but rejected, but the numbers allowed on the river at any one time were restricted. During this time the toilet and camp facilities along the river were extended and refurbished in order to 'contain' the tourists, and limit their impact on the surrounding nature and other activities associated with the river (fishing, hiking, etc.). Activities are restricted upstream of Tørring, and only 50 canoes are allowed to set out from Tørring each week. The canoe season runs from 16 June to 28 February, and activity is restricted to between 08.00 and 18.00 during this period, to limit disturbance to wildlife. Landing is only allowed at designated areas such as campsites. Up to three-person canoes are allowed, and groups may consist of a maximum of five canoes. The Gudenå River is viewed as one of the most precious natural areas in Denmark; nature conservation is a top priority and the above restrictions ensure that other activities along the river are not unnecessarily disturbed by canoes.

Exploring the Gudenå River by canoe can be described as a transport-as-tourism experience. Participants physically engage with the environment in a very direct way that makes them co-producers of the tourist experience. The trip is also inherently social, being shared with other participants, and produces many memorable stories. As trips can be adapted to suit the ability level of the group, it can be embraced by families with young children as well as more competent adults. While the skill level required is low, given the high level of self-reliance, the Gudenå River provides tourists with a unique slow travel opportunity.

Sea kayaking tours in British Columbia

Sea kayaking tours are available in many parts of the world, such as Scotland, Oman, Fiji, Australia and British Columbia. Trips are organized either independently by participants with their own equipment, or tourists can join a tour organized over a few hours to several days. Some tours are essentially small-scale expeditions, and may involve scientific data collection such as monitoring wildlife. Given that much of the activity is undertaken by individuals, small groups or small tourism operators, there is very little formal data available on sea kayaking. Data that exists provides estimates of numbers, but there is only anecdotal evidence on how kayakers access regions for tours, and it is assumed transport modes will reflect general trends of car travel and air travel over longer distances. That said, as for any tourism product, there is much potential for those engaging in kayaking tours to access the region by other forms of slow travel.

British Columbia provides opportunities for sea kayaking around its extensive coastline and islands. This is frequently integrated with opportunities for wildlife watching, and tours are sold as Orca trips (sea kayaking with killer whales) and whale-watching tours more generally.

Although recent data are not available, a survey of activity during the 1990s suggested sea kayaking was a growth activity. Between 1991 and 1995 the proportion of British Columbia residents participating grew from 3 per cent to 7 per cent, and since 1995 estimated participation has grown at a rate of 20 per cent per year (Gill et al, 2003). Some 30,000 kayakers stayed at least one night on the coast, for a total of 140,000 user days in 1996. The most popular area is the Gulf Islands, with 7340 kayakers recorded in 1996. Other popular locations include Johnstone Strait, Broken Islands, Clayoquot Sound, Nootka Sound and the Broughton Archipelago, which each attracted between 1000 and 3500 kayakers in 1996 (Gill et al, 2003).

In 2000 there were approximately 250 kayak service-providers, mostly small operators, although there were 30 to 40 large operations, offering a wide range of services including rental, instruction, touring and sales of associated equipment (Gill et al, 2003). Some 10–12 per cent of overnight trips are guided (Coastal Community Network, 2005), the remainder being conducted independently or by club groups. Gill et al (2003), while acknowledging that kayakers generally have minimal environmental impact, comment on the potential for increasing numbers to cause localized damage to the natural environment through human waste, litter and vegetation damage. However, no attention has been paid to the wider global impacts that might result from travel to access kayak tours. About 50 per cent of kayakers rent their equipment (Gill et al, 2003), which minimizes the need for car-based travel to the area in order to transport kayaks. In their travel information, tour operators do mention Greyhound bus access as well as travel by air and car. From a wider sustainable tourism perspective, sea kayaking has provided opportunities for cultural heritage development; the Heiltsuk, a First Nation community, are developing a kayaking business (Ministry of Small Business, Tourism and Culture, 2001).

Sea kayaking tours in British Columbia provide extensive opportunities for travel and destination experiences. Travel is at a slow pace, taking in multiple destinations. As an active traveller, kayakers co-create the experience through their intense physical involvement in both movement and the environment. There is much engagement with other people on the tour with whom an adventure is shared and friendships forged. Kayaking in such a wilderness setting is an extreme activity for most participants, which creates memorable stories. Given the connection to the environment visited and wildlife observed, participants are likely to share environmental concerns, something industry might encourage through promotion of slow travel to the kayaking base. Sea kayaking therefore encompasses much of the slow travel ingredients and could be developed in other regions.

Lessons learned

Both sea kayaking and inland canoe tours have been developed by small tourism operators or individual enthusiasts. Unlike many other forms of slow travel there is no requirement for substantial infrastructure, and therefore investment has come from the small businesses offering a niche product. There is relatively little regulation, although in many countries strict health and safety and insurance regulations will impact on operators. The development of canoeing and kayaking is therefore very dependent on current fashion and the entrepreneurial skills of small operators. However, canoeing and kayaking are clearly aligned with the ingredients of slow travel, and in a variety of coastal and inland waterway settings there is considerable potential for further development. As a carbon-neutral tourism activity there is scope for government investment in appropriate locations, where access by other forms of slow travel is feasible. Such a strategy would develop a low-carbon tourism product with a significant experiential element, where participants develop skills and a close contact with the natural environment.

10
The Future of Slow Travel

Walton (2009, p783) argues that 'work in tourism studies tends to be present-minded and instrumental in its approaches, schematic rather than grounded or contextualized when gesturing towards the potential significance of change over time'. Our ambitious aim has been to define slow travel from the outset and to present a case as to how this might provide a new form of sustainable tourism development in the future. In order to do this we began with an analysis of the contextual issues and approaches to sustainable development and tourism impact over the past decades. This was achieved through an exploration of impacts at a local destination level and within a wider global context. Even when examined at a destination level, tourism cannot be considered a 'green' industry, on several counts. More than this, there is clearly a contestation of the notion that tourism is invariably a positive agent for change.

At a global level it is now recognized that the tourism sector makes a significant contribution to GHG emissions and therefore climate change. Analysis of tourism data illustrates the major role played by transport in the use of finite resources and generation of tourism's share of GHG emissions. Thus, it is the travel component that warrants further scrutiny. International and national policy options are currently emerging that will help to reshape tourism demand and provision in the future. The sector is responding, if rather slowly, to these challenges. Lane (2009, p19), for example, comments:

> ... how the linear growth of tourism was first challenged by the concept of sustainable tourism, how the challenge went largely unheeded, and how only now, thirty years on, is the industry beginning to fear the unsustainable future.

Should the tourism sector choose to ignore the issues being flagged up by a succession of research studies and by policy-makers, and it has a relatively poor record to date, then it will struggle to meet the challenges of an emerging green and dynamic economy.

The question is whether the response from the tourism sector will follow the current pattern of tokenism, or be sufficiently far-reaching to bring about real change. Analysis of the sector response to a low-carbon future, in Chapter 2, indicates that most mechanisms in situ have only limited likelihoods of success, given the dominant paradigm of growth, profit and consequent increase of externalities. Weaver (2009, p35) argues that the roll-out of sustainable tourism during the past decades has amounted to no more than a paradigm nudge, rather than a fundamental shift in the tourism system:

> It may be ... that industry (and government) is engaging in a 'veneer sustainability' version of paradigm nudge primarily as a response to the veneer environmentalism exhibited by the general public itself, in high per capita GNP societies at least.

Therein lies a real danger: inertia will dominate the current system at the expense of innovation. The book has also explored the drivers of tourism and theoretical perspectives that seek to explain tourism demand. Tourism consumption has been analysed and increasingly represented as bringing potential problems in recent years; it has thus attracted the attention of academics from various disciplines. They seek to re-appraise the societal processes that have facilitated the rise of tourism. It is also clear that tourism has attracted the attention of theorists interested in its complexity as a social phenomenon, one which has particular significance in western society. Therefore, it is timely to propose a new tourism system which would embrace the principles of slow travel; a system that has the potential to bring about a paradigmatic shift, rather than the incremental nudge referred to earlier.

Our thesis for slow travel revolves around a number of core processes and ingredients that come together to facilitate lower-carbon tourism. There is clearly a task of refining and modifying what can best be described as an emerging theory. The core elements are: a process which brings about a modal shift away from air and car travel; a behavioural shift to the rediscovery of travel for its own sake to facilitate slower, but more carbon-efficient, journeys that engender engagement with people encountered and places en route, as well as at the destination; and an increasing expression of environmental concern by tourists conscious of a need to reduce their carbon footprint whilst maintaining the benefits of travel. These core elements have been the subject of investigation in the preceding case study chapters. The potential of slow travel is explored. This is essentially a discussion focusing on behavioural change, not just of individuals and groups which make up the market, but also policy-makers and tourism structures that supply the tourism offering; change is the subject of this final chapter.

Future scenarios

There have been surprisingly few published articles that seek to predict the future of tourism, but authors who address this topic lend support to the view that it is fraught with uncertainty (Faulkner, 2001; Formica and Kothari, 2008). In particular, it is argued that the greatest difficulty for tourism organizations is the assessment of future environmental impacts (Pechlaner and Fuchs, 2002). Nor does tourism stand alone; it has well-defined links with the communications, transport and hospitality sectors (Farrell and Twining-Ward, 2004). In turn, it is dependent on the health of other business sectors that generate income and the desire to travel among the population.

With regard to the welfare of societies, one external factor reigns above all else; it is the need to respond with urgency to the challenges of resource depletion and climatic change. The current global strategy of economic growth (about 4 per cent per annum, in recent decades) continues to realize pessimistic scenarios of resource depletion and climate change, which have been presented as serious dangers some time ago (Daly, 1996; Meadows et al, 1972). Transport is no exception. It is estimated that the world's citizens travelled 23 billion km in total in 2000, and this is expected to rise to 105 billion km by 2050 (Schafer and Victor, 2000). Tourism could well account for 15–20 per cent of this projected additional distance; there is also a very uneven distribution of travel patterns between developed and developing countries (Gilberg and Perl, 2008). However, there is no certainty that the current development patterns will continue, as limits may be reached (e.g. through peak oil), or tipping points might occur which bring about a radical restructuring of systems we currently depend upon (Urry, 2008).

One such tipping point relates to carbon reduction and climatic change. There is substantial consensus around the need to limit a global temperature rise to no more than 2°C; the debate now is how to achieve the right prescription. The 'business as usual' scenario is no longer tenable. Unless all sectors of the economy act together, there will be unavoidable consequences; not only could there be devastation in some parts of the world, but also tourism will wither. Butler (2008) argues that the role of external agents has been systematically underestimated in future scenarios for tourism and that prediction should engage chaos theory in order to better understand random events and the turbulence that might occur. Thus, environmental impact is now the major agent of change in a move to a new paradigm in tourism, not supply sector innovation. The consequences of not changing to meet climatic challenge are unthinkable. Some authors point to the social consequences of mass unemployment, poverty and disorder if the world collapses into involuntary recession (Schriefl et al, 2008). This was avoided, but only narrowly, following the economic crisis of 2008–09 through unprecedented government intervention to retain the integrity of a global banking system in collapse (Jackson, 2009). Dennis and Urry (2007, p66) paint a potentially bleaker scenario which envisages a nexus system coming into place, featuring database and digital manipulation:

> *Are we 'predicting' a dystopic digital Orwellisation of self and society with more or less no movement without digital tracing and tracking with almost no-one within at least rich societies outside a digitical panopticon and with a carbon database as the*

public measure of worth and status? Maybe. Yet possible future(s) are just that: they are possible.

Such stark deterministic predictions are made in the light of the potential consequences of not responding to resource depletion, ecological damage and climatic change. Scientific opinion, based on a recent agglomeration of evidence, has now hardened; atmospheric concentration of CO_2 should be limited to the lower end of the range 450–550 parts per million by volume if the world is to avoid the avoidable. The problem has been diagnosed, solutions are less clear. A good starting point, in building a slow travel scenario, is perhaps to review the present.

The current tourism scenario

It is often said that tourism is remarkably robust. It has, after all, recovered speedily from regional and global crises in the past three decades. In the face of one of the worst recessions since the 1930s, coupled with the greatest environmental challenge ahead, the initial response from the UNWTO on the matter was to set out a *Roadmap to Recovery* (UNWTO, 2009a, p2), which highlighted seven points:

- Organizations need to realize that the crisis is significant and transforming.
- Markets will change and 'future operating patterns for global economies will be vastly different from the past'.
- There is a need to harness technology to become more efficient and reduce costs.
- Engagement in public/private partnerships should be encouraged.
- Advocate to governments that tourism is important.
- Help the poorest countries to grow tourism and to fight climatic change, especially in Africa. They should do this by 'growing their flights, revenues, technology, skills and financing in an increasingly climate neutral world'.
- Advocate that tourism and travel packages are at the core of stimulus packages and the new green deal.

The language of the document implies that the apparent contradictions have not as yet been reconciled. This is typified by the call to grow aviation in a carbon-neutral world. As Butler (2008, p350) notes:

> ... *sustainable tourism has often been tied to a worthy but somewhat impractical social and economic goals such as poverty alleviation, often running counter to environmental aspects of sustainability.*

The UNWTO (2009a, p1) has also made several calls for more governmental support for tourism, which, at the same time, is described as being a sector 'synonymous with resilience'. According to the UNWTO, tourism has the power to bring about a long-term transformation to a Green Economy, a term used to describe a proposed change in the way governments direct their economies. Tourism, it is argued, will also be a major job creator which will help to alleviate poverty in developing countries (UNWTO, 2009b; World Travel and Tourism Council, 2009). These are bold claims. The UNWTO indicates that this transformation will occur principally through 'responsible energy related consumption' and 'anti-poverty operation patterns' (UNWTO, 2009a, p1). There are, as yet, only sketchy notes as to how this might occur.

The Green Economy Initiative (UNEP, 2009) does, however, hold great promise, as it seeks to encourage governments and pan-global organizations to re-shape, refocus and invest in a new economic order, which will act as an engine of recovery and transform production and consumption patterns. There are two or possibly three approaches to this new theoretical base for development. Critical theorists argue that the only way forward is to remove a marketing approach which fosters consumption without recourse to sustainable development; this requires a paradigmatic change to the wider economic order, and equally to the tourism system. Development theorists argue that policy advice which guides governments, consumers and producers towards more sustainable ways of operating and consuming will bring considerable environmental gain. There is not necessarily a need to bring about major changes to the tourism system, but just to make the necessary changes within it. The third way is to accept that these two perspectives are not entirely mutually exclusive (Mittelstadt and Kilborne, 2008).

UNEP sets out the strands of the Green Economy initiative which will involve more of the following across all sectors, including tourism:

- clean technologies
- renewable energies
- water services
- green transportation
- waste management
- green buildings
- sustainable agriculture and forests.

The aim is to achieve better returns on investment based on reducing GHG emissions, using fewer resources, creating less waste and reducing social disparities. The initiative clearly has a vision, but how will it be realized? Firstly, it should be noted that there have been a multitude of limited projects in tourism spanning at least two decades now, with little or no effect other than adoption by a number of small-scale individual businesses or destinations (Weaver, 2007). Nevertheless, sustainable tourism development as a conceptual framework is widely recognized as what societies want (Lafferty, 2004). Dwyer et al (2009) reported considerable commitment to the concept by destination managers and tourist organizations located in Australia. Unfortunately, despite this broad consensus, there has not been widespread adoption of the principles of sustainable development into practice; the sector is still moving in the wrong direction (Sharpley, 2009). This message has been reinforced by the EU (COM, 2003, p18):

> *Despite these many initiatives, which exist from international down to local level and are available everywhere, there is still no significant change from unsustainable patterns of consumption and production in European tourism.*

The issues, response and approaches presented by UNEP are to be detailed in a report to be published in late 2010. The gathering of data and analysis for the report is referred to as an 'open architecture' framework to reach consensus on transforming scenarios. We hope that this book offers a contribution as to how tourism might be re-shaped to meet the requirements of a new green economic order.

Currently, tourism is not only a social phenomenon, which has continued to flourish in most societies, but it is also a complex mesh of public and private organizations delivering production and consumption of leisure. We are referring primarily to domestic tourism, which is estimated to be ten times the size of the international market to which most scholars refer. Academic interest has predominantly focused on western tourism development, and much less is written about domestic tourism in the context of a developing world. The growth of domestic tourism in Brazil, China and India might take a different form to western societies. For example, Urry's (2007) new mobilities paradigm (seen as so important to recast the social sciences) explains the multiplicity of connections in societies which are essentially at a distance, fast and often involving physical movement. This is essentially a western outlook. While the five interdependent mobilities described by Urry (see Chapter 3) are growing in the developing world, given the widespread levels of poverty, they play a much less significant role in the structure of everyday life. Hall (2010) comments:

> *... the concept of 'vacation rights' highlights massive global inequality in access to such mobility. For much of the world's population, and notably those in the least developed countries ... the concept is meaningless and irrelevant by virtue of the majority of people's poverty, powerlessness and immobility.*

It is also important to note that within developed countries there is considerable inequality, and significant sections of the population for whom international and even domestic tourism plays little part in their lives.

There is no overall estimate of tourism's worth in terms of social value set against environmental impact. The international market has grown from 25 million arrivals in 1950 to 842 million in 2006; this amounts to an average increase of 7 per cent per annum. Thus, the combination of domestic and international tourism forms a major economic sector which consumes an increasing level of finite resources. It is also a substantial and increasing polluter, especially in relation to the production of GHGs. The contribution of transport to this process has been underestimated; over 50 per cent of annual travel distance can be attributed to leisure travel in developed countries (Holden, 2007). There are increasing calls for transport not only to reduce CO_2 emissions, but also to enhance liveability across communities (Hickman and Banister, 2007).

There are three driving forces fuelling the existing tourism system; these are not significantly different from Krippendorf's diagnosis in the 1980s (Krippendorf, 1984). This system has proved its resilience and has continued to achieve growth, despite international epidemics, financial crises, wars and terrorism in the intervening 25 years. The processes are as follows:

1   Socio-cultural values continue to favour travel as a leisure pursuit.
     The combination of increased leisure time in many western societies, and amongst the mercantile classes of the developing economies, coupled with a propensity to spend disposable income on travel, are two constant determinants. The advances in technology, changes in the procurement of information and advice and attitudes towards mobility are also important stimulants within the current tourism sector. Marketing is more than a simple brochure highlighting distribution channels; it is a labyrinth of societal interfaces including media representation, viral communications and a general hub of promotional messages about speed, distance, aeromobility and automobility, which Urry refers to as the essential elements of mobilities.
2   A reduction in travel costs has changed perceptions of travel.
     The travel time budget of people has remained relatively constant in recent years (Metz, 2008). However, improved transport technology and government investment in infrastructure and reduced energy prices have enabled access to a wider range of destinations within this overall budget. This real reduction in cost, associated with low-cost airlines and falling petrol prices (in real terms), is compounded by a perceived reduction in travel cost in the market place. This has fuelled a demand for shorter-stay tourism over longer distances.
3   The tourism supply sector is still growing, and choice of destination has become almost infinite.
     Local and national governments, pan-governmental organizations and the media have continued to encourage the supply of new destinations (and equally resist the decline of resorts in other places). The rationale behind destination development is to stimulate economic activity led by powerful, upstream institutional drives. Other factors, such as environmental externalities accruing from such developments, have been far less important. The process of increased supply is uneven and has been undertaken regardless of competitive advantage or disadvantage in a global market.

The result is that the tourism system has enjoyed almost continued growth, but there have been losses attributed to this process too. They are best summarized as a degradation of the 'public goods' associated with many destinations, a loss of diversity (and biodiversity) across destination regions coupled with a plethora of externalities affecting the environment (Mowforth and Munt, 2009). Given the preference for micro-studies in tourism, it is only now that we have counted the total sum of resource use and degradation attributable to tourism development. These negative outcomes continue to increase as the system links extended multi-markets to more destinations through a multiplicity of marketing and distribution channels; it is a process which is unlikely to change, partly because the externalities have not been internalized by the supply sector and partly through inertia in the system. It is instructive to note the way in which Urry (2007, p268) refers to the automobile as a central lynchpin of mobilities:

> *Such locked-in institutional processes are extremely difficult to reverse as billions of agents around the world co-evolve and adapt to it and built their lives around its strange mixture of coercion and flexibility.*

The same prognosis readily applies to tourism. Given the interdependencies of organizational and governmental systems which promulgate growth as a panacea, we are seemingly locked into the current tourism system. The group of institutions which develop policy guidance, offer investment opportunities, represent tourism business interests and include a myriad of tourist associations around the world therefore tend to be guided by the following tenets of tourism:

- Reduce the perceived cost of travel in order to stimulate higher levels of demand than hitherto, even though the returns may be marginal.
- Avoid the internalization of externalities, including CO_2 emissions.
- Stimulate increased supply as an economic goal, regardless of saturation of demand.
- Encourage a travel culture across societies through partnerships with media, government and tourist associations.
- Promulgate sustainable tourism and pro-poor tourism as a response to a critique of tourism as neo-colonialism.

The current tourism system is imbued with these values. It offers unlimited travel opportunities for those with the wherewithal, ironically at the expense of those who will bear the initial thrust of adverse climatic change. It perpetuates a system which is profligate of the world's resources, especially in relation to public goods where there is a wider ecological significance at stake. It is also one which perpetuates the inequalities between western and other societies (Mowforth and Munt, 2009). There are exceptions to this generalization, but many pro-environmental tourism schemes are small-scale, and thus whilst they may show the way ahead, they do not, even collectively, provide an answer. The reality is constant degradation of the base on which tourism relies.

The TEEB (The Economics of Ecosystems and Biodiversity) report (2009) has referred to the way in which the world's natural capital is being continually run down without societies knowing its true value. The report, for example, cites the irrevocable damage to coral reefs and loss of biodiversity in many countries. Tourism has had its part to play in this process. It is also reliant on transport for its existence and thus has a derived heavy dependency on fossil fuels; it is a system which happens to be increasing carbon emissions when other sectors are reversing the trend. How does this square with a world order which is attempting to come to terms with challenged economic and ecological systems? Jackson (2009, p15) describes the scenario as follows:

> *The uncomfortable reality is that we find ourselves faced with the imminent end of the era of cheap oil, the prospect of steadily rising commodity prices, the degradation of air, water and soil, conflicts over land use, resource use, water use, forestry and fishing rights, and the momentous challenge of stabilizing the global climate. And we face these tasks with an economy that is fundamentally broken, in desperate need of renewal. In these circumstances, a return to business as usual is not an option.*

Even if there are technological breakthroughs in the development of fuels with low ecological footprints, it is argued that there will also be a need to substitute and reduce car and air travel to achieve long-term sustainability (Holden and Høyer, 2005; Jackson, 2005). In summary, external agents of change will bring these shifts if the institutions and supply sectors within the tourism system fail to be proactive. If governments and private sector organizations plan with due diligence for a transition, then there will be opportunities to reap benefits for some if not most communities. That is the assumption made in developing the following scenario.

Transition to slow travel

Paradigmatic shifts are associated with moments of change rather than incrementalism. However, there is often a series of factors which build momentum for change. There are signs that a morphology in the tourism system is already in motion. Policy adjustment is in the making. There are steps to encourage major players in the tourism sector to be more proactive (rather than a small number of organizations currently dealing with the issues in a holistic manner). Secondly, there is evidence of a convergence of consumer values, two of which are particularly important: becoming more environmentally aware; and becoming increasingly cost-conscious in a less certain economic outlook. These core underlying factors are likely to combine to bring about a change in attitudes. Experience tells us, however, that awareness does not always translate into action and hence lead to lower carbon consumption (Midden and McCalley, 2002). Weaver (2007), for example, presents a scenario which suggests that people are becoming increasingly aware of climatic change and even lend support to the idea of doing things differently. However, in reality, he argues, they are not ready to make major shifts in their own lifestyles. Given a marginal consumer response, there will be a reluctance to change within the supply sector. Suppliers will adopt minor changes which pay lip service to the greening of tourism (Bianchi, 2004). Many suppliers are currently gaining from this equivocal position. Furthermore, resistance will persist in the system as some destinations would stand to lose. For example, island tourism, which relies on long-haul flights, is predicted to decline as oil prices increase (Becken, 2008, p696):

> *Initially, a peak in oil production would manifest itself as rapidly escalating prices followed by worldwide oil shortage.*

It may even spell near total decline for such destinations, as markets dwindle. Thus, a scenario which outlines new approaches and including some reduction in tourism supply signifies uncertainty and most probably risk for some suppliers. It will therefore almost certainly be denounced as unworkable by core institutions. Lobbying by advocates seeking to maintain a semblance of the current mainstream, high-carbon tourism economy will continue to work to avoid change; the stance of the aviation sector alone provides evidence to support this argument (Gössling and Upham, 2009).

This type of shift in market or supply condition is, of course, not a new phenomenon. Destinations have always suffered from the vagaries of changing fashions and the consequences of economic disparities. Many destinations in Central and Eastern Europe took a severe blow with the demise of the Soviet bloc. The transition period has not been easy for the fledgling Central and Eastern European states. Many Latin American states have reorganized tourism in the face of economic collapse. There are also examples of external climatic impacts affecting many tourism destinations, such as New Orleans, in the USA, which was seriously damaged by a hurricane in 2005. In almost every case, destinations have set out plans to seek recovery. Thus, there is a degree of flexibility within the existing tourism system to meet natural, institutional and market challenges to tourism. After an initial shock and disrupted demand, many tourism providers will be able to respond to a changing tourism system.

There is another key matter worth reiteration at this point in the discussion. Much of the tourism that occurs across the world involves primarily short- to medium-distance travel and is essentially domestic or cross-border in nature. There are many examples of where short-distance, longer-stay tourism has remained an essential part of social life. For example, in Scandinavia the practice of staying at a holiday home for several weeks in the summer is still commonplace, although, as 95 per cent of these trips are by car, the travel element remains unsustainable (All et al, 2008). There are also aspirations to encourage a renewed domestic market in some countries (Dwyer et al, 2009). This is where slow travel can be developed to good effect in the world of domestic tourism. It is where the greatest potential lies to move to a low-carbon tourism economy.

Markets are nurtured by global companies in the tourism system. Thus, these companies will have an important role as an agent of change in the transition phase to a new green tourism order. Governmental incentives to adopt low-carbon approaches will bring a response to meet changing consumer expectations and for opportunities to reduce costs (Lynes and Dredge, 2006). There are a few cases of this happening now, but the price of resources will determine a decidedly different pace of change. The alternative will be to continue to compromise ecological systems to the point of collapse.

It is probable that if the tourism sector cannot reach for new solutions, governments will increase intervention to secure the welfare of their citizens by introducing regulation to avoid worst-case scenarios (TEEB, 2009). Thus, real changes to the current system (the moment of change) will happen in response to a cluster of external factors: an increasingly rapid decline of ecological systems, an intensity of use of finite resources and greater tangible impacts of climatic change. The extent, pattern and nature of the change will depend on a wide range of variables. Of these, three will be of utmost importance: the pace in which the effects of climatic change impinge on tourism destinations (as the evidence to date indicates that it is a sector which is slow to react); the extent to which governments introduce regulation regarding use of resources such as carbon/energy quotas or trading certificates; and, finally, shifts in market behaviour will occur partly as a response to economic events (the trigger), but also in relation to environmental concerns. In the face of more risk-laden travel, people are likely to opt for more secure, less demanding holidays. The period of transition will involve the following inputs into the system, many of which will be parallel or overlapping in nature.

Policy

Policy development will be essential in the process of directing change. One prelude to a progressive emerging policy framework can be seen with regard to an example from the European Union. Within recent EU policy development there has been some attempt to specifically address wider sustainable development issues within the tourism sector; for example, in a communication on sustainable tourism (COM 2003). This was followed by the establishment of an advisory group on sustainable tourism, launched in 2004. This culminated in a report from the group which highlighted the climate change impacts of tourism and made a number of recommendations (see Table 10.1). These endorse slow travel.

Clearly, such a document does not represent formal policy; however, it offers a parallel to that being adopted by UNEP. The gestation time for the formalization of such policy frameworks remains a cause for concern. Five years on from the initial thrust of policy advice on tourism in 2001, the EU reported that tourism businesses have barely embraced sustainable development (Commission for the European Communities, 2006).

The principal and fundamental change likely to be seen in all policy frameworks will be the framing of all tourism development within the ecological limits of climatic change. Reduced use of resources has been advised in previous pronouncements, but there is likely to be a hardening line as forecasted depletion becomes reality. The ecological principles of conservation, resource reduction and carbon reduction will become imperatives, as will the

Table 10.1 *European Commission Tourism Sustainability Group recommendations to address the impact of tourism transport*

Aviation sector

- Research, support and regulation leading to improvements in vehicle, aircraft and fuel technology and traffic management (including air traffic control).
- Participation by the aviation sector in an EU emissions trading system, and encouragement of all international airlines to participate in similar systems.
- Actively promoting carbon-offsetting schemes to travellers, with the support of operators.

Modal shift to more environmentally-friendly forms of transport for tourism (train, coach/bus, water, cycle, foot)

- Adjusting taxation and pricing mechanisms to reflect environmental cost.
- Actively and creatively promoting alternative transport options (equally for the enjoyable experience they offer as well as for their low impact) and providing high-quality information to tourists on them.
- Investing in appropriate infrastructure and services (cycle trails, rail services, coach and car parking, etc.), using revenue from environmental taxes where appropriate.
- Continuously improving integration between different types of transport service and ease of use by tourists.
- Careful location of new tourism development with respect to accessibility.

A further approach is to seek to reduce distances travelled, while retaining total visitor spending. This may require:

- Adjusting target markets and promotion towards more local and domestic source markets.
- Encouraging fewer but longer holidays, while recognizing that this goes against recent market trends.
- Promoting attractions and activities within and around the destination rather than longer excursions.

Source: European Commission Tourism Sustainability Group, 2007, pp9–10

precautionary principle; these will replace current voluntary guidance supported by best practice examples.

Travel costs

Policy frameworks may also lead to more formal regulations to shape demand and supply. For example, personal carbon allowances may play a role in the future. However, before this occurs, it is likely that escalating cost structures will increase the price of travel. High-carbon elements will witness price rises, such as airline and car travel, in response to taxation regimes based on the 'polluter pays' principle. Some researchers doubt the efficacy of some regulations or taxes to deliver significant reductions in emissions (Mayor and Tol, 2009). There will nevertheless be an increase in travel costs simply because of market forces and possibly through regulation such as energy quota certificates. These combined factors will bring a return to the consumer perception that spatial distance is, once again, an important rule of thumb in estimating cost and hence demand. In developing countries, this fundamental rule has not been lost, as motorized transport remains scarce and non-motorized transport is appropriate for shorter trips. There will obviously be differential applications in accordance with regional or local circumstances, as well as all manner of trade-offs and synergies.

Travel behaviour

The transition will also be marked with a change in behaviour in some of the markets. There is already mounting evidence of a green consciousness among some market segments in developed countries (Dolnicar and Leisch, 2008; Dolnicar et al, 2008). Pro-environmental behaviour is dependent on attitudes towards the environment (Nilsson and Küller, 2000). It is estimated that 30 per cent of the population are already green supporters and 40 per cent described as neutrals who could become engaged. Only 30 per cent of the market is averse or rejects outright the need to be more attuned to environmental concerns (KMR, 2008). This is likely to become more diffused as the problems of climatic change become more tangible. However, Jackson (2005) points out that behavioural change requires more than information, and Moser and Dilling (2007) note that people rationalize their aversion to take action and present discourses accordingly to justify their approach. In the context of slow travel, the rationale is not so much about reduction or removal of travel, but about choice that is still within the comfort, convenience and cost zones of a wide range of the population.

There is likely to be another fundamental driver. It is argued that travel reduction is more likely to come from reduced levels of affluence than pro-environmental behaviour. Jackson (2009, p187) estimates that this level of adjustment will be an enormous task:

> In a world of 9 billion people all aspiring to western lifestyles, the carbon intensity of every dollar of output must be at least 130 times lower in 2050 than it is today. By the end of the century, economic activity will need to be taking carbon out of the atmosphere not adding to it.

As economies seek to reduce the carbon intensity in the economic system, growth may not be axiomatic and there could well be less disposable income available across communities. This is another principal reason why a slow travel paradigm is possible. It is based on an assumption that modest shifts of behaviour, driven by an emotional need for holiday-taking, but with recourse to the rational boundaries of economics and ecology, can take place within most tourism markets. Consumers will expect to influence tourism development and changing supply of tourism. There is, however, already a slow travel movement which is advocating a different way to take holidays; the question is about the pace and breadth of its growth.

There are three possible scenarios for slow travel during this period of transition.

Slow travel as a niche market

Slow travel is currently a niche market favoured by sections of the middle class in developed economies and by lower socio-economic groups who have little alternative. One possible option is that this niche will continue to grow, but at a relatively modest rate. Thus, it would remain as a small market segment in comparison to mainstream tourism. It will nevertheless enjoy a status similar to alternative, eco- and responsible tourism, which are becoming more diffuse. Some of the characteristics of the market will include people taking advantage of revitalized overland passenger transport networks, staying at destinations located within closer proximity to the place of origin and re-kindling the resurgence of interest in local food and beverages.

Slow travel destinations emerge

A second scenario might be that slow travel emerges as a more mainstream market. This will require commitment on the part of destinations to become future-makers rather than takers (Ellyard, 2006). An emergent market in Europe has been reported by Euromonitor (2008, p15):

> Slow travel in Western Europe is forecast by Euromonitor International to record healthy growth over the next five years, at an estimated 10% Compound Annual Growth Rate (CAGR), becoming a significant alternative to 'sun and sea' and cultural tourism. Consumers are expected to regard slow travel as the most relaxing – and possibly rewarding – holiday option. This type of tourism will attract consumer segments such as baby boomers as well as health and socially-conscious people. Slow travel's increasing popularity is expected to produce a noticeable impact on travel and tourism worldwide.

In response to this growing trend, it is envisaged that some destinations will re-invent themselves as slow travel places. Dolnicar et al (2009), for example, argue that destinations will need to look beyond their own borders to achieve low-carbon tourism. They suggest, for example, that destinations will need to encourage short-haul tourism by train travel, offering added value for visitors such as free circulatory buses and cycle hire so as to reduce the necessity to carry equipment to the destination by car.

The potential for small- to medium-size resorts across all continents is enormous; there will be a revitalization of place and regions (Arnesto and Martin, 2006). Some examples of development point to this happening already. The Alpine Pearl resorts, for example, is an attempt by 22 destinations to sustain nature and reduce impacts on the environment by offering soft mobility holidays (Matos, 2004). These focus on car-free holidays and involve investment in other more sensitive modes (walking, cycling and electric cars) and the integration of public transport. Verbeek and Mommaas (2008) argue that it is an environmentally sound product, but that it is still in the development stage. The institutional barriers between transport and tourism providers, across borders and sectors of tourism have not entirely been overcome. The authors comment that there is also a need to design slow travel products and destinations according to different time and spatial settings to meet the requirements of the slow traveller. The European Environment

Agency (EEA, 2003) estimated that of the 100 million tourists who visit the Alpine region of Europe, some 80 per cent travel by car, and that there has been a considerable increase in car travel during the past decade. The impact of the slow travel destinations, the Alpine Pearls, will be small, but it offers a model for other destinations to follow.

Slow travel as a set of principles applied to all types of tourism

A third scenario is that the values and approaches to slow travel will be adopted on a far wider scale than at a number of progressive destinations. The transition to a low-carbon tourism system would encourage both markets and suppliers to change the production and consumption of tourism, in line with the principles set out in Chapter 4, but principally involving those outlined in the next section. Here we propose a slow travel paradigm, drawing inspiration from the conceptual development of sustainable consumption (Jackson, 2005). It offers a way of decoupling speed, distance and unacceptable levels of environmental degradation from the tourist experience.

Some authors suggest that this mainstream approach will happen through a process of reflexive shared mobility (thinking about the consequences of travel on others), leading to what has been described as ecomobility (Beckmann, 2002; Nielsen, 2005). It has the potential to deliver core elements of the tourist experience, such as wellbeing, relaxation and social relationships (including hedonism), without enduring the externalities of high-carbon mobility. It is a scenario which hinges on the design of travel experience, which is characterized by being local and pushed forward in a bottom-up manner by transitional communities; it would be bounded within ecological limits and offer greater social equity.

A new paradigm of slow travel

There is an argument, drawn essentially from ecology, that dominant forms or systems are eventually replaced by sub-systems and this, in turn, strengthens a new or modified system. However, Weaver (2009, p35) notes that the dominant paradigm can often absorb selected elements of an emergent paradigm and hence deflect consequential change. He describes this process as 'a paradigm nudge that diabolically reinforces the incumbent worldview'. This perspective could well happen in the transition from high- to low-carbon tourism; the way to avoid this negative symbiosis is, among other factors, through greater consumer power within the system (Lane, 2009). In this final section, attention is paid to how a slow travel paradigm might form the basis of a new tourism system. This would involve changes to the current assumptions, values and principles discussed throughout the book.

The system would have a goal of achieving sustainable tourism, but it would remain in the form of an ideal; in reality, ideals are difficult to achieve, but they are essential in providing aims and direction. The system would be designed as a coherent entity with tourists, as agents of consumption, interacting with new structures of provision (Verbeek and Mommaas, 2008). The processes imbued in the system would reverse the current emphasis on intense use of resources, speed, immediacy and consumption of as many attractions and destinations as possible within a time compression.

It would, on the contrary, interface with the values of slowness, feature a relaxed approach to time as enrichment, and focus on exploration and relationships with other actors in the performance of the tourist experience (Ryan, 1997; Woehler, 2004). It would also emphasize localness and locality, rather than distance and intensity; the system might involve a myriad of localized mass markets and destinations which would have interfaces with a smaller intra- and interregional travel market (North, 2009). Finally, it would be a system which positions itself to appeal to lifestyles, rather than stacking up products or destinations for sale.

The system would therefore be underpinned by a different set of values than the current one. This point responds directly to the axiom of the critical theorists; that is, that replacement of the existing tourism system (driven by marketing and to the exclusion of other factors) is the only way forward.

Accordingly, there are six key principles of slow travel which would underpin a new tourism system:

- A reduction of resources in the supply of tourism.
- A reduction in the CO_2 emissions from tourism, especially in relation to the transport element.
- An increase in travel cost to reflect the reality of carbon intensity in tourism.
- A renaissance of travel (i.e. the journey) as part of the tourist experience.
- Time spent well is associated with experience and relaxation rather than speed.
- The experience is as much about locality, diversity and culture, as well as slow food.

This can only be brought about by a series of related changes which would occur during a period of transition. A modal shift away from air and car travel is fundamental to the achievement of lower CO_2 emissions in tourism. Consumers and providers will need to seek out substitutes such as trains, coaches and, in the future, low-carbon vessels at sea. This will entail a re-envisaging of ideas about speed, distance and time in tourism; recreating an imagery of romantic travel. Travel will take longer and tourists will travel lesser distances. Based on current tourism transport models, this is counter-intuitive: the contemporary drivers are speed, efficiency and reduced costs. Currently, destinations that fail to deliver a cheap, rapid transit system that connects to core markets are not considered realistic propositions by distribution sectors.

In a slow travel paradigm this will remain a constraint and it is likely that some destinations will have limited scope for further development. Destinations will need to re-shape to become lower-carbon places and thus seek to attract more local markets. This recognizes the potential of existent domestic tourism across the world. It is self-evident that most people are content with travelling shorter distances to achieve the same benefits and satisfactions.

The second major change is therefore a renewed focus on the travel experience. In terms of contemporary mass tourism, travel is seen as a discomfort, an element of tourism to be tolerated in order to arrive at a destination, a place deemed appropriate for relaxation and pleasure. However, the joy of travel has not entirely been lost. There are many who travel to experience the journey, to see new places, meet new people and to socialize with family and friends. The journey needs to be restored as a core component of tourism.

Finally, as climate change impacts become apparent, there will be wider acknowledgement of the role played by individual consumers in the process of carbon reduction. This will drive demand for lower-carbon tourism products, and see increasing rejection of high-carbon consumption as much on the grounds of cost as in ethical terms. Ultimately, slow travel will provide a much lower carbon tourism system, and may even reach the ideal of carbon neutrality (Gössling, 2009).

There are several fundamental differences between mainstream contemporary tourism and slow travel (see Table 10.2). The revised tourism system (Figure 10.1) illustrates that slow travel refers to the whole tourist experience. It is a holistic idea that embraces both destination-based and travel experiences. More than this, it especially resituates travel as a fundamental part of tourism. As such, it facilitates tourist engagement with multiple places en route, as well as at the destination, with a growing environmental consciousness. Slow travel also recognizes the essential sociability of tourism. A re-evaluation of modal choice emerges from the core ingredients, but equally, as with a low-carbon outcome, modal choice might be the main motivation for some.

In order that slow travel might develop successfully in the future, there is a need for further research in a number of areas that have been alluded to already. There is scope for regions to be envisioned as slow-travel destinations, but this will require significant research to understand the adaptation factors and processes required for a slow-travel path. Destinations will also need further knowledge to understand how they might achieve emissions targets currently being set at an international level and the impact that changing travel

Table 10.2 *The differences between mainstream tourism and slow travel*

Contemporary tourism	Slow travel
Speedy transit	Slower travel times
Prevailing modes of the car and airline dominate	Wider range of modes including bus and train
Immediacy	Slowness
Resource intensive	Resource reduction
Journey is a corridor	Journey is the thing
Consumption of many attractions	Localness
Maximizing visits	Staying awhile
High-carbon	Low-carbon
Commoditization	De-commoditization
Standardized hospitality dominates	Slow food and beverages

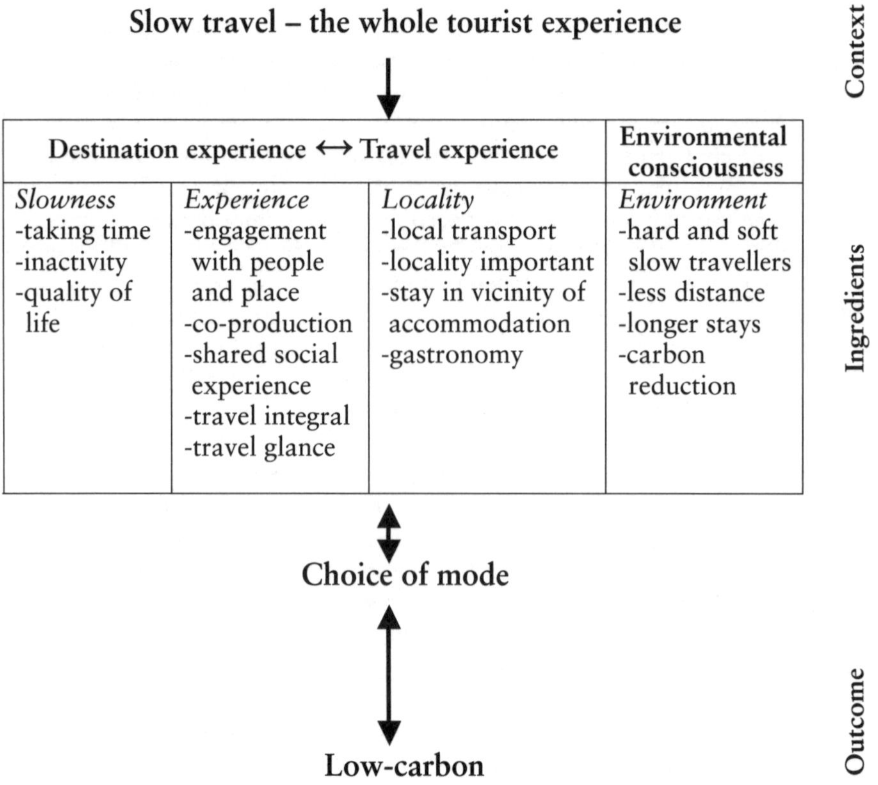

Slow travel – the whole tourist experience

Destination experience ↔ Travel experience			Environmental consciousness
Slowness -taking time -inactivity -quality of life	*Experience* -engagement with people and place -co-production -shared social experience -travel integral -travel glance	*Locality* -local transport -locality important -stay in vicinity of accommodation -gastronomy	*Environment* -hard and soft slow travellers -less distance -longer stays -carbon reduction

Context

Ingredients

Choice of mode

Low-carbon

Outcome

Figure 10.1 *Conceptual diagram of slow travel*

costs might bring. There is also a need to understand more about slow travel consumption. There are questions of tourist identity and the role of identity formation in tourism consumption and a need to understand new market segments as they emerge. However, Chapter 3 has drawn attention to the need to focus not only on consumers, but to take a more holistic view of the tourism system to understand the interaction between provision structures and the consumer. It is also clear that further analysis needs to consider the social processes that are fundamentally interlinked with travel.

The slow travel paradigm offers one path, among a choice of many routes, towards the overall goal of sustainable development in tourism. The complexities of the existing world economic system and unfolding dynamics likely to be experienced within the next decade(s) preclude neat solutions based on the past. However, if societies are assailed by external impacts of the magnitude that scientists now foresee, there is scope for bolder approaches. Slow travel seeks to meet the bottom line of ecological survival, whilst delivering welfare measures that many have become accustomed to in commonplace lifestyles. Slow travel responds to these needs as it is designed on the basis of lower-carbon input, less but enriched travel, renewed expectations and enhanced experiences within proximate localities. It could well, in time, become the epiphany of low-carbon tourism.

References

Adams, J. (1997) 'Can technology save us?' *World Transport Policy and Practice* 2(3), 417

Adler, J. (1989) 'Travel as performed art'. *American Journal of Sociology* 94, 1366–1391

Agnew, M. and Viner, D. (2001) 'Potential impact of climate change on international tourism'. *Tourism and Hospitality Research* 3, 37–60

Agrawal, A.W. and Schimek, P. (2007) 'Extent and correlates of walking in the USA'. *Transportation Research Part D* 12, 548–563

Aitken, S.R and Leigh, C.H. (1986) 'Land use conflicts and rain forest conservation in Malaysia and Australia: The Endau-Rompin and Gordon Franklin controversies'. *Land Use Policy* 13(3), 161–179

Ajzen, I. (1991) 'The theory of planned behavior'. *Organizational Behavior and Human Decision Processes* 50, 179–211

Ajzen, I. and Fishbein, M. (1980) *Understanding Attitudes and Predicting Social Behaviour*. London: Prentice Hall

Albers, S., Bühne, J.-A. and Peters, H. (2009) 'Will the EU-ETS instigate airline network reconfigurations?' *Journal of Air Transport Management* 15, 1–6

All, C., Holden, E., Grimstad-Klepp, F. and Høyer-Leivestad, H. (2008) 'Leisure time consumption: Part of the problem or part of the solution in transforming into sustainable consumption'. In *Proceedings: Sustainable Consumption and Production, A Framework for Action*. 10–11 March, Brussels

Amato, J. (2004) *On Foot – A History of Walking*. New York: New York University Press

Amelung, B. and Viner, D. (2006) 'Mediterranean tourism: Exploring the future with the Tourism Climatic Index'. *Journal of Sustainable Tourism* 14(4), 349–366

Amelung, B., Nicholls, S. and Viner, D. (2007) 'Implications of global climate change for tourism flows and seasonality'. *Journal of Travel Research* 45(3), 285–296

Anable, J. (2005) '"Complacent car addicts" or "aspiring environmentalists"? Identifying travel behaviour segments using attitude theory'. *Transport Policy* 12, 65–78

Anable, J. and Gatersleben, B. (2005) 'All work and no play? The role of instrumental and affective factors in work and leisure journeys by different travel modes'. *Transportation Research Part A* 39, 163–181

Anable, J., Lane, B. and Kelay, T. (2006) *An Evidence Base Review of Public Attitudes to Climate Change and Transport Behaviour.* London: Department for Transport

Andereck, K., Valentine, K., Knopf, R. and Vogt, C. (2005) 'Residents' perceptions of community tourism impacts'. *Annals of Tourism Research* 32, 1056–1076

Anderson, J. (2004) 'Walking whilst walking: a geographical archaeology of knowledge'. *AREA* 36(3), 254–261

Andreassen, T.W. (1995) 'Dissatisfaction with public services: the case of public transport'. *Journal of Services Marketing* 9(5), 30–41

Andrews, C. (2006) *Slow is Beautiful.* Gabriola Island: New Society Publishers

Anon (2008) 'Environmental protection train service'. *China Post.* Available on: www.chinapots.com.tw/taiwan/2008/03/09/146244/TRA-launches.htm

Ap, J. (1990) 'Residents' perceptions research on the social impacts of tourism'. *Annals of Tourism Research* 17, 610–616

Archer, B. and Fletcher, J. (1996) 'The economic impact of tourism in the Seychelles'. *Annals of Tourism Research* 23(1), 32–47

Arellano, A. (2007) 'Religion, pilgrimage, mobility and immobility'. In R. Raj and N.D. Morpeth (eds) *Religious Tourism and Pilgrimage Management: An International Perspective.* Wallingford: CAB International, 89–97

Arlt, W.G. and Feng, G. (2009) 'The Yangzi River Tourism Zone'. In B. Prideaux and M. Cooper (eds) *River Tourism.* Wallingford: CABI, 117–130

Arnesto, L. and Martin, B.G. (2006) 'Tourism and quality agro-food products: an opportunity for the Spanish countryside'. *Tidjschrift voor Economishe en Social Geografie* 97(2), 166–177

Arnould, E.J. and Price, L.L. (1993) 'River magic: Extraordinary experience and the extended service encounter'. *Journal of Consumer Research* 20, 24–45

Asensio, J. (2000) 'The success story of Spanish suburban railways: and determinants of demand and policy implications'. *Transport Policy* 7, 295–302

Aspen Global Change Institute (2006) *Climate Change and Aspen: An Assessment of Potential Impacts and Responses.* Available on: http://www.agci.org/aspenStudy.html

Assi, E. (2000) 'Searching for the concept of authenticity: implementation guidelines'. *Journal of Architectural Conservation* 6(2), 60–69

Aycart, C. (2004) 'Greenways, the Spanish experience: The Rever project'. *Ingeneria y Territorio* 69, 1–19

Bachram, H. (2004) 'Climate fraud and carbon colonialism; the new trade in greenhouse gases'. *Capitalism Nature Socialism* 15(4), 5–20

Bærenholdt, J.O., Haldrup, M., Larsen, J. and Urry, J. (2004) *Performing Tourist Places.* Aldershot: Ashgate

Baloglu, S. and Shoemaker, S. (2001) 'Prediction of senior traveler's motorcoach use for demographic, psychological and psychographic characteristics'. *Journal of Travel Research* 40, 12–18

Banister, D., Stead, D., Steen, P., Akerman, K., Dreberg, P., Nijkamp, P. and Scleirer-Tappeser, R. (2000) *European Transport Policy and Sustainable Mobility.* London: Spon

Barr, S. (2004) 'Are we all environmentalists now? Rhetoric and reality in environmental action'. *Geoforum* 35, 231–249

Barr, S., Ford, N.J. and Gilg, A.W. (2003) 'Attitudes towards recycling household waste in Exeter, Devon: quantitative and qualitative approaches'. *Local Environment* 8(4), 407–421

Barr, S., Shaw, G., Coles, T. and Prillwitz, J. (2010) '"A holiday is a holiday": practicing sustainability, home and away'. *Journal of Transport Geography* 18(3), 474–481

Becken, S. (2002) 'Analysing international tourist flows to estimate energy use with air travel'. *Journal of Sustainable Tourism* 10(2), 114–131

Becken, S. (2004) 'How tourists and tourism experts perceive climate change and carbon-offsetting schemes'. *Journal of Sustainable Tourism* 12(4), 332–344

Becken, S. (2005) 'Towards sustainable tourism transport: An analysis of coach tourism in New Zealand'. *Tourism Geographies* 7(1), 23–42

Becken, S. (2007) 'Tourists' perception of international air travel's impact on the global climate and potential climate change policies'. *Journal of Sustainable Tourism* 15(4), 351–368

Becken, S. (2008) 'Developing indicators for managers in the face of peak oil'. *Tourism Management* 29, 695–705

Becken, S. (2009) *The Carbon Footprint of Domestic Tourism: Technical report.* Wellington, New Zealand: LEAP. Available on: http://researcharchive.lincoln.ac.nz/dspace/bitstream/10182/1216/1/becken_carbon_footprint.pdf (accessed 22.01.09)

Becken, S. and Gnoth, J. (2004) 'Tourist consumption systems among overseas visitors: reporting on American, German and Australian visitors to New Zealand'. *Tourism Management* 25, 375–385

Becken, S. and Hay, J.E. (2007) *Tourism and Climate Change: Risks and Opportunities.* Clevedon: Channel View Publications

Becken, S. and Patterson, M. (2006) 'Measuring national carbon dioxide emissions from tourism as a key step towards achieving sustainable tourism'. *Journal of Sustainable Tourism* 14(4), 323–338

Becken, S. and Simmons, D.G. (2002) 'Understanding energy consumption patterns of tourist attractions and activities in New Zealand'. *Tourism Management* 23(4), 343–354

Becken, S., Simmons, D. and Frampton, C. (2003a) 'Energy use associated with different travel choices'. *Tourism Management* 24(3), 267–277

Becken, S., Simmons, D. and Frampton, C. (2003b) 'Segmenting tourists by their travel pattern for insights into achieving energy efficiency'. *Journal of Travel Research* 42, 48–56

Beckmann, J. (2003) 'Sustainable transport and reflexive mobility. Definitely economically feasible and always socially acceptable'. In *Proceedings of European Conference of Ministers of Transport Managing the Fundamental Drivers of Transport Demand.* Paris: ECMT

Beeton, S. (2003) *An Economic Analysis of Rail Trails in Victoria, Australia.* Melbourne: La Trobe University

Beirão, G. and Sarsfield Cabral, J.A. (2007) 'Understanding attitudes towards public transport and private cars: a qualitative study'. *Transport Policy* 14(6) 478–489

Bem, D.J. (1967) 'Self-perception: an alternative interpretation of cognitive dissonance phenomena'. *Psychological Review* 74(3), 183–200

Bernhofer, F. and Miglbauer, E. (2008) 'Donau Radweg-Erfahrungen und Zukunftsperspectiven'. In *EUROBIKE conference.* 25 January, Friedrichshafen

Bessiere, J. (1998) 'Local development and heritage: Traditional food and cuisine as tourist attractions in rural areas'. *Sociologica Ruralis* 38(1), 21–34

Bestard, A.B. and Font, A.R. (2009) 'Environmental diversity in recreational choice modelling'. *Ecological Economics* 68, 2743–2750

Bhatia, A.K. (2002) *Tourism Development Principle and Practice.* New Delhi: Sterling

Bianchi, R.V. (2004) 'Tourism restructuring and the politics of sustainability: A critical view from the European periphery (the Canary Islands)'. *Journal of Sustainable Tourism* 12(6), 495–529

Bianchini, F. and Schwengel, H. (1991) 'Re-imagining the city'. In J. Corner and S. Harvey (eds) *Enterprise and Heritage: Crosscurrents of National Culture*. London: Routledge, 212–230

Bickerstaff, K., Simmons, P. and Pidgeon, N. (2008) 'Constructing responsibilities for risk: Negotiating citizen–state relationships'. *Environment and Planning A* 40, 1312–1330

Bigano, A., Hamilton, J.M., Lau, M., Tol, R.J. and Zhou, Y. (2004) *A Global Database of Domestic and International Tourist Numbers at National and Subnational Level*. Working Paper FNU 54, Research Unit Sustainability and Global Change, Centre for Marine and Atmospheric Science, Hamburg University

Billig, M. (1996) *Arguing and Thinking: A Rhetorical Approach to Social Psychology*. Cambridge: Cambridge University Press

Billig, M., Condor, S., Edwards, D., Gane, M., Middleton, D. and Radley, A. (1988) *Ideological Dilemmas: A Social Psychology of Everyday Thinking*. London: Sage

Binkhorst, E. and Den Dekker, T. (2009) 'Agenda for co-creation tourist experience research'. *Journal of Hospitality, Marketing and Management* 18, 311–327

Blake, J. (1999) 'Overcoming the value-action gap in environmental policy: Tensions between national policy and local experience'. *Local Environment* 4(3), 257–278

Blum, U., Gercek, H. and Viegas, J. (1992) 'High Speed Railways and the European Periphery'. *Transportation Research A* 26, 211–221

Böhler, S., Grischkat, S., Haustein, S. and Hunecke, M. (2006) 'Encouraging environmentally sustainable holiday travel'. *Transportation Research Part A* 40, 652–670

Boon, B., Schroten, A. and Kampman, B. (2007) 'Compensation schemes for air transport'. In P. Peeters (ed) *Tourism and Climate Change Mitigation: Methods, Greenhouse Gas Reductions and Policies*. Breda: Stichting NHTV Breda, 77–90

Boorstin, D. (1987) *The Image. A Guide to Pseudo Events in America*. New York: Atheneum

Bord Failte (1998) *Perspectives on Irish Tourism*. Dublin: Bord Failte

Borgnat, P, Fleury, E., Robardet, C. and Scherver, A. (2009) 'Spatial Analysis of dynamic movements of Vélo V, Lyon's shared bicycle programme'. In *Dans European Conference on Complex Systems ECCS 2009*. Warwick: UK

Borrie, W.T. and Roggenbach, J.W. (2001) 'The dynamic, emergent and multi-plex nature of a site wilderness experience'. *Journal of Leisure Research* 33(2), 202–228

Bowker, J.M., Bergstrom, J.C. and Gill, J. (2007) 'Estimating the economic value and impacts of recreational trails: a case study of the Virginia Creeper Rail Trail'. *Tourism Economics* 13(2), 241–260

Bows, A. and Anderson, K. (2007) 'Policy clash: Can projected aviation growth be reconciled with the UK Government's 60% carbon-reduction target?' *Transport Policy* 14, 103–110

Bows, A., Anderson, K. and Footitt, A. (2009a) 'Aviation in a low-carbon EU'. In S. Gössling and P. Upham (eds) *Climate Change and Aviation: Issues, Challenges and Solutions*. London: Earthscan, 89–109

Bows, A., Anderson, K. and Peeters, P. (2009b) 'Air transport, climate change and tourism'. *Tourism and Hospitality Planning & Development* 6(1), 7–20

Bramwell, B. and Lane, B. (1993) 'Sustainable tourism: An evolving global approach'. *Journal of Sustainable Tourism* 1(1), 1–5

Bramwell, B. and Lane, B. (2008) 'Priorities in sustainable tourism'. *Journal of Sustainable Tourism* 16(1), 1–4

Brand, C. and Boardman, B. (2008) 'Taming of the few – unequal distribution of greenhouse gas emissions from personal travel in the UK'. *Energy Policy* 36, 224–238

Breakell, B. (1999) 'Moorbus – on the Right Road'. *Countryside Recreation* 7(2), 11–14

Breiling, á M. and Charamza, P. (1999) 'The impact of global warming on winter tourism and skiing: a regionalised model for Austrian snow conditions'. *Regional Environmental Change* 1(1), 4–14

Britton, S. (1991) 'Tourism, capital, and place: towards a critical geography of tourism'. *Environment and Planning D: Society and Space* 9, 451–478

Broderick, J. (2009) 'Voluntary carbon offsetting for air travel'. In S. Gössling and P. Upham (eds) *Climate Change and Aviation: Issues, Challenges and Solutions.* London: Earthscan, 329–346

Bryman, A. (1999) 'Theme parks and McDonalization'. In B. Smart (ed) *Resisting McDonaldization.* London: Sage, 101–116

Brynes, T.A. and Warnken, J. (2006) 'Greenhouse gas emission from marine tourism: A case study of Australian tour boat operators'. *Journal of Sustainable Tourism* 14(3), 255–270

Bryson, B. (1998) *A Walk in the Woods, Re-discovering America on the Appalachian Trail.* New York: Broadway Books

Bührmann, S. (2008) 'Bicycles as public-individual transport-European developments'. Paper presented to MEETBIKE, European Conference on Bicycle Transport and Networking. 3–4 April, Dresden

Bull, A. (1991) *The Economics of Travel and Tourism.* Melbourne: Longman

Bull, C.J. (2006) 'Reviewing cyclists as sports tourists: The experience and behaviours of a case study group of cyclists in East Kent'. *Journal of Sports Tourism* 11, 259–274

Burch, W.R. Jnr (1979) 'The long distance trail as significant cultural creation'. In W.R. Burch Jnr (ed) *Long Distance Trails: The Appalachian Trail as a Guide to Future Research and Management.* New Haven: Yale University, 9–10

Bureau of Transport Statistics (2009) *US Passenger Miles.* Available on: www.bts.gov/publications/national_transportation_statistics/html/table_01_37.html

Bureau of Transportation Statistics (1995) *Long Distance Leisure Travel in the US.* Available on: www.bts.gov.travel/leisure_travel/United_States/index.html (accessed 10.09.09)

Butler, R. (2008) 'Tourism in the future: Cycles, waves or wheels'. *Futures* 41, 346–352

CABE (2009) *Open Space Strategies: Best Practice Guide.* Available on: www.cabe.org.uk/publications/open-space-strategies (accessed 05.10.09)

Can Europe (2008) *Transport.* Available on: http://www.climnet.org/publicawareness/transport.html#faq7

Cao, X., Mokhtarian, P. and Handy, S.R. (2009) 'The relationship between the built environment and non work travel'. *Transportation Research Part A* 43, 548–559

Car Free Walks (2009) *Car Free Walks.* Available on: www.carfreewalks.org.walking_tips-php (accessed 21.11.09)

CARIBSAVE Partnership (2009) *Caribsave.* Available on: http://caribsave.org/ (accessed 16.11.09)

Carù, A. and Cova, B. (2003) 'Revisiting consumption experience: A more humble but complete view of the concept'. *Marketing Theory*, 3(2), 267–286

Cass, N., Shove, E. and Urry, J. (2004) 'Transport infrastructures: A social-spatial-temporal model'. In D. Southerton, H. Chappells and B. van Vliet (eds) *Sustainable Consumption: The Implications of Changing Infrastructures of Provision.* Cheltenham: Edward Elgar, 113–129

Cassidy, T. (1997) *Environmental Psychology: Behaviour and Experience in Context.* Hove: Psychology Press

Caulkins, P.P., Bishop, R.C. and Bouwes, N.W. (1986) 'The travel cost model for lake recreation: A comparison of two methods for incorporating site quality and substitution effects'. *American Journal of Agricultural Economics* 68, 291–297

Cavill, N. and Bauman, A. (2004) 'Changing the way people think about health enhancing physical activity: Do mass media campaigns have a role?' *Journal of Social Sciences* 22(8), 771–790

Cavill, N., Kahlmeier, S. and Racioppi, F. (eds) (2006) *Physical Activity and Health in Europe: Evidence for Action.* Copenhagen: World Health Organization Regional Office for Europe

Cerin, E., Leslie, E., de Toit, L., Owen, N. and Lawrence, D.F. (2007) 'Destinations that matter: Associations with walking for transport'. *Health & Place* 13, 713–724

Ceron, J.P. and Dubois, G. (2007) 'Limits to tourism? A backcasting scenario for sustainable tourism mobility in 2050'. *Tourism and Hospitality Planning & Development* 4(3), 191–209

Cessford, G.R. (2002) 'Perception and reality of conflict: Walkers and mountain bikers on the Queen Charlotte Track, New Zealand'. In *Conference Proceedings Monitoring and Management of Visitor Flows in Recreational and Protected Areas.* 30 January–2 February , Bodenkultur University, Vienna, Austria

Chamon, M., Mauro, P. and Okawa, Y. (2008) 'Cars, mass ownership in the emerging market giants'. *Economic Policy* 23(54), 243–296

Chan, W.W. and Lam, J.C. (2003) 'Energy-saving supporting tourism: A case study of hotel swimming pool heat pump'. *Journal of Sustainable Tourism* 11(1), 74–83

Chapin, D.M., Cohen, K.P., Davis, W.K., Kintner, E.E., Koch, L.J., Landis, J.W., Levenson, M., Mandil, I.H., Pate, Z.T., Rockwell, T., Schriesheim, A., Simpson, J.W., Squire, A., Starr, C., Stone, H.E., Taylor, J.J., Todreas, N.E., Wolfe, B. and Zebroski, E.L. (2002) 'Nuclear safety: Nuclear power plants and their fuel as terrorist targets'. *Science* 297(5589), 1997–1999

Chapman, L. (2007) 'Transport and climate change: a review'. *Journal of Transport Geography* 15, 354–367

Chappells, H., Van Vliet, B. and Southerton, D. (2004) 'Conclusions'. In D. Southerton, H. Chappells and B. Van Vliet (eds) *Sustainable Consumption: The Implications of Changing Infrastructures of Provision.* Cheltenham: Edward Elgar, 144–150

Charles, M.B., Barnes, P. and Ryan, N. (2007) 'Airport futures, Towards a critique of the aerotropolis model'. *Futures* 39(9), 1009–1028

Charlton, C. (1998) 'Public transport and sustainable tourism: the case of the Devon and Cornwall Rail Partnership'. In C.M. Hall and A.A. Lew (eds) *Sustainable Tourism.* Harlow: Addison Wesley Longman, 132–145

Chase, J.B. (2005) *Backpacker's Guide to the Appalachian Trail.* Mechanicsburg, PA: Stackpole Books

Chettri, P., Arrowsmith, C. and Lawrence, D.F. (2004) 'Determining hiking experiences of nature-based tourist destinations'. *Tourism Management* 25, 31–43

Chin, C.B.N. (2008) *Cruising in the Global Economy: Profits, Pleasure and Work at Sea.* Aldershot: Ashgate

Chok, S., Macbeth, J. and Warren, C. (2007) 'Tourism as a tool for poverty alleviation: A critical analysis of "pro-poor tourism" and implications for sustainability'. *Current Issues in Tourism* 10(2&3), 144–165

Chrzan, J. (2004) 'Slow food, what, why and where?' *Food Culture and Society: An International Journal of Multidisciplinary Research* 17(2), 17–132

Civil Aviation Authority (2006) *No-frills Carriers: Revolution or Evolution?* CAP 770. London: Civil Aviation Authority

Clark, G., Darrall, J., Grove-White, R., Macnaghten, P. and Urry, J. (1994) *Leisure Landscapes: Leisure, Culture and the English Countryside: Challenges and Conflicts.* Background Papers. London: Council for the Preservation of Rural England

Clawson, M. and Knetsch, J.L. (1966) *Economics of Outdoor Education*. Baltimore: The Johns Hopkins University Press

Clearwater Paddling (2009) *Clearwater Paddling*. Available on: http://www. clearwaterpaddling.com/index.asp (accessed 11.09.09)

Climatecare (2009) *Reducing Carbon Emissions*. Available on: http://www. jpmorganclimatecare.com/ (accessed 21.10.09)

Cloke, P. and Perkins, H.C. (1998) '"Cracking the canyon with the awesome foursome": representations of adventure tourism in New Zealand'. *Environment and Planning D: Society and Space* 16, 185–218

Cloke, P., Milbourne, P. and Thomas, C. (1996) 'The English National Forest: Local reaction to plans for re-negotiated nature-society relations in the countryside'. *Transcripts of the Institute of British Geographers* 21, 552–571

Coastal Community Network (2005) *Charting a Marine Trail for BC*. Available on: https://www.confmanager.com/communities/c122/files/pdf/marine_trail_bc.pdf (accessed 08.09.09)

Collins-Kreiner, N. and Kliot, N. (2000) 'Pilgrimage tourism in the Holy Land, the behavioural characteristics of Christian pilgrims'. *Geo Journal* 50(1), 55–67

COM (2001) *EU White Paper: European Transport Policy for 2010: Time to Decide*. Available on: http://ec.europa.eu/transport/strategies/2001_white_paper_ en.htm

COM (2003) *Basic Orientations for the Sustainability of European Tourism*. COM 716. Available on: http://eur-lex.europa.eu/LexUriServ/LexUriServ.do?uri=COM: 2003:0716:FIN:en:PDF (accessed 16.09.09)

COM (2006) *Keep Europe Moving – Sustainable Mobility For Our Continent. Mid-Term Review of the European Commission's 2001 Transport White Paper*. Available on: http://eur-lex.europa.eu/LexUriServ/LexUriServ.do?uri=COM:2006: 0314:FIN:EN:PDF (accessed 21.10.09)

COM (2007) *Limiting Global Climate Change to 2 degrees Celsius: The way ahead for 2020 and beyond*. Available on: http://eur-lex.europa.eu/LexUriServ/site/en/com/ 2007/com2007_0002en01.pdf (accessed 19.11.09)

COM (2009a) *White Paper: Adapting to Climate Change: Towards a European Framework for Action*. Available on: http://eur-lex.europa.eu/LexUriServ/LexUri Serv.do?uri=COM:2009:0147:FIN:EN:PDF (accessed 05.08.09)

COM (2009b) *A Sustainable Future for Transport: Towards An Integrated, Technology-Led and User-Friendly System*. Available on: http://ec. europa.eu/ transport/publications/doc/2009_future_of_transport.pdf (accessed 21.10.09)

COM (2009c) *Towards a Comprehensive Climate Change Agreement in Copenhagen*. Available on: http://eur-lex.europa.eu/LexUriServ/LexUriServ.do?uri=COM:2009: 0039:FIN:EN:PDF (accessed 07.12.09)

Commission of European Communities (2006) *A Renewed EU Tourism Policy: Towards a Stronger Partnership for European Tourism*, COM 2006, 134 Final. Commission of European Communities

Committee on Climate Change (2009) Meeting the UK Aviation Target – Options for Reducing Emissions to 2050. Available on: http://www.theccc.org.uk/reports/ aviation-report (accessed 10.12.09)

Community of European Railways and Infrastructure Companies and International Union of Railways (2008) *Rail Transport and Environment, Facts and Figures*. Paris: Community of European Railways and Infrastructure Companies and International Union of Railways

Confederation of Passenger Transport (2008) *Britain's Coaches: Partnerships and Passengers*. London: Confederation of Passenger Transport

Conrady, R. and Buck, M. (2008) *Trends and Issues in Global Tourism*. New York: Springer

Cooper, C., Fletcher, J., Fyall, A., Gilbert, D. and Wanhill, S. (2008) *Tourism: Principles and Practice*, 4th edn. Harlow: Prentice Hall

Cope, A., Doxford, D. and Probert, C. (1999) 'Monitoring visitors to the UK countryside resources. The approaches of land and recreation resource management to visitor monitoring.' *Land Use Policy* 17, 59–66

Corbett, J.J. and Farrell, A. (2002) 'Mitigating air pollution impacts of passenger ferries'. *Transportation Research Part D* 7, 197–211

Corbett, J.J. and Koehler, H.W. (2003) 'Updated emissions from ocean shipping'. *Journal of Geophysical Research* 108(D20), 4650–4666

Croall, J. (1995) *Preserve or Destroy: Tourism and the Environment*. London: Calouste Gulbenkian Foundation

Crompton, J.L. (1979) 'Motivations for pleasure vacation'. *Annals of Tourism Research*, Oct/Dec, 408–424

Crompton, J.L. (2001) 'Perception of how the presence of Greenway Trails affects the value of proximate properties'. *Journal of Park and Recreation Administration* 19(3), 114–130

Csikszentmihalyi, M. (2000) 'The costs and benefits of consuming'. *Journal of Consumer Research* 27, 267–272

Culinane, S. (1997) 'Traffic management in Britain's National Parks'. *Transport Reviews* 17(3), 267–279

Currie, G. and Wallis, I. (2008) 'Effective ways to grow urban bus markets – a synthesis of evidence'. *Journal of Transport Geography* 16, 419–429

Curry, N. and Ravenscroft, N. (2001) 'Countryside recreation provision in England: exploring a demand-led approach'. *Land Use Policy* 18, 281–291

Curry, N.R., Joseph, D.H. and Slee, W. (2001) 'To climb a mountain? Social inclusion and outdoor recreation in Britain'. *World Leisure Journal* 43(2), 13–15

Curtin, S. (2009a) 'What makes for memorable wildlife encounters? Revelations from "serious" wildlife tourists'. *Journal of Ecotourism* (In press)

Curtin, S. (2009b) 'Wildlife tourism: The intangible, psychological benefits of human-wildlife encounters'. *Current Issues in Tourism* 12(5), 451–474

Curtin, S. and Wilkes, K. (2005) 'British Wildlife Tourism Operators: Current Issues and Typologies'. *Current Issues in Tourism* 8(6), 455–478

Cwerner, S. (2009) 'Introducing aeromobilities'. In S. Cwerner, S. Kesselring and J. Urry (eds) *Aeromobilities*. Abingdon: Routledge, 1–21

Daley, B. and Preston, H. (2009) 'Aviation and climate change: Assessment of policy options'. In S. Gössling and P. Upham (eds) *Climate Change and Aviation: Issues, Challenges and Solutions*. London: Earthscan, 347–372

Dallen, J. (2007) 'Sustainable transport, market segmentation and tourism: The Looe Valley branch line railway, Cornwall, UK'. *Journal of Sustainable Tourism* 15(2), 180–199

Dalton, G.J., Lockinton, D.A. and Baldock, T.E. (2007) 'A survey of tourist operator attitudes to renewable energy supply'. *Renewable Energy* 32(4), 567–586

Dalton, G.J., Lockinton, D.A. and Baldock, T.E. (2008) 'Feasibility analysis of stand-alone renewable energy supply options for a large hotel'. *Renewable Energy* 33(7), 1475–1490

Daly, H. (1996) *Beyond Growth. The Economics of Sustainable Development*. Boston: Beacon Press

Dann, G. (1977) 'Anomie, ego-enhancement and tourism'. *Annals of Tourism Research*, Mar/Apr, 184–194

Dann, G. (1992) 'Travelogs and the management of the unfamiliar'. *Journal of Travel Research* 30(4), 59–63

Dann, G. (1994) 'Travel by train: keeping nostalgia on track'. In A.V. Seaton (ed) *Tourism: The State of the Art*. Chichester: Wiley, 775–782

Dann, G. (1999) 'Writing the tourist in space and time'. *Annals of Tourism Research* 26(1), 159–187

Danziger, N. (1992) *Danziger's Adventures: From Miami to Kabul*. London: Harper-Collins

Darker, C.D., French, D.P. and Larkin, M. (2007) 'An exploration of walking behaviour. An interpretative phenomenological approach'. *Social Science and Medicine* 65, 2172–2183

Davies, D. (2006) 'Emissions trading for ships – a European perspective'. *Naval Engineers Journal* 3, 131–138

De Botton, A. (2002) *The Art of Travel*. New York: Pantheon Books

de Fraiture, C., Giordano, M. and Liao, Y. (2008) 'Biofuels and implications for agricultural water use: Blue impacts of green energy'. *Water Policy* 10(1), 67–81

de Freitas, C.R. (2003) 'Tourism climatology: Evaluating environmental information for decision making and business planning in the recreation and tourism sector'. *International Journal of Biometeorology* 48(1), 45–54

De Maio, P. and Gifford, J. (2004) 'Will smart bikes succeed as public transportation in the U.S.?' *Journal of Public Transportation* 7(2), 1–16

De Paul University (2007) *The Return of the Intercity Bus: The decline and recovery of the scheduled service to American cities 1960–2007*. Available on: www.capitolpub.com/media/pdf/Intercity_bus_study.pdf (accessed 30.11.09)

Dean, C.J. (1993) 'Travel by excursion coach in the UK'. *Journal of Travel Research* 31(4), 59–64

Den Breejen, L. (2007) 'The experience of long distance walking: A case study of the West Highland Way in Scotland'. *Tourism Management* 28, 1417–1427

Dennis, K. and Urry, J. (2007) *The Digital Nexus of Post-Automobility*. Lancaster: University of Lancaster (Department of Sociology)

Dennis, K. and Urry, J. (2009) *After the Car*. Cambridge: Polity Press

Dennis, N. (2007) 'We're all going on a summer holiday! The impact of low-cost scheduled airlines on charter operations and the inclusive tour holiday market'. In *Proceedings of Association for European Transport Conference*. Leiden

Department for Environment Food and Rural Affairs (2008) *Climate Change Act 2008 – key provisions/milestones*. Available on: http://www.defra.gov.uk/environment/climatechange/uk/legislation/provisions.htm (accessed 18.06.09)

Department for Environment Food and Rural Affairs (2009) *Climate Change Act 2008*. Available on: http://www.defra.gov.uk/environment/climatechange/uk/legislation/index.htm (accessed 18.06.09)

Department for Transport (2002) *A Review of the Effectiveness of Personalised Journey Planning Techniques*. London: The Stationery Office

Department for Transport (2006) *National Travel Survey: 2006*. London: National Statistics

Department for Transport (2008) *Public Experiences of and Attitudes to Air Travel*. Available on: http://www.dft.gov.uk/pgr/statistics/datatablespublications/trsnstatsatt/airtravel (accessed 12.02.09)

Department for Transport (2009) *National Travel Survey: 2008*. London: National Statistics

Dickinson, J. (2008) 'Travelling slowly: An exploration of the discourse of holiday travel'. In *Proceedings of the Universities' Transport Studies Group Annual Conference*. 3–5 January, Portsmouth

Dickinson, J. (2009) 'Slow Travel as a Holiday Experience'. Working paper, Bournemouth University

Dickinson, J.E. and Dickinson, J. (2006) 'Local transport and social representations: Challenging the assumptions for sustainable tourism'. *Journal of Sustainable Tourism* 14(2), 192–208

Dickinson, J.E. and Robbins, D. (2007) 'Using the car in a fragile rural tourist destination: A social representations perspective'. *Journal of Transport Geography* 15, 116–126

Dickinson, J.E. and Robbins, D. (2008) 'Representations of tourism transport problems in a rural destination'. *Tourism Management* 29, 1110–1121

Dickinson, J.E. and Robbins, D. (2009) '"Other people, other times and special places": A social representations perspective of cycling in a tourism destination'. *Tourism and Hospitality: Planning and Development* 6(1), 69–85

Dickinson, J.E., Calver, S., Watters, K. and Wilkes, K. (2004) 'Journeys to heritage attractions in the UK: A case study of National Trust property visitors in the south west'. *Journal of Transport Geography* 12, 103–113

Dickinson, J.E., Robbins, D. and Fletcher, J. (2009) 'Representation of transport: A rural destination analysis'. *Annals of Tourism Research* 36, 103–123

Dickinson, J.E., Robbins, D. and Lumsdon, L. (2010a) 'Holiday travel discourses and climate change'. *Journal of Transport Geography* 18, 482–489

Dickinson, J.E., Robbins, D. and Lumsdon, L. (2010b) 'Slow travel'. Working paper, Bournemouth University

Dietz, T., Stern, P.C. and Guagnano, G.A. (1998) 'Social structural and social psychological bases of environmental concern'. *Environment and Behavior* 30(4), 450–471

Dignance, J. (2006) 'Religion and secular pilgrimage journeys'. In J.T. Dallen and D.H. Olsen (eds) *Tourism, Religion and Spiritual Journeys*. London: Routledge, 36–50

Dolnicar, S. and Leisch, F. (2008) 'An investigation of tourists patterns of obligation to protect the environment'. *Journal of Travel Research* 46(4), 63–71

Dolnicar, S., Crouch, G. and Long, P. (2008) 'Environmentally friendly tourists: What do they really know about them?' *Journal of Sustainable Tourism* 16(2), 197–210

Donati, K. (2005) 'The pleasure of diversity in slow food's ethic of taste'. *Food Culture and Society: An International Journal of Multidisciplinary Research* 8(2), 227–242

Dowling, R.K. (2006) 'The cruising industry'. In R.K. Dowling (ed) *Cruise Ship Tourism*. Wallingford: CABI, 3–17

Downward, P. and Lumsdon, L. (2001) 'The development of recreational cycle routes: An evaluation of user needs'. *Managing Leisure* 6(1), 50–60

Downward, P. and Lumsdon, L. (2004) 'Tourism transport visitor spending: A study in the North York Moors National Park, UK'. *Journal of Travel Research* 42, 415–420

Dubois, G. and Ceron, J.P. (2006a) 'Tourism and climate change: Proposals for a research agenda'. *Journal of Sustainable Tourism* 14(4), 399–415

Dubois, G. and Ceron, J.P. (2006b) 'Tourism/leisure greenhouse gas emissions forecasts for 2050: Factors for change in France'. *Journal of Sustainable Tourism* 14(2), 172–191

Duffy, R. (2004) 'Ecotourists on the beach'. In M. Sheller and J. Urry (eds) *Tourism Mobilities: Places To Play, Places In Play*. London: Routledge, 32–43

Duval, D.T. (2007) *Tourism and Transport*. Clevedon: Channel View Publications

Duval, D.T. (2009) 'Aeropolitics and economics of aviation emissions mitigation'. In S. Gössling and P. Upham (eds) *Climate Change and Aviation: Issues, Challenges and Solutions*. London: Earthscan, 179–192

Dwyer, L., Edwards, D., Mistilis, N., Roman, C. and Scott, N. (2009) 'Destination and enterprise management for a tourism future'. *Tourism Management* 30, 63–74

Economic and Social Council (2009) *Methodological Development and Harmonization of Transport Statistics*. Geneva: Task Force on Buses and Coaches of the Working Party on Transport Statistics

Edensor, T. (2000) 'Walking in the British Countryside: Reflexivity, embodied practices and ways to escape'. *Body and Society* 6(3–4), 81–106

Edensor, T. and Holloway, J. (2008) 'Rhythm analysing the coach tour: the Ring of Kerry, Ireland'. *Transactions of the Institute of British Geographers* 33(4), 483–501

EEA (2003) *Europe's Environment, Third Assessment*. Copenhagen: EEA

Eiser, J.R. and van der Pligt, J. (1988) *Attitudes and Decisions*. London: Routledge

Elkington, J. (1997) *Cannibals with Forks: The Triple Bottom Line of 21st Century Business*. Stony Creek, CT: New Society Publishers

Elkington, J. (2004) *The Triple Bottom Line. Does it Add Up?* Available on: johnelkingon.com/TBL-elkington-chapter.pdf. (accessed 01.10.09)

Ellyard, P. (2006) 'Societal changes–impacts and opportunities for tourism'. In *Proceeding of the Tourism Futures Conference 21st Century Responses to 21st Century Realities*

English Historic Towns Forum (1994) *Getting it Right: A Guide to Visitor Management in Historic Towns*. Bath: English Historic Towns Forum

English Tourist Board (1999) *Tool Kit Walking Holidays*. London: English Tourist Board

Entrikin, N. (1991) *The Betweeness of Places*. Baltimore, MD: The Johns Hopkins University Press

Environment Agency (2009) *EU Emissions Trading Scheme – Aviation*. Available on: http://www.environment-agency.gov.uk/business/topics/pollution/107596.aspx (accessed 27.11.09)

Erfurt-Cooper, P. (2009) 'European waterways as a source of leisure and recreation'. In B. Prideaux and M. Cooper (eds) *River Tourism*. Wallingford: CABI, 95–116

Esbester, M. (2008) 'Mapping the way? Maps, emotion, gender'. In G. Letherby and G. Reynolds (eds) *Gendered Journeys, Mobile Emotions*. Farnham: Ashgate, 33–44

Essex, S., Kent, M. and Newnham, R. (2004) 'Tourism development in Mallorca: Is water supply a constraint?' *Journal of Sustainable Tourism* 12(1), 4–28

Euromonitor International (2007) *WTM Global Trends Report 2007*. London: Euromonitor

Europa (2009) *Emission Trading System (EU ETS)*. Available on: http://ec.europa.eu/environment/climat/emission/index_en.htm (accessed 27.11.09)

European Commission (2001) *European Transport Policy for 2010: Time to Decide*

European Commission Tourism Sustainability Group (2007) *Action for More Sustainable European Tourism*. Available on: http://ec.europa.eu/enterprise/sectors/tourism/files/docs/tsg/tsg_final_report_en.pdf (accessed 16.11.09)

European Parliament, Directorate-General for Internal Policies, Policy Department B Structural and Cohesion Policies (2009) *The European Cycle Route Network EuroVelo*. Available on: http://www.europarl.europa.eu/activities/committees/studies/download.do?language=en&file=26868

Eurostar (2008) *Greener than Flying*. Available on: http://www.eurostar.com/UK/uk/leisure/about_eurostar/environment/greener_than_flying.jsp (accessed 19.06.08)

Eurostar (2009) *Tread Lightly*. Available on: www.eurostar.com/pdf/treadlightly/reports/treadlightlyreport_uk_uk.pdf (accessed 18.11.09)

Eves, F., Hoppé, R. and McLaren, L. (2003) 'Prediction of different types of physical activity using the theory of planned behaviour'. *Journal of Applied Behavioural Research* 8(2), 77–95

Eyring, V. and Corbett, J. (2007) *Comparing Fuel Consumption, Carbon Dioxide and Other Emissions from International Shipping and Aircraft: A Summary of Recent Research Findings.* Available on: http://www.pa.op.dlr.de/SeaKLIM/Fuel_Emissions_International_Shipping.html (accessed 17.09.09)

Farrell, B.H. and Twining-Ward, L. (2004) 'Reconceptualizing tourism'. *Annals of Tourism Research* 31(2), 274–295

Faulkner, B. (2001) 'A societal marketing approach to national tourism planning: Evidence from the South Pacific'. *Tourism Management* 22(2), 135–147

Fayos-Solá, E. (1996) 'Tourism policy: a midsummer's night's dream'. *Tourism Management* 17(6), 405–412

Fennell, D.A. (2006) *Tourism Ethics.* Clevedon: Channel View Publications

Festinger, L. (1957) *A Theory of Cognitive Dissonance.* Stanford, CA: Stanford University Press

Filimonau, V., Dickinson, J., Robbins, D. and Reddy, V. (2010) 'A critical review of environmental impact assessment of tourism: Life cycle assessment as a new approach'. *Journal of Sustainable Tourism,* forthcoming

Fleming, W.R. and Toepper, L. (1990) 'Economic impact studies: Relating the positive and negative impacts to tourism development'. *Journal of Travel Research* 29(1), 35–42

Fonte, M. (2006) 'Slow food's presidia. What do small producers do with big retailers'. *Research in Rural Sociology and Development* 12, 203–240

Foresight (2006) *Intelligent Information Futures. Project Overview.* London: Department of Trade and Industry

Foresta, R. (1987) 'Transformation of the Appalachian Trail'. *Geographical Review* 77(1), 77–85

Formica, S. and Kothari, T.H. (2008) 'Strategic destination planning: Analyzing the future of tourism'. *Journal of Travel Research* 46, 355–362

Foster, C., Hillsdon, M. and Thorogood, M. (2004) 'Environmental perceptions and walking in English adults'. *Journal of Epidemiol Community Health* 58, 924–928

Foster, J. (2005) 'Northward, upward: Stories of train travel, and the journey to white South African nationhood, 1895–1950'. *Journal of Historical Geography* 31, 296–315

Frändberg, L. (2005) 'Tourism as victim, problem or solution: story lines of a complex industry-environment relation'. In C.M. Hall and J. Higham (eds) *Tourism, recreation and climate change.* Clevedon: Channel View Publications, 273–285

Frändberg, L. (2008) 'Paths in transnational time-space: Representing mobility biographies of young Swedes'. *Geogr. Ann. B* 90(1), 17–28

Franklin, A. and Crang, M. (2001) 'The trouble with tourism and travel theory?' *Tourist Studies* 1(1), 5–22

Freeman, M. (1999) 'The railway as cultural metaphor'. *Journal of Transport History* 20(2), 160–166

Freighter World Cruises Inc (2009) *About us.* Available on: http://www.freighterworld.com/aboutfwc.html (accessed 29.10.09)

Freund, P. and Martin, G. (2004) 'Walking and motoring: Fitness and social organisation of movement.' *Sociology of Health and Illness* 36(3), 273–286

Frykman, J. (2000) 'Slow Cities – mednigeln som signum'. *oo-tal* 4, 34–39

Galani-Moutafi, V. (2000) 'The self and the other: Traveler, ethnographer, tourist'. *Annals of Tourism Research* 271(1), 203–224

Gardner, N. (2009) 'A manifesto for slow travel'. *Hidden Europe Magazine* 25, 10–14

Gärling, T., Fujii, S., Garling, A. and Jakobsson, C. (2003) 'Moderating effects of social value orientation on determinants of proenvironmental behavior intention'. *Journal of Environmental Psychology* 23, 1–9

Gärling, T., Garling, A. and Johansson, A. (2000) 'Household choices of car-use reduction measures'. *Transportation Research Part A* 34, 309–320

Gayeton, D. (2009) *Slow Life in a Tuscan Town*. New York: Welcome Books

Gehl, J. (1996) *Life Between Buildings: Using Public Space*. Copenhagen: Arkitektens Forlag

Germann Molz, J.G. (2009) 'Representing pace in tourism mobilities: staycations, Slow Travel and The Amazing Race'. *Journal of Tourism and Cultural Change* 7(4) 270–286

Giddens, A. (1990) *The Consequences of Modernity*. Cambridge: Polity Press

Gilberg, R. and Perl, A. (2008) *Transport Revolutions. Moving People and Freight Without Oil*. London: Earthscan

Giles-Corti, B. and Donovan, R.J. (2002) 'The relative influence of individual, social and physical environment determinants of physical activity'. *Social Science and Medicine* 54, 1793–1812

Gill, A., Kriwoken, L.K., Dobson, S. and Fallon, L.D. (2003) 'The challenges of integrating tourism into Canadian and Australian coastal zone management'. *Dalhousie Law Journal* 26(1), 85–147

Gillespie, E. (2008) 'The slow traveller'. *The Observer*, Sunday 6 April

Givoni, M. (2006) 'Development and impact of modern high speed trains: A review'. *Transport Reviews* 26(5), 593–612

Givoni, M., Brand, C. and Watkiss, P. (2008) 'Are railways "climate friendly"?' *Built Environment* 35(1), 70–86

Gnoth, J. (1997) 'Tourism motivation and expectation formation'. *Annals of Tourism Research* 24(2), 283–304

Goffman, E. (1963) *Behaviour in Public Places*. New York: Free Press

Golob, T.F. and Hensher, D.A. (1998) 'Greenhouse gas emissions and Australian commuters' attitudes and behavior concerning abatement policies and personal involvement'. *Transport Research D* 3(1), 1–18

González-Savignat, M. (2004) 'Competition in air transport, the case of the high speed train'. *Journal of Transport Economics and Policy* 38(1), 77–108

Goodwin, H. and Francis, J. (2003) 'Ethical and responsible tourism: Consumer trends in the UK'. *Journal of Vacation Marketing* 9(3), 271–284

Gössling, S. (2002) 'Global environmental consequences of tourism'. *Global Environmental Change* 12, 283–302

Gössling, S. (2009) 'Carbon neutral destinations: A conceptual analysis'. *Journal of Sustainable Tourism* 17(1), 17–37

Gössling, S. and Hall, M. (2006) 'Wake up, this is serious'. In S. Gössling and M. Hall (eds) *Tourism and Global Environmental Change*. Routledge: New York, 305–320

Gössling, S. and Peeters, P. (2007) '"It does not harm the environment!" An analysis of industry discourses on tourism, air travel and the environment'. *Journal of Sustainable Tourism* 15(4), 402–417

Gössling, S. and Upham, P. (2009) 'Introduction: aviation and climate change in context'. In S. Gössling and P. Upham (eds) *Climate Change and Aviation: Issues, Challenges and Solutions*. London: Earthscan, 1–23

Gössling, S., Hall, C.M. and Lane, B. (2008) *Sustainable Tourism Futures, Perspectives on Systems, Restructuring and Innovations*. London: Routledge

Gössling, S., Hall, C.M. and Weaver, D.B. (2009) 'Sustainable tourism futures'. In S. Gössling, C.M. Hall and D.B. Weaver (eds) *Sustainable Tourism Futures, Perspectives on Systems, Restructuring and Innovations.* New York: Routledge, 1–19

Gössling, S., Peeters, P. and Scott, D. (2008) 'Consequences of climate policy for international tourist arrivals in developing countries'. *Third World Quarterly* 29(5), 873–901

Gössling, S., Ceron, J.P., Dubois, G. and Hall, M.C. (2009) 'Hypermobile travellers'. In S. Gössling and P. Upham (eds) *Climate Change and Aviation: Issues, Challenges and Solutions.* London: Earthscan, 131–150

Gössling, S., Hansson, C.B., Horstmeier, O. and Saggel, S. (2002) 'Ecological footprint analysis as a tool to assess tourism sustainability'. *Ecological Economics* 43(2–3), 199–211

Gössling, S., Peeters, P., Ceron, J.P., Dubois, G., Patterson, T. and Richardson, R.B. (2005) 'The eco-efficiency of tourism'. *Ecological Economics* 54, 417–434

Graburn, N. (1983) 'To pray, pay and play. The cultural structure of Japanese domestic tourism'. *Cahiers du Tourisme, serie B* 26, 1–89

Greene, D.L., Hopson, J.L. and Li, J. (2006) 'Have we run out of oil yet? Oil peaking analysis from an optimist's perspective'. *Energy Policy* 34, 515–531

Grimshaw, J. (1998) cited in Woods, M.J. *A Strategic and Environmental Assessment of the National Cycle Network.* Cheddar, UK: J. Woods and Associates

Gronau, W. and Kagermeier, A. (2007) 'Key factors for leisure and tourism successful public transport provision'. *Journal of Transport Geography* 15, 127–135

Guiver, J. (2007) 'Modal talk: Discourse analysis of how people talk about bus and car travel'. *Transportation Research Part A* 41, 233–248

Guiver, J., Lumsdon, L. and Morris, K. (2007) 'The role of scheduled buses in reducing car journeys in tourist areas'. In P. Peeters (ed) *Tourism and Climate Change Mitigation: Methods, greenhouse gas reductions and policies.* Breda: Stichting NHTV Breda, 119–131

Guiver, J., Lumsdon, L., Weston, R. and Ferguson, M. (2007) 'Do buses help to meet tourism objectives? The contribution and potential of scheduled buses in rural destination areas'. *Transport Policy* 14, 275–282

Gursoy, D. and Rutherford, D.G. (2004) 'Host attitudes toward tourism: An improved structural model'. *Annals of Tourism Research* 31(3), 495–516

Gursoy, D., Jurowski, C. and Uysal, M. (2002) 'Resident attitudes: A structural modeling approach'. *Annals of Tourism Research* 29(1), 79–105

Guthold, R., Ono, T., Strong, K.L., Chatterji, S. and Mobaria, A. (2008) 'Worldwide variability in physical activity: A 51 country survey'. *American Journal of Preventive Medicine* 34(6), 486–494

Gutiérrez, J. (2001) 'Location, economic potential and daily accessibility: An analysis of the accessibility impact of the high speed line Madrid–Barcelona–French Border'. *Journal of Transport Geography* 9(4), 229–242

Hadfield, P. (2001) 'Slip, sliding away'. *New Scientist,* 7 March. Available on: www.newscientist.com/article/dn191-slip-sliding-away.html

Halager A. and Richards, G. (eds) (2002) *Tourism and Gastronomy.* London: Routledge

Haldrup, M. (2004) 'Laid-back mobilities: Second home holidays in time and space'. *Tourism Geographies* 6(4), 434–454

Hall, C.M. (2006) 'Introduction: Culinary tourism and regional development: from slow food to slow tourism'. *Tourism Review International* 9(4), 1–4

Hall, C.M. (2007a) 'The possibilities of slow tourism: Can the slow movement help develop sustainable forms of tourism consumption?' Paper presented at *Achieving Sustainable Tourism Conference.* 11–14 September, Helsingborg, Sweden

Hall, C.M. (2007b) 'Pro-poor tourism: do "tourism exchanges benefit primarily the countries of the South"?' *Current Issues in Tourism* 10(2&3), 111–118

Hall, C.M. (2009) 'Degrowing tourism: Décroissance, sustainable consumption and steady-state tourism'. *Anatolia: An International Journal of Tourism and Hospitality Research* 20(1), 46–61

Hall, C.M. and Page, S.J. (2006) *The Geography of Tourism and Recreation: Environment, Place and Space*. London: Routledge

Hall, D. (2010) 'Transport geography and new European realities: a critique'. *Journal of Transport Geography* 18(1), 1–13

Halsall, D.A. (1992) 'Transport for Tourism and Recreation'. In B.S. Hoyle and R.D. Knowles (eds) *Modern Transport Geography*. London: Belhaven, 155–177

Halsall, D.A. (2001) 'Railway heritage and the tourist gaze: Stoomtram Hoorn-Medemblik'. *Journal of Transport Geography* 9, 151–160

Hammitt, W.E., Kaltenborn, B.P., Vistad, O.I., Emmelin, L. and Teigland, J. (1992) 'Common access tradition and wilderness management in Norway: a paradox for managers'. *Environmental Management* 16(2), 149–156

Hannam, K., Sheller, M. and Urry, J. (2006) 'Editorial: mobilities, immobilities and moorings'. *Mobilities*, 1(1), 1–22

Hardin, G. (1968) 'The tragedy of the commons'. *Science* 162(3859), 1243–1248

Hares, E., Dickinson, J. and Wilkes, K. (2010) 'Climate change and the air travel decisions of UK tourists'. *Journal of Transport Geography* 18(3), 466–473

Harrison, R., Newholm, T. and Shaw, D. (eds) (2006) *The Ethical Consumer*. London: Sage

Hawes, M., Candy, S. and Dixon, G. (2006) 'A method for surveying the condition of extensive walking track systems'. *Landscape and Urban Planning* 78(3), 275–287

Haywood, R. (2007) 'Britain's national railway network: fit for purpose in the 21st century'. *Journal of Transport Geography* 15, 198–216

Hellmund, P.C. and Smith, D.S. (2006) *Designing Greenways: Sustainable Landscapes for Nature and People*. Washington, DC: Island Press

Hensher, D.A. and Brewer, A.M. (2002) 'Going for gold at the Sydney Olympics: how did transport perform?' *Transport Reviews* 22(4), 381–399

Hensher, D.A., Stopher, P. and Bullock, P. (2003) 'Service quality – developing a service quality index in the provision of commercial bus contracts'. *Transportation Research Part A* 37(6), 499–517

Herlihy, D. (2004) *Bicycle: The History*. New Haven: Yale University Press

Hickman, R. and Banister, D. (2007) 'Looking over the horizon: Transport and reduced CO2 emissions in the UK by 2030'. *Transport Policy* 14, 377–387

Hill, W. and Pickering, C.A. (2006) 'Vegetation associated with different walking track types in the Koscuszki Alpine area, Australia'. *Journal of Environment Management* 78(1), 24–34

Hillman, M. and Whalley, A. (1979) *Walking is Transport*. London: Policy Studies Institute

Hoegh-Guldberg, O. (1999) 'Climate change, coral bleaching and the future of the world's coral reefs'. *Marine and Freshwater Research* 50, 839–866

Hoenninger, P. (2003) 'MobiHarz project: Integrated mobility management and services for visitors'. In *ECOMM Conference Proceedings Managing Transport Demand to Attain Sustainable Transport Demand and Economic Effectiveness – Why and How?* 21-23 May, Karlstad

Hogg, M.A. and Abrams, D. (1988) *Social Identifications: A Social Psychology of Intergroup Relations and Group Processes*. London: Routledge

Holden, A. (2000) *Environment and Tourism*. London: Routledge

Holden, E. (2007) *Achieving Sustainable Mobility: Everyday and Leisure-time Travel in the EU*. Aldershot: Ashgate

Holden, E. and Høyer, K.G. (2005) 'The ecological footprints of fuels'. *Transportation Research Part D* 10(5), 395–403

Holding, D. (2001) 'The Sanfte Mobilitaet project. Achieving reduced car dependence in European report areas'. *Tourism Management* 22(4), 411–417

Holding, D.M. and Kreutner, M. (1998) 'Achieving a balance between "carrots" and "sticks" for traffic in National Parks: the Bayerischer Wald project'. *Transport Policy* 5, 175–183

Holloway, C. (2006) *The Business of Tourism*, 7th edn. Harlow: Pearson Education Limited

Holmgren, K., Belhaj, M., Gode, J., Särnholme, E., Zetterberg, L. and Åhman, M. (2006) *Greenhouse Gas Emission Trading For The Transport Sector*. Stockholm: Swedish Environmental Research Institute

Honore, C. (2004) *In Praise of Slowness: How a Worldwide Movement is Challenging the Cult of Speed*. San Francisco: Harper

Horton, D. (2007) 'Fear of cycling'. In D. Horton, P. Rosen and P. Cox (eds) *Cycling and Society*. Aldershot: Ashgate, 133–152

Horton-Salway, M. (2001) 'The construction of M.E.: The discursive action model'. In M. Wetherell, S. Taylor and S.J. Yates (eds) *Discourse as Data: A Guide For Analysis*. Milton Keynes: The Open University, 147–188

Howkins, T.J. (2005) 'Changing hegemonies and new external pressures: South East European railway networks in transition'. *Journal of Transport Geography* 13, 187–197

Høyer, K.G. (2000) 'Sustainable tourism or sustainable mobility? The Norwegian case', *Journal of Sustainable Tourism* 8(2), 147–160

Høyer, K.G. (2009) 'A conference tourist and his confessions: An essay on life with conference tourism, aeromobility and ecological crisis'. *Tourism and Hospitality Planning & Development* 6(1), 53–69

Høyer, K.G. and Aall, C. (2005) 'Sustainable mobility and sustainable tourism'. In M.C. Hall and J. Higham (eds) *Tourism, Recreation And Climate Change*. Clevedon: Channel View Publications, 260–272

Hoyle, B. (2002) 'Urban waterfront revitalization in developing countries: the example of Zanzibar's Stone Town'. *Geographical Journal* 168(2), 141–162

Hugo, M.L. (1999) 'A comprehensive approach to the planning, grading and auditing of hiking trails as ecotourism products'. *Current Issues* 2(2–3), 138–173

Hull, R.B., Stewart W.P. and Li, Y.K. (1992) 'Experience patterns, capturing the dynamic nature of the recreation experience'. *Journal of Leisure Research* 24(3), 240–252

Hunter, C. (2002) 'Sustainable tourism and the touristic ecological footprint'. *Environment, Development and Sustainability* 4, 7–20

Hunter, C. and Shaw, J. (2007) 'The ecological footprint as a key indicator of sustainable tourism'. *Tourism Management* 28, 46–57

IATA (2008a) *Aviation Carbon Offset Programmes: IATA guidelines and toolkit*. Available on: http://www.iata.org/NR/rdonlyres/22669B08–918C-4AB7–8D8F-8F9743BA8FE6/61823/Carbon_Offset_Guidelines_May2008.pdf

IATA (2008b) *Building a Greener Future: 3rd edition – October 2008*. Available on: http://www.iata.org/nr/rdonlyres/c5840acd-71ac-4faa-8fee-00b21e9961b3/0/building_greener_future_oct08.pdf (accessed 18.06.09)

I-ce. (2000) *The Significance of Non-Motorized Transport for Developing Countries*. Utretch: I-ce

IFAD (2001) *Rural Poverty Report 2001: The Challenge Of Ending Rural Poverty.* Oxford: Oxford University Press

Institute of Transport and Tourism (2008) *The Shropshire Hills Shuttles Surveys.* Preston: Institute of Transport and Tourism

Institute of Transport and Tourism, Downward, P. and Sustrans (2007) *The Economic Impact of Cycle Tourism in North East England.* Preston: Institute of Transport and Tourism

Intergovernmental Panel on Climate Change (2007) *IPCC Fourth Assessment Report.* Available on: http://www.ipcc.ch/ (accessed 06.10.09)

International Association of Passenger Transport (2003) *Leisure and Tours: an opportunity for public transport.* Available on: http://www.uitp.org/nos/corebrief/CB_L&T-en.pdf (accessed 23.10.09)

International Association of Passenger Transport (2009) *Leisure and Tours: an opportunity for public transport.* Available on: http://www.uitp.org/knowledge/statistics.cfm (accessed 23.10.09)

International Union of Railways (2009) *Railways Statistics Synopsis.* Available on: http://www.uic.org.spip.php?article1347 (accessed 17.09.09)

Irion, J.B. and Ball, D.A. (2001) 'The New York and Josephine: Two steamships of the Charles Morgan Line'. *The International Journal of Nautical Archaeology* 30(1), 48–56

Jackson, J.B. (1994) *A Sense of Place, A Sense of Time.* New Haven, CT: Yale University Press

Jackson, T. (2005) 'Live better by consuming less. Is there a double dividend in sustainable consumption?' *Journal of Industrial Ecology* 9, 19–36

Jackson, T. (2009) *Prosperity without Growth.* Earthscan: London

Jafari, J., Pizam, A. and Przeclawski, K. (1990) 'A sociocultural study of tourism as a factor of change'. *Annals of Tourism Research* 17(3), 469–472

Jani, M. (1999) 'Aviation and externalities: The accomplishments and problems'. *Transportation Research Part D* 4, 159–180

Jani, M. (2003) 'The potential for modal substitution'. In P. Upham, J. Muaghan, D. Raper and C. Thomas (eds) *Towards Sustainable Aviation.* London: Earthscan

Jenner, P. and Smith, C. (2008) *The Green Travel Guide.* Richmond: Crimson

Jennings, G. (2003) 'Marine tourism'. In S. Hudson (ed) *Sport and Adventure Tourism.* London: Haworth Hospitality Press, 125–164

Jensen, A. (1998) 'Competition in railway monopolies'. *Transportation Research E* 34, 267–287

Jivén, G. and Larkham, P.J. (2003) 'Sense of place, authenticity and character. A commentary'. *Journal of Urban Design* 8(1), 67–81

Johnson, C. (2007) *Freighter Cruises: No Buffet or Floor Show, But No Crowds Either!* Available on: http://www.buzzle.com/articles/freighter-cruises-no-buffet-or-floor-show-but-no-crowds-either.html (accessed 29.10.09)

Johnson, J.D., Snepenger, D.J. and Akis, S. (1994) 'Residents' perceptions of tourism development'. *Annals of Tourism Research* 21(3), 629–642

Jones, P., Shears, P., Hillier, D., Comfort, D. and Lowell, J. (2003) 'Return to traditional values? A case study of slow food'. *British Food Journal* 105(4–5), 297–304

Kahler, M. (2009) *Cruising with the Cargo: Low Costs on the High Seas.* Available on: http://budgettravel.about.com/cs/cruisesdeals/a/cruise_cargo.htm (accessed 29.10.09)

Kane, M. and Zink, R. (2004) 'Package adventure tours: markers in serious leisure careers'. *Leisure Studies* 23(4), 329–345

Karadeniz, D. (2008) *The Impact of the Little Miami Scenic Trail on Single Family Residential Property Values*. Unpublished Masters degree thesis, Cincinatti, University of Cincinatti

Kay, G. (1999) 'Routes for recreational walking'. *Town and Country Planning* 58, 78–81

Kay, G. and Moxham, N. (1996) 'Path for whom? Countryside access for recreational walking'. *Leisure Studies* 15, 171–183

Kendle, A. (2008) *Really Slow Travel: Walking Your Way Around the World*. Available on: www.vagabondish.com/slow-travel-walking-around-world/ (accessed 14.10.09)

Kennedy, F. (2000) 'Why life is sweeter in the slow lane'. *The Independent*, 3 July

King, B., Pizam, A. and Milman, A. (1993) 'Social impacts of tourism: Host perceptions'. *Annals of Tourism Research* 20, 650–665

Klein, R.A. (2005) *The Cruise Ship Squeeze: the new pirates of the seven seas*. Gabriola Island, BC: New Society Publishers

KMR Group (2008) *Global Marketing Insights from TGI, Green Values, Consumers and Branding*. London: KMR Group

Knoflacher, H. (2007) 'Problems caused by motorway/railway freight traffic share in the Tyrol'. *Proceedings of the Institute of Mechanical Engineers, Part F Journal of Rail and Rapid Transit* 215(1), 45–51

Knox, P. (2005) 'Creating ordinary places: Slow cities in a fast world'. *Journal of Urban Design* 10(1), 1–11

Koetse, M.J. and Rietveld, P. (2009) 'The impact of climate change and weather on transport. An overview of empirical findings'. *Transportation Research Part D* 14, 205–221

Kokkranikal, J., McLellan, R. and Baum, T. (2003) 'Island tourism and sustainability: A case study of the Lakshadweep Islands'. *Journal of Sustainable Tourism* 11(5), 426–447

Kollmuss, A. and Agyeman, J. (2002) 'Mind the gap: Why do people act environmentally and what are the barriers to pro-environmental behaviour?' *Environmental Education Research* 8(3), 239–260

Koucky, M. (2007) *Cykelturismen i Europa*. Sweden: Koucky & Partners AB

Krippendorf, J. (1984) *The Holiday Makers*. London: Heinemann

Kuniyal, J.C., Jain, A.P. and Shanningrahi, A.S. (1998) 'Public involvement in solid waste management in the Himalayan trails in and around the Valley of the Flowers, India'. *Resources, Conservation and Recycling* 24, 299–322

Kurz, T., Donaghue, N., Rapley, M. and Walker, I. (2005) 'The ways that people talk about natural resources: Discursive strategies as barriers to environmentally sustainable practices'. *British Journal of Social Psychology* 44, 603–620

Kyle, G. and Chick, G. (2004) 'Enduring leisure involvement: The importance of personal relationships'. *Leisure Studies* 23(3), 243–266

Lacho, K.J. and Kiefer, A. (2008) 'The use of trade association services to develop a low cost promotion budget', Allied Academies International Internet Conference. Available on: http://www.alliedacademies.org/Public/Proceedings/Internet Proceedings/paai-10.pdf#page=30 (accessed 19.06.09)

Lafferty, W.M. (2004) *Governance for Sustainable Development*. Cheltenham: Edward Elgar

Lambert, D., Martins, L. and Ogbon, M. (2006) 'Currents, visions and voyages: historical geographies of the sea'. *Journal of Historical Geography* 32, 479–493

Lamers, M. and Amelung, B. (2007) 'The environmental impacts of tourism in Antarctica. A global perspective'. In P. Peeters (ed) *Tourism and Climate Change*

Mitigation: Methods, greenhouse gas reductions and policies. Breda: Stichting NHTV Breda, 51–62

Landry, C. and Bianchini, F. (1995) *The Creative City*. London: Demos

Lane, B. (1999) *Trails and Tourism: The Missing Links*. Available on: www. americantrails.org/resources/economics/tourismukecon.html (accessed 21.09.09)

Lane, B. (2009) 'Thirty years of sustainable tourism, drivers, progress, problems – and the future'. In S. Gössling, C.M. Hall, and D.B. Weaver (eds) *Sustainable Tourism Futures, Perspectives on Systems, Restructuring and Innovations*. London: Routledge, 19–33

Lankford, S.V. (1994) 'Attitudes and perceptions toward tourism and rural regional development'. *Journal of Travel Research* 32(3), 35–43

Lanzendorf, M. (2000) 'Social change & Leisure Mobility'. *World Transport Policy and Practice* 6(3), 21–25

Larsen, J., Urry, J. and Axhausen, K.W. (2006) *Mobilities, Networks, Geographies*. Aldershot: Ashgate

Larsen, J., Urry, J. and Axhausen, K.W. (2007) 'Networks and tourism: mobile social life'. *Annals of Tourism Research* 34(1), 244–262

Larson, J. (2001) 'Tourism mobilities and the travel glance: experiences of being on the move'. *Scandinavian Journal of Hospitality and Tourism* 1(2), 80–98

Lassen, C. (2009) 'A life in corridors: Social perspectives on aeromobility and work in knowledge organization'. In S. Cwerner, S. Kesselring and J. Urry (eds) *Aeromobilities*. Abingdon: Routledge, 177–193

Lea, J. (1988) *Tourism and Development in the Third World*. London: Routledge

Lee, C. and Moudon, V. (2006) 'Correlates of walking for Transportation or Recreation Purposes'. *Journal of Physical Activity and Health* 3(1), 77–98

Lee, C.-C. and Chang, C.P. (2008) 'Tourism development and economic growth: A closer look at panels'. *Tourism Management* 29, 180–192

Leitch, A. (2003) 'Slow food and the politics of pork fat: Italian food and European identity'. *Ethnos* 168(4), 437–462

Letherby, G. and Reynolds, G. (2009) 'Afterword: Destination unknown'. In G. Letherby and G. Reynolds (eds) *Gendered Journeys, Mobile Emotions*. Farnham: Ashgate, 201–208

Lindberg, K. and Johnson, R.L. (1997) 'Modeling resident attitudes towards tourism'. *Annals of Tourism Research* 24(2), 402–424

Lindsey, G. (1999) 'Use of urban greenways: insights from Indianapolis'. *Landscape and Urban Planning* 45, 145–157

Lindsey, G., Man, J., Poynton, S. and Dickson, K. (2004) 'Property values, recreation values and urban greenways'. *Journal of Park and Recreation Administration* 22(93), 69–90

Liu, J.C., Sheldon, P.J. and Var, T. (1987) 'Resident perception of the environmental impacts of tourism'. *Annals of Tourism Research* 14, 17–37

Löfgren, O. (2000) *On Holiday: a history of vacationing*. Berkeley: University of California Press

Lopéz-Pita, A. (2003) 'The effects of high speed rail on the reduction of air traffic congestion'. *Journal of Public Transportation*, 6(1), 37–49

Lorenzoni, I. and Pidgeon, N.F. (2006) 'Public views on climate change: European and USA perspectives'. *Climatic Change* 77, 73–95

Lorenzoni, I., Nicholson-Cole, S. and Whitmarsh, L. (2007) 'Barriers perceived to engaging with climate change among the UK public and their policy implications'. *Global Environmental Change* 17, 445–459

Lumsdon, L. (1997) *Tourism Marketing*. London: Thompson International

Lumsdon, L. (2000a) 'Investigating the needs of recreational cycling: the experience of the Peak District National Park'. *Transport Planning Review* 71(3), 379–389

Lumsdon, L. (2000b) 'Transport and tourism: Cycle tourism – a model for sustainable development?' *Journal of Sustainable Tourism* 8(5), 361–377

Lumsdon, L. (2004) 'Walking and tourism: The imagery of European cities'. In *Proceedings – Walk 21 V Cities for People, Fifth International Conference on Walking in the 21st century.* 9–11 June, Copenhagen, Denmark

Lumsdon, L.M. (2006) 'Factors affecting the design of tourism bus services'. *Annals of Tourism Research* 33(3), 748–766

Lumsdon, L. and Mitchell, J. (1999) 'Walking, transport and health: do we have the right prescription?' *Health Promotion International* 14(3), 271–280

Lumsdon, L. and Page, S.J. (2004) 'Progress in transport and tourism research: Reformulating the transport-tourism interface and future research agendas'. In L. Lumsdon and S.J. Page (eds) *Tourism and Transport: issues and agenda for the new millennium.* London: Elsevier, 1–28

Lumsdon, L. and Spence, J. (2004) 'Rationale and design of urban recreational walking in several cities in the UK'. In *Proceedings-Walk 21 III Steps Third International Conference – Steps Towards Liveable Cities.* 4–5 September, Donostia-San Sebastian, Spain

Lumsdon, L. and Swift, J.S. (2001) *Latin American Tourism.* New York: Continuum

Lumsdon, L., Downward, P. and Rhoden, S. (2006) 'Transport for tourism. Can public transport encourage a modal shift in the day visitor market'. *Journal of Sustainable Transport* 14(2), 139–156

Lynes, J.K. and Dredge, D. (2006) 'Going green: Motivations for environmental commitment in the airline industry. A case study of Scandinavian Airlines'. *Journal of Sustainable Tourism* 14(2), 116–138

Lyons, G. and Urry, J. (2005) 'Travel time use in the information age'. *Transportation A* 39, 257–276

Lyons, G., Jain, J. and Holley, D. (2007) 'The use of travel time by rail passengers'. *Transportation A* 39, 257–276

Macbeth, J. (2000) 'Utopian tourists – cruising is not just about sailing'. *Current Issues in Tourism* 3(1), 20–34

MacCannell, D. (1989) *The Tourist.* Columbia and Princeton: University of California Press

Mackaye, B. (1921) 'An Appalachian Trail: A project in regional planning'. *Journal of American Institute of Architects* 9, 325–330

Macnaghten, P. (1993) 'Discourses of nature: argumentation and power'. In E. Burman and I. Parker (eds) *Discourse analytic research: repertoires and readings of texts in action.* London: Routledge, 52–72

Macnaghten, P. (1995) 'Public attitudes to countryside leisure: a case study on ambivalence'. *Journal of Rural Studies* 11(2), 135–147

Macnaghten, P., Brown, R. and Reicher, S. (1992) 'On the nature of nature: experimental studies in the power of rhetoric'. *Journal of Community and Applied Social Psychology* 2, 43–61

Macquarie Dictionary (2009) *Macquarie Dictionary: Australia's National Dictionary Online.* Available on: http://www.macquariedictionary.com.au/anonymous@9c98889861952/-/p/dict/index.html (accessed 23.06.09)

Maddison, D. (2001) 'In search of a warmer climate? The impact of climate change on flows of British tourists'. *Climatic Change* 49(1–2), 193–208

Mahoney, M. and Potter, J-L. (2004) 'Integrating health impact assessment into the triple bottom line concept'. *Environmental Impact Assessment Review* 24(2), 150–160

Mander, S. and Randles, S. (2009) 'Aviation coalitions: Drivers of growth and implications for carbon dioxide emissions reduction'. In S. Gössling and P. Upham (eds) *Climate Change and Aviation: Issues, Challenges and Solutions*. London: Earthscan, 273–290

Manente, M., Minghetti, V. and Celotto, E. (2000) 'Visitor and mobility management in tourism destinations: a cross analysis of strategies, projects and practices'. *The Tourism Review* 2, 5–19

Manning, E., Valliere, W., Bacon, J.J., Graefe, A., Kyle, G. and Hennessey, R. (2000) *Use and Users of the Appalachian Trail*. Burlington: University of Vermont

Marchetti, C. (1994) 'Anthropological invariants in travel behaviour'. *Technological Forecasting and Social Change* 47(1), 75–88

Markwell, K., Stevenson, D. and Rowes, D. (2004) 'Footsteps and memories: Interpretation of Australian urban landscape through the medium of walking tours'. *International Journal of Heritage Studies* 10(5), 457–473

Marris Freighter Cruises (2009) *Passenger Firsthand Stories*. Available on: http://www.freightercruises.com/frames.php (accessed 29.10.09)

Marshall, G. (2007) *Carbon Detox*. London: Gaia Publishing

Marshall, I. (1998) *Story Line, Exploring the Literature of the Appalachian Trail*. Charlottesville, VA: The University Press of Virginia

Martins, N. (2009) 'Parque patrimonial do Montego'. Presentation at *O Lazer e o Turismo Ciclável em Portugal*. 6 November, Aveiro, University of Aveiro

Mason, P. (2003) *Tourism Impacts, Planning and Management*. Oxford: Butterworth-Heinemann

Massot, M.H., Armoogum, J., Bonnel, P. and Carrbel, D. (2006) 'Potential for car use reduction through a simulation approach: Paris and Lyon case studies'. *Transport Reviews* 26(1), 25–42

Mathieson, A. and Wall, G. (2006) *Tourism: Changes, impacts and opportunities*. Harlow: Pearson Prentice Hall

Matos, W. (2004) 'Can slow travel bring new life to the Alpine regions'. In K. Weiermair and C. Mathies (eds) *The Tourism and Leisure Industry*. New York: Haworth, 93–103

Mayer, H. and Knox, P.L. (2006) 'Slow cities: Sustainable places in a fast world'. *Journal of Urban Affairs* 28(4), 321–334

Mayer, H. and Knox, P.L. (2009) 'Pace of life and quality of life: The slow city charter'. In M.J. Sirgy, R. Phillips and D. Rahtz (eds) *Community Quality of Life Indicators: Best Cases III*. New York: Springer Communications, 21–40

Mayor, K. and Tol, R.S.J. (2009) 'The impacts of European climate change regulations in international tourist markets'. *Transportation Research Part D* 15(1), 26–36

McCauley, R. (1949) *The Fabled Shore*. London: Penguin

McCool, S.F. and Martin, S.R. (1994) 'Community attachment and attitudes toward tourism development'. *Journal of Travel Research* 32(3), 29–34

Mckercher, B. (1992) 'Tourism as conflicting land use'. *Annals of Tourism Research* 19(3), 467–481

Mckercher, B. and Lau, G. (2008) 'Movement patterns of tourists within a destination'. *Tourism Geographies* 10(3), 355–374

Meadows, D.H., Meadows, D.L., Randers, J. and Behrens, W. (1972) *Limits to Growth – A report to the Club of Rome project on the predicament of mankind*. New York: Universe Books

Meek, S., Ison, S. and Enoch, M. (2009) 'Stakeholder perspectives on the current and future roles of UK bus based park & ride'. *Journal of Transport Geography* 17, 468–475

Met Office (2009) *Warming: Climate change – the facts*. Available on: http://www. metoffice.gov.uk/climatechange/guide/downloads/quick_guide.pdf (accessed 21.07.09)

Metz, D. (2008) *The Limits to Travel*. London: Earthscan

Metz, D. (2009) *The Limits To Travel; How Far Will You Go?* London: Earthscan

Meyer, D. (2009) 'Pro-poor tourism: Is there actually much rhetoric? And, if so, whose?' *Tourism Recreation Research* 34(2), 197–199

Michaelova, A. and Krause, K. (2000) 'International maritime transport and climate change'. *Intereconomics* 35(3), 127–136

Michaels, M. (2000) 'These boots are made for walking ... mundane technology, the body and human-environment relations'. *Body and Society* 6(3–4), 107–126

Midden, C.J.H. and McCalley, L.T. (2002) 'Energy conservation through product-integrated feedback. The roles of goal setting and social orientation'. *Journal of Economic Psychology* 23, 589–603

Midgley, P. (2009) 'The role of smart bike-sharing systems in urban mobility'. *Journeys*, May, 23–31

Miele, M. (2008) 'Cittáslow: Producing slow against the fast life'. *Space and Polity* 12(1), 135–156

Miele, M. and Murdoch, J. (2002) 'The practical aesthetics of traditional cuisines: Slow food in Tuscany'. *Sociologia Ruralis* 42(4), 312–328

Mill, C.R. and Morisson, A.M. (1985) *The Tourism System: An Introductory Text*. Englewood Cliffs NJ: Prentice Hall

Millinog, A. and Schechtner, K. (2006) 'City tourism-pedestrian orientation behaviour'. Paper presented at Walk 21 VII, 7th International Conference on Walking & Liveable Cities, 23–25 October, Melbourne, Australia

Ministry of Small Business, Tourism and Culture (2001) *Mid Coast Tourism Opportunity Strategy*. British Columbia: Marlyn Chisholm & Associates in association with Geoscape Environmental Planners, Catherine Berris Associates and Sunderman and Associates

Mintel (2003) *Cycling Holidays in Europe*. London: Mintel

Mintel (2004) *Backpacking: UK*. London: Mintel

Mintel (2006) *Watersports Holidays – Europe*. London: Mintel

Mintel (2007) *Cycling Holidays UK*. London: Mintel

Mintel (2008a) *Bicycles-UK*. London: Mintel

Mintel (2008b) *Rail Travel-Europe*. London: Mintel

Mintel (2008c) *Active Leisure Pursuits – UK – April 2008*. London: Mintel

Mintel (2008d) *Adventure Tourism – Europe*. London: Mintel

Mintel (2009a) *Bus and Coach Travel Europe*. London: Mintel

Mintel (2009b) *Slow Travel Special Report*. London: Mintel

Mittelstaedt, J.D. and Kilbourne, W.E. (2008) 'Macromarketing Perspectives on Sustainable Consumption'. In *Proceedings: Sustainable Consumption and Production, A Framework for Action*. 10–11 March, Brussels

Moen, J. and Fredman, P. (2007) 'Effects of climate change on Alpine skiing in Sweden'. *Journal of Sustainable Tourism* 15(4), 418–437

Mordue, T. (2005) 'Tourism, performance and social exclusion in "Olde York"'. *Annals of Tourism Research* 32(1), 179–198

Morris, R.V. (2006) 'The land of hope: Third Grade student use of a walking tour to explain the community'. *Social Studies* 97(3), 129–132

Morrow, S. (2005) 'Continuity and change: the planning and management of long distance walking routes in Scotland'. *Managing Leisure* 10, 237–250

Moscovici, S. (1981) 'On social representations'. In J. Forgas (ed) *Social Cognition*. London: Academic Press, 181–209

Moser, S.C. and Dilling, L. (eds) (2007) *Creating a Climate for Change: Communicating Climate Change and Facilitating Social Change*. Cambridge: Cambridge University Press

Mota, J.C. (2009) 'Cycling in rural areas – sustainable mobility and strategic planning'. Presentation at *Contemporary Society and Cultural Shifts in Public Policy*. 22–23 June, Aveiro, University of Aveiro

Mowforth, M. and Munt, I. (2009) *Tourism and Sustainability: Development and New Tourism in the Third World*, 3rd edn. London: Routledge

Müller, H. (1999) 'Verkehrsmanagement in ferienorten'. *Tourism Review* 54(2), 65–77

Muniz, A.M. and O'Guinn, T.C. (2001) 'Brand Community'. *Journal of Consumer Research* 27, 412–432

Murray, M. and Graham, B. (1997) 'Exploring the dialectics of route-based tourism: The Camino de Santiago'. *Tourism Management* 18(8), 513–524

Mustonen, P. (2006) 'Volunteer tourism: postmodern pilgrimage'. *Journal of Tourism and Cultural Change* 3(3), 160–177

Nathan Associates (2007) *Impacts of the Motor Coach Industry on Society and the Economy: An Industry that Binds the Nation Together*. Available on: atwww.buses.org/files/download/2006%20Impact%20of%20Motorcoaches.pdf (accessed 30.11.09)

National Express (2008) *National Express, Carbon Calculator*. Available on: http://www.nationalexpress.com/coach/OurService/CarbonEmissionsCalculator.cfm (accessed 19.06.08)

National Statistics (2005) *Travel Trends 2004*. Basingstoke: Palgrave Macmillan

National Travel Survey (2006) *National Travel Survey*. Available on www.gov.uk/gtr/statistics/ (accessed 03.12.09)

Nawijn, J., Peeters, P. and Van der Sterren, J. (2008) 'The ST-EP programme and least developed countries: is tourism the best alternative?' In P.M. Burns and M. Novelli (eds) *Tourism Development: Growth, Myths and Inequalities*. Wallingford: CAB International, 1–10

NERA Consulting (2005) *Economic Instruments for Reducing Ship Emissions in the European Union*. Available on: http://ec.europa.eu/environment/air/pdf/task3_final.pdf (accessed 03.12.09)

Nickerson, R.S. (2003) *Psychology and Environmental Change*. Mahwah, NJ: Lawrence Erlbaum Associates Inc

Nilsson, J.H. (2009) 'Low-cost aviation'. In S. Gössling and P. Upham (eds) *Climate Change and Aviation: Issues, Challenges and Solutions*. London: Earthscan, 113–129

Nilsson, J.H., Svärd, A.C., Widarsson, A. and Wirell, T. (2007) 'Slow destination marketing in small Italian Towns'. In *16th Nordic Symposium in Tourism and Hospitality Research*. 27–29 September, Helsingborg

Nilsson, M. and Küller, M. (2000) 'Travel behaviour and environmental concern'. *Transportation Research Part D* 5(3), 211–234

Norman, W. and MacDonald, C. (2003) 'Getting to the bottom of the Triple Bottom Line'. *Business Ethics Quarterly* 14(2), 243–262

North, P. (2009) 'Eco-localisation as a progressive response to peak oil and climate change – A sympathetic critique'. *Geoforum* (2009), doi:10.1016/j.geoforum.2009.04.013

O'Connor, M. (2006) 'The "Four Spheres" framework for sustainability'. *Ecological Complexity* 3, 285–292

Office for National Statistics (2009) *Travel Trends 2008: Data and commentary from the International Passenger Survey*. London: OPSI

Ogara, I. (1998) 'History of Amusement Park Construction by Private Railway Companies in Japan'. *Japanese Railway and Transport Review*. March, 28–34

Oktar, L. (2001) 'The ideological organization of representational processes in the presentation of us and them'. *Discourse and Society* 12(3), 313–346

Önüt, S. and Soner, S. (2006) 'Energy efficiency assessment for Antalya Region hotels in Turkey'. *Energy and Buildings* 38(8), 964–971

Orbaşli, A. (2000) *Tourist in Historic Towns: Urban Conservation and Heritage Management*. London and New York: Spon

Orbaşli, A. and Shaw, S. (2004) 'Transport and visitors in historic cities'. In L. Lumsdon and S. Page (eds) *Tourism and Transport*. Oxford: Elsevier, 93–105

Ory, D.T. and Mokhtarian, P.L. (2005) 'When is getting there half the fun? Modeling the liking for travel'. *Transportation Research Part A* 39(2/3), 97–123

Otero, J.G. (2002) 'Greenways: from autonomous itineraries to networks: The REVER (Red Verte Europea) experience and projects'. In *Proceedings of the Walk 21 3rd International Conference*. 9–10 May, San Sebastian

Ouellette, J.A. and Wood, W. (1998) 'Habit and intention in everyday life: The multiple processes by which past behaviour predicts future behaviour'. *Psychological Bulletin* 124(1), 54–74

Outdoor Industry Foundation (2009) *Outdoor Recreation Participation Study 2009.* Available on: http://outdoorindustry.org/images/researchfiles/

Outforadventure (2009) *Sea Kayaking British Columbia.* Available on: http://www.outforadventure.com/ (accessed 11.09.09)

Page, S.J. (1999) *Transport for Tourism*. London: Routledge

Page, S.J., Brunt, P., Busby, G. and Connell, J. (2001) *Tourism: A Modern Synthesis*. London: Thomson

Parkins, W. (2004) 'Out of time: fast subjects and slow living'. *Time and Society* 13(2–3), 363–382

Parry, M. (2009) 'Climate change is a development issue, and only sustainable development can confront the challenge'. *Climate and Development* 1, 5–9

Parry, M.L., Rozenzweig, C., Iglesias, A., Livermore, M. and Fisher, G. (2004) 'Effects of climate change on global food production under SRES emissions and socioeconomic scenarios'. *Global Environmental Change* 14(1), 53–67

Paul Watkiss Associates (2009) *Updating of Eurostar CO2 Emissions using Energy Logging Train Data.* Available on: www.eurostar.com/pdf/treadlightly/reports/treadlightlyreport_uk_uk.pdf (accessed 18.11.09)

Pearce, P.L. (1998) 'The relationship between residents and tourists: the research literature and management directions'. In W.F. Theobald (ed) *Global tourism*. 2nd edn. Oxford: Butterworth-Heinemann, 129–149

Pearce, P.L., Moscardo, G. and Ross, G.F. (1996) *Tourism Community Relationships*. Oxford: Elsevier

Peattie, K. (1999) 'Trappings versus substance in the greening of marketing planning'. *Journal of Strategic Marketing* 7(2), 131–148

Peeters, P. (2007) 'Mitigating tourism's contribution to climate change – an introduction'. In P. Peeters (ed) *Tourism and Climate Change Mitigation: Methods, greenhouse gas reductions and policies*. Breda: Stichting NHTV Breda, 11–26

Peeters, P. (2009) 'Pro-Poor Tourism, Climate Change and Sustainable Development'. *Tourism Recreation Research* 34(2), 203–205

Peeters, P. and Schouten, F. (2006) 'Reducing the Ecological Footprint of Inbound Tourism and Transport to Amsterdam'. *Journal of Sustainable Tourism* 14(2), 157–171

Peeters, P., Gössling, S. and Becken, S. (2006) 'Innovation towards tourism sustainability: Climate change and aviation'. *Int. J. Innovation and Sustainable Development* 1(3), 184–200

Peeters, P., Gössling, S. and Lane, B. (2008) 'Moving towards low-carbon tourism: New opportunities for destinations and tour operators'. In S. Gössling, C.M. Hall and D.B. Weaver (eds) *Sustainable Tourism Futures: Perspectives on Systems, Restructuring and Innovations*. New York: Routledge, 240–257

Peeters, P., Szimga, E. and Duijnisveld, M. (2007) 'Major environmental impacts of European tourist transport'. *Journal of Transport Geography*, 15, 83–93

Peeters, P., Williams, V. and de Haan, A. (2009) 'Technical and management reduction potentials'. In S. Gössling and P. Upham (eds) *Climate Change and Aviation: Issues, Challenges and Solutions*. London: Earthscan, 293–307

Peisley, T. (2008) *2020 Vision: New Focus for the Global Cruise Industry*. Colchester: Seatrade Communications Ltd

Perdue, R.R., Long, P.T. and Allen, L. (1990) 'Resident support for tourism development'. *Annals of Tourism Research* 17, 586–599

Peters, P. (2006) *Time, Innovation And Mobilities: Travel in Technological Cultures*. London: Taylor & Francis

Petrini, C. (2001) *Slow Food: The Case For Taste*. New York: Columbia University Press

Pfeffer, J. and Salancik, G.R. (1978) *The External Control of Organizations*. New York: Harper and Row

Pickering, C.M. and Hill, W. (2007) 'Impacts of recreation and tourism on plant diversity and vegetation in protected areas in Australia'. *Journal of Environmental Management* 85(4), 791–800

Pietryowski, B. (2004) 'You are what you eat: the social economy of the Slow Food Economy'. *Review of the Social Economy* 62(3), 307–321

Pine, B.J. and Gilmore, J.H. (1999) *The Experience Economy*. Boston: Harvard Business School Press

Pink, S. (2007) 'Sensing Cittáslow: slow living and the constitution of the sensory city'. *The Senses and Society* 2(1), 59–74

Pisani, C. (2002) 'Fair at sea: the design of a future legal instrument on marine bunker fuels emissions within the climate change regime'. *Ocean Development & International Law*, 33, 57–76

Pizam, A., Neumann, Y. and Reichel, A. (1979) 'Tourist satisfaction: uses and misuses'. *Annals of Tourism Research*, April/June, 195–197

Plog, S.C. (1974) 'Why destination areas rise and fall in popularity'. *Cornell Hotel and Restaurant Administration Quarterly* 14(4), 55–58

Pollan, M. (2007) *In Defense of Food*. New York: Penguin Press

Pooley, C.G. and Turnbull, J. (2000) 'Modal choice and modal change: the journey to work in Britain since 1890'. *Journal of Transport Geography* 8, 11–24

Poon, A. (1993) *Tourism, Technology, and Competitive Strategies*. Wallingford: CAB International

Porter, G. (2002) 'Living in the walking world: Rural mobility and social equity issues in sub-saharan Africa'. *World Development* 30(2), 285–300

Potter, J. and Wetherell, M. (1987) *Discourse and Social Psychology: Beyond Attitudes and Behaviour*. London: Sage

Pralong, J-P. (2007) 'Geotourism: A new form of tourism utilising natural landscapes and based on imagination and emotion'. *Tourism Review* 61(3), 20–27

Prideaux, B. (2000) 'The role of the transport system in destination development'. *Tourism Management* 21, 53–63

Pro-Poor Tourism Partnership (2009) *What is pro-poor tourism?* Available on: http://www.propoortourism.org.uk/what_is_ppt.html (accessed 22.09.09)

Prud'homme, R. and Bocarejo, J.P. (2006) 'The London congestion charge: a tentative economic appraisal'. *Transport Policy* 12(3), 279–287

Psaraftis, H.N. and Kontovas, C.A. (2009) 'CO2 emission statistics for the World Commercial Fleet'. *WMU Journal of Maritime Affairs* 8(1), 1–25

Pucher, J. and Buehler, R. (2008) 'Making cycling irresistible: Lessons from the Netherlands, Denmark and Germany'. *Transport Reviews* 28(4), 495–528

Pucher, J. and Dijkstra, L. (2000) 'Making walking and cycling safer: Lessons from Europe'. *Transportation* 54(3), 25–50

Rails to Trails Conservancy (1998) *Rail Trails and Safe Communities.* Available on: www.railstotrails.org/resources/documents/ (accessed 25.11.09)

Randles, S. and Mander, S. (2009a) 'Aviation, consumption and the climate change debate: "Are you going to tell me off for flying?"' *Technology Analysis and Strategic Management* 21(1), 93–113

Randles, S. and Mander, S. (2009b) 'Practice(s) and ratchet(s): a sociological examination of frequent flying'. In S. Gössling and P. Upham (eds) *Climate Change and Aviation: Issues, Challenges and Solutions.* London: Earthscan, 245–271

Raux, C., Traisnel, J.P., Nicholas, J.P. and Delvert, K. (2005) *Bilans énergétiques transport-habitats et méthodologie BETEL.* Lyon: LET, ETHEL project R2 Report

Ravenscroft, N. (2004) 'Tales from the tracks. Discourses of constraint in the use of mixed cycle and walking routes'. *International Review for the Sociology of Sport* 39(1), 27–44

Ravindranath, N.H. and Sathaye, J.A. (2002) *Climatic Change and Developing Countries.* Dordrecht: Kluwer Academic Publishers

Regulation (EC) 443/2009 on setting emission performance standards for new passenger cars as part of the Community's integrated approach to reduce CO2 emissions from light-duty vehicles [2009] OJ L14, 5.6.09

Rhoden, S. and Lumsdon, L. (2006) 'A conceptual classification of the transport-tourist experience'. In *Proceedings of Association for European Transport Conference.* Strasbourg

Ritchie, B.W. (1998) 'Bicycle tourism in the South Island of New Zealand: planning and management issues'. *Tourism Management* 19, 567–582

Ritzer, G. (1993) *The McDonaldization of Society.* Thousand Oaks, CA: Pine Forge Press

Ritzer, G. (2004) *The Globalization of Nothing.* London: Sage

Robbins, D. (1996) 'A sustainable transport policy for tourism on small islands: a case study of Malta'. In L. Briguglio, R. Butler, D. Harrison and W.L. Filho (eds) *Sustainable Tourism In Islands And Small States: Case Studies.* London: Pinter, 180–198

Robbins, D. and Dickinson, J.E. (2007) 'Can domestic tourism growth and reduced car dependency be achieved simultaneously in the UK'. In P. Peeters (ed) *Tourism and Climate Change and Mitigation: Methods, greenhouse gas reductions and policies.* Breda: Stichting NHTV Breda, 169–187

Roberson, D.N. Jnr and Babic, V. (2009) 'Remedy for modernity: Experiences of walkers and hikers on Medvednica mountain'. *Leisure Studies* 28(1), 105–112

Roberts, L. and Hall, D. (2001) *Rural Tourism and Recreation: Principles to Practice.* Wallingford: CABI Publishing

Rodaway, P. (1994) *Sensuous Geographies. Body, Sense and Place.* London: Routledge

Rogers, E.M. (1995) *Diffusion of Innovations,* 4th edn. New York: The Free Press

Romilly, P. (1999) 'Substitution of bus and car travel in urban Britain: An economic evaluation of bus and car exhaust emissions and other costs'. *Transportation Research Part D* 4, 109–125

Russell, J. (2007) 'Measuring the impact of transport modes: Are railways really greener than flying?' *Focus* 10(4), 28–33

Russell, J.A. (1980) 'The circumplex model of affect'. *Journal of Personality and Social Psychology* 39, 1161–1178

Ryan, C. (2000) 'Tourist experiences, phenomenographic analysis, post positivism and neural network software'. *International Journal of Tourism Research* 2, 119–131

Ryan, C. (ed) (2002) *The Tourist Experience*. London: Continuum

Saelens, B.E., Sallis, J.F. and Frank, L.D. (2003) 'Environmental Correlates of walking and cycling: Findings from transportation, urban design and planning literatures'. *Annals of Behavioural Medicine* 25(2), 80–91

Sallis, J.F., Frank, L.D., Saeleno, B.E. and Kraft, M.K. (2004) 'Active transportation and physical activity: opportunities for collaboration on transportation and public health research'. *Transportation Part A* 38, 249–268

Salomon, I. and Mokhtarian, P.L. (1998) 'What happens when mobility-inclined market segments face accessibility enhancing policies?' *Transportation Research D* 3(3), 129–140

Santarelli, M.G.L., Calì, M. and Bertonasco, A. (2003) 'Different fuelling technologies for urban transport bus services in an Italian big town: economic, environmental and social considerations'. *Energy Conservation and Management* 44, 2353–2370

Sasidharan, V., Sirakaya, E. and Kerstetter, D. (2002) 'Developing countries and tourism ecolabels'. *Tourism Management* 23(2), 161–174

Sauer, C. (1925) *The Morphology of Landscapes*. Berkeley: University of California

Schafer, A. and Victor, D.G. (2000) 'The future mobility of the world population'. *Transportation Part A* 34, 171–205

Schafer, C.S., Lee, B.K. and Turner, S. (2000) 'A tale of three greenway trails: user perceptions related to the quality of life'. *Landscape and Urban Planning* 49, 163–178

Scheyvens, R. (2009) 'Pro-poor tourism: is there value beyond the rhetoric?' *Tourism Recreation Research* 34(2), 191–196

Schilcher, D. (2007) 'Growth versus equity: the continuum of pro-poor tourism and neoliberal governance'. *Current Issues In Tourism* 10(2&3), 166–193

Schlich, R., Schonfelder, S., Hanson, S. and Axhausen, K.W. (2004) 'Structures of leisure travel: Temporal and spatial variability'. *Transport Reviews* 24(2), 219–237

Schriefl, E., Exner, A., Lauk, C. and Kulterer, K. (2008) 'On the way towards degrowth society: a review of transformation scenarios and desirable visions of the future'. In *Proceedings of Economic De-Growth for Ecological Sustainability and Social Equity*. 18–19 March, Paris

Scott, D., McBoyle, G. and Mills, B. (2003) 'Climate change and the skiing industry in southern Ontario (Canada): exploring the importance of snowmaking as a technical adaptation'. *Climate Research* 23, 171–181

Sethi, A. (2007) 'All aboard for Sydney'. *The Guardian*, 29 September. Available on: www.Guardian.co.uk/travel/series/londontosydneybybus. (accessed on 03.12.09)

Shailes, A., Senior, M.L. and Andrew, B.P. (2001) 'Tourists' travel behaviour in response to congestion: the case of car trips to Cornwall, United Kingdom'. *Journal of Transport Geography* 9(1), 49–60

Sharma, S. (2009) 'The great American staycation and the risk of stillness'. *Journal of Media and Culture* 12(1), 1–3

Sharpley, R. (1999) *Tourism, Tourists and Society*, 2nd edn. Huntington: ELM publications

Sharpley, R. (2009) *Tourism Development and the Environment: Beyond Sustainability?* London: Earthscan

Shaw, S. and Thomas, C. (2006) 'Social and cultural dimensions of air travel demand: Hyper-mobility in the UK?' *Journal of Sustainable Tourism* 14(2), 209–215

Sheller, M. and Urry, J. (2004) 'Places to play, places in play'. In M. Sheller and J. Urry (eds) *Tourism Mobilities: Places To Play, Places In Play*. London: Routledge, 1–10

Sheller, M. and Urry, J. (2006) 'The new mobilities paradigm'. *Environment and Planning A* 38, 207–226

Sheridan, L. and Teal, G. (2006) 'Fantasy and reality: tourist and local experiences of cruise ship tourism in Ensenada, Baja California, Mexico'. In R.K. Dowling (ed) *Cruise Ship Tourism*. Wallingford: CABI, 315–326

Shivelbusch, W. (1977) *The Railway Journey: the Industrialization of Time and Space in the Nineteenth Century*. Berkeley CA: University of California Press

Shove, E. (2003) 'Converging conventions of comfort, cleanliness and convenience'. *Journal of Consumer Policy* 26(4), 395–428

Shove, E. and Pantzar, M. (2005) 'Nordic walking, understanding the invention and re-invention of Nordic walking'. *Journal of Consumer Culture* 5(11), 43–64

Shropshire Hills AONB (2009) *Shropshire Hills Area of Outstanding Natural Beauty: Management Plan 2009–2014*. Available on: wwwshropshirehillsaonb.co.uk/partnerships/management_plan.html (accessed 30.11.09)

Siegel, P.Z., Brackbill, R.M. and Heath, G.W. (1995) 'The epidemiology of walking for exercise – Implications for promoting activity among sedentary groups'. *American Journal of Public Health* 85(5), 706–710

Silkeborg Turistbureau (2009) *Silkeborg: Canoeing*. Available on: http://old.silkeborg.com/sw3703.asp (accessed 11.09.09)

Simmel, G., Frisby, D. and Featherstone, M. (1997) *Simmel on Culture: Selected Writings*. London: Sage

Simmons, J. (1984) 'Railways, hotels and tourism in Great Britain 1839–1914'. *Journal of Contemporary History* 19(2), 201–222

Simonsen, P. and Jorgensen, B. (1996) *Cycle Tourism: Environmental and Economic Sustainability*. Unpublished report. Bornholm: Bornholm Research Centre

Simpson, M.C., Gössling, S., Scott, D., Hall, C.M. and Gladin, E. (2008) *Climate Change Adaptation and Mitigation in the Tourism Sector: Frameworks, Tools and Practices*. Paris: UNEP, University of Oxford, UNWTO, WMO

Skinner, D. and Rosen, P. (2007) 'Hell is other cyclists: rethinking transport and identity'. In D. Horton, P. Rosen and P. Cox (eds) *Cycling and Society*. Aldershot: Ashgate, 83–96

Slow Food (2009) *Slow Food*. Available on: http://www.slowfood.com/ (accessed 18.11.09)

Slow Movement (2009) *Slow Movement*. Available on: www.slowmovement.com (accessed 14.10.09)

Slow Moves (2009) *Slow Moves*. Available on: http://slowmovesblog.blogspot.com/2009/01/biarritz-to-barcelona-cycle.html (accessed 14.10.09)

Slowplanet.com (2009) *Slow Travel*. Available on: http://www.slowplanet.com/travel

Slowtravel.com (2007) *Slow Transportation, Slow Destination, Slow Recreation*. Available on: http://www.slowtravel.com/slow-travel-sections/ (accessed 06.11.07)

Smith, M. (2008) *The Man in Seat 61, A Guide to taking the train through Europe*. London: Transworld Publishers

Smith, M. and Kelly, C. (2006) 'Wellness tourism'. *Tourism Recreation Research* 31(1), 1–4

Smith, R.A. (2003) 'Railways: how they may contribute to a sustainable future'. *Proceedings of the Institution of Mechanical Engineers Part F. Journal of Rail and Rapid Transport* 217, 243–248

Smith, V.L. (1989) *Hosts and Guests: The Anthropology of Tourists,* 2nd edn. Philadelphia: University of Pennyslvania

Solnit, R. (2001) *Wanderlust: A history of walking.* London: Verso

Solyu, S. (2007) 'Estimation of Turkish road emissions'. *Energy Policy* 35, 4088–4094

Southerton, D., van Vliet, B. and Chappells, H. (2004a) 'Introduction: consumption, infrastructures and environmental sustainability'. In D. Southerton, H. Chappells and B. van Vliet (eds) *Sustainable Consumption: The implications of changing infrastructures of provision.* Cheltenham: Edward Elgar, 1–11

Southerton, D., Warde, A. and Hand, M. (2004b) 'The limited autonomy of the consumer: implications for sustainable consumption'. In D. Southerton, H. Chappells and B. van Vliet (eds) *Sustainable Consumption: The implications of changing infrastructures of provision.* Cheltenham: Edward Elgar, 32–48

South West Climate Change Impacts Partnership (2008) *Climate Change and Tourism in The South Of England: What Can Your Tourism Business Do To Adapt?* Available on: http://www.oursouthwest.com/climate/registry/tourism-leaflet-2007.pdf

Sovacool, B.K. (2009) 'Early modes of transport in the United States: Lessons for modern energy policymakers'. *Policy and Society* 27, 411–427

Spaargaren, G. (2004) 'Sustainable consumption: a theoretical and environmental policy perspective'. In D. Southerton, H. Chappells and B. van Vliet (eds) *Sustainable Consumption: The implications of changing infrastructures of provision.* Cheltenham: Edward Elgar, 15–31

Spaargaren, G. and van Vliet, B.J.M. (2000) 'Lifestyles, consumption and the environment: the ecological modernisation of domestic consumption'. *Environmental Politics* 9(1), 50–77

Speakman, C. (2005) 'Tourism and transport: future prospects'. *Tourism and Hospitality Planning & Development* 2(2), 129–136

Stead, D. (1999) 'Relationships between transport emissions and travel patterns in Britain'. *Transport Policy* 6, 247–258

Stebbins, R.A. (2005) 'Choice and experiential reflection of leisure'. *Leisure Science* 27, 349–352

Stebbins, R.A. (2007) *Serious Leisure: A perspective of our time.* Piscataway NJ: Transaction Publishers

Steiner, T.J. and Bristow, A.L. (2000) 'Road pricing in National Parks: a case study of the Yorkshire Dales National Park'. *Transport Policy* 7, 93–103

Sterl, P., Brandenburg, C. and Arnberger, A. (2008) 'Visitors' awareness and assessment of recreation disturbance of wildlife in the Donau-Auen National Park'. *Journal of Nature Conservation* 16, 135–145

Stern, N. (2006) *Stern Review: the economics of climate change.* Available at: http://www.hm-treasury.gov.uk/sternreview_index.htm (accessed 06.10.09)

Stettler, J. (2009) *The Future of Mobility and its Impact on Tourism.* Luzern: Luzern Business School

Stevenson, K. (2009) 'Women and young girls dare not travel alone: the dangers of sexual encounters on Victorian railways'. In G. Letherby and G. Reynolds (eds) *Gendered Mobilities.* Farnham: Ashgate, 189–200

Stoll-Kleemann, S., O'Riordan, T. and Jaeger, C.C. (2001) 'The psychology of denial concerning climate mitigation measures: evidence from Swiss focus groups'. *Global Environmental Change* 11, 107–117

Stradling, S. and Anable, J. (2008) 'Individual transport patterns'. In R. Knowles, Shaw, J. and Docherty, I. (eds) *Transport Geographies: mobilities, flows and spaces.* Oxford: Blackwell Publishing, 179–195

Stradling, S., Carreno, M., Rye, T. and Noble, A. (2007) 'Passenger perceptions and the ideal bus journey experience'. *Transport Policy* 14, 283–292

Su, M.M. and Wall, G. (2009) 'Destination and en-route experiences among train travellers to Tibet'. *Tourism Recreation Research* 34(2), 181–190

Swanson, J., Ampt, L. and Jones, P. (1997) 'Measuring bus passenger preferences'. *Traffic Engineering & Control* 38(6), 330–336

Sweeting, J.E.N. and Wayne, S.L. (2006) 'A shifting tide: environmental challenges and cruise industry responses'. In R.K. Dowling (ed) *Cruise Ship Tourism*. Wallingford: CABI, 327–337

Tao, C.H. and Wall, G. (2009) 'Tourism as a sustainable livelihood strategy'. *Tourism Management* 30, 90–98

TEEB (2009) *The Economic of Ecosystems and Biodiversity for National and International Policy Makers*. Available on: www.unep.org/greeneconomy/

Tertoolen, G., van Kreveld, D. and Verstraten, B. (1998) 'Psychological resistance against attempts to reduce private car use'. *Transportation Research Park A: Policy and Practice* 32(3), 171–181

The Travel Foundation (2006) *Insider Guide: Climate Change And Tourism – A Guide For Managers*. Bristol: The Travel Foundation

Theroux, P. (1979) *The Old Patagonian Express, By Train Through the Americas*. London: Penguin

Thompson, A.S. (2003) 'Changing railway structure and ownership: is anything working?' *Transport Reviews* 23(3), 311–355

Thompson, K. and Schofield, P. (2007) 'An investigation of the relationship between public transport performance and destination satisfaction'. *Journal of Transport Geography* 15, 136–144

Thrift, N. (1996) *Spatial Formations*. London: Sage

Thrift, N. (2004) 'Intensities of feeling: towards a spatial politics of affect'. *Geografiska Annaler Series B* 86, 57–78

Tolley, R. and Walker, J. (2004) 'Conference conclusions: Walk 21 V Cities for People, Fifth International Conference on Walking in the 21st century'. Available on: www.walk21.com/papers/copehagen%20conclusions.pdf (accessed 07.10.09)

Tolley, R., Lumsdon, L. and Bickerstaff, K. (2001) 'The future of walking in Europe: A Delphi project to identify expert opinion on future walking scenarios'. *Transport Policy* 8, 307–315

Tomes, P.A. and Knoch, C. (2009) *Rail Trail Users Surveys and Economic Impact: A Comparison of Trail User Expenditures*. Available on: www.railstotrails.org/resources/documents/ (accessed 25.11.09)

Torkildsen, G. (1999) *Leisure and Recreation Management*. London: E & FN Spon

Torres, R. and Momsen, J.H. (2007) 'Holiday package tourism and the poor in The Gambia'. *Development South Africa* 24(3), 445–464

Tosun, C. (2001) 'Challenges of sustainable tourism development in the developing world: the case of Turkey'. *Tourism Management* 22, 289–303

Towner, J. (1985) 'The Grand Tour: A key phase in the history of tourism'. *Annals of Tourism Research* 12(3), 297–333

Towner, J. (2002) 'Literature, tourism and the Grand Tour'. In M. Robinson and H-L. Andersen (eds) *Literature and Tourism Essays in the Reading and Writing of Tourism*. London: Thomson, 226–238

Transport New South Wales (2002) *Sydney Bus Users*. Available on: www.transport.nsw.gov/au/tlc/documents

Transport Regeneration Limited (2009) *The Value of Community Rail Partnerships*. Bury St Edmunds: Transport Regeneration Limited

Trendscope (2008) *Radreisen der Deutschen.* Cologne, Germany: Trendscope GbR

TUI Travel PLC (2009) *Sustainable Development Report 2008.* Available on: http://sd2008.tuitravelplc.com/tui-sd/pages/sectors/tuinorthernregion/nordic? whoareyou=add&ngo=true&submit=Submit (accessed 18.11.09)

Turnbull, K.F. (2000) 'Visitor transportation at US National Parks: Increasing accessibility but preserving the environment'. *Transportation Research Board* 9(210), 3–8

Turner, V. and Turner, E. (1978) *Image and Pilgrimage in Christian Culture.* New York: Columbia University Press

Tyler, N. (ed) (2002) *Accessibility and the Bus System.* London: Thomas Telford

Tyndall Centre for Climate Change Research (2009) *What's Atmospheric CO_2?* Available on: http://www.tyndall.ac.uk/widgets/co2-ppm (accessed 21.10.09)

United Nations Environment Programme (2009) *Kick the Habit.* Available on: www.unep.org/publish/ebooks/kick-the-habit/Default.aspx?bid=1DOT1MAC (accessed 20.07.09)

United Nations World Tourism Organization (2005) *Declaration: 'Harnessing Tourism for the Millennium Development Goals'.* Available on: http://www. unwto.org/sdt/fields/en/pdf/decla-ny-mdg-en.pdf (accessed 05.08.09)

United Nations World Tourism Organization (2007) *Davos Declaration: Climate change and tourism responding to global challenges.* Available on: http://www. unwto.org/pdf/pr071046.pdf (accessed 14.11.07)

United Nations World Tourism Organization (2009a) *Roadmap to Recovery, a message from the World Tourism Organization.* Available on: www.unwto.org/ pdf/brochure_TRC_roadmap.pdf (accessed 10.07.09)

United Nations World Tourism Organization (2009b) *Sustainable Tourism – Eliminating Poverty: About ST-EP.* Available on: http://www.unwto.org/ step/about/en/step.php?op=1 (accessed 22.09.09)

United Nations World Tourism Organization (2009c) *Tourism Highlights: 2009 Edition.* Available on: http://www.unwto.org/facts/eng/highlights.htm (accessed 01.10.09)

Unwin, N.C. (1995) 'Promoting the public health benefits of cycling'. *Public Health* 109, 41–46

Upham, P., Tomei, J. and Boucher, P. (2009) 'Biofuels, aviation and sustainability: prospects and limits'. In S. Gössling and P. Upham (eds) *Climate Change and Aviation: Issues, Challenges and Solutions.* London: Earthscan, 309–328

Urry, J. (1990) *The Tourist Gaze: Travel, Leisure and Society.* London: Sage

Urry, J. (2000) *Sociology Beyond Societies: Mobilities For The Twenty-First Century.* London: Routledge

Urry, J. (2002) 'Mobility and proximity'. *Sociology* 36(2), 255–274

Urry, J. (2005) 'The "system" of automobility'. In M. Featherstone, N. Thrift and J. Urry (eds) *Automobilities.* London: Sage, 25–39

Urry, J. (2007) *Mobilities.* Cambridge: Polity Press

Urry, J. (2008) 'Governance, flows, and the end of the car system?' *Global Environmental Change* 18, 343–349

Urry, J. (2009) 'Aeromobilities and the global'. In S. Cwerner, S. Kesselring and J. Urry (eds) *Aeromobilities.* Abingdon: Routledge, 25–38

US Environmental Protection Agency (2009) *US Climate Policy and Actions.* Available on: http://www.epa.gov/climatechange/policy/index.html (accessed 15.09.09)

Utiger, M. and Richardson, A.J. (2000) *Veloland Schweiz: Resultante der Zählungen und Befragungen 1999.* Bern, Switzerland: Stiftung Veloland Schweiz

Van Dijk, J. (1997) 'Political discourse and racism: describing others in western parliaments'. In S.H. Riggins (ed) *The language and politics of exclusion: Others in discourse*. London: Sage, 31–64

Van Goeverden, C.D. (2007) 'Long distance travel in Europe: the potential of the train'. In P. Peeters (ed) *Tourism and Climate Change Mitigation: Methods, greenhouse gas reductions and policies*. Breda: Stichting NHTV Breda, 105–117

Van Goeverden, C.D. (2009) 'Explaining factors for train use in European long-distance travel'. *Tourism and Hospitality Planning & Development* 6(1), 21–37

Vaughan, A. (1997) *Railway Men, Politics and Money*. London: John Murray

Vaughan, D.R., Farr, H. and Slee, R.W. (2000) 'Estimating and interpreting the local economic benefits of visitor spending: an explanation'. *Leisure Studies* 19, 95–118

Verbeek, D.H.P. (2009) *Sustainable Tourism Mobilities: A Practice Approach*. Thesis, The Brabant Centre for Sustainable Development, University of Tilberg, The Netherlands

Verbeek, D.H.P. and Mommaas, H. (2007) 'Sustainable tourism mobility: the social practices approach'. In P. Peeters (ed) *Tourism and Climate Change Mitigation: Methods, greenhouse gas reductions and policies*. Breda: Stichting NHTV Breda, 63–74

Verbeek, D.H.P. and Mommaas, H. (2008) 'Transitions to sustainable tourism mobility: The social practices approach'. *Journal of Sustainable Tourism* 16(6), 629–644

Vidal, J. (2008) 'True scale of CO_2 emissions from shipping revealed'. *The Guardian*, 13 Feb. Available on: http://www.guardian.co.uk/environment/2008/feb/13/climate-change.pollution (accessed 19.06.08)

Voelklein, C. and Howarth, C. (2005) 'A review of controversies about social representations theory: a British debate'. *Culture & Psychology* 11, 431–454

Wackernagel, M. and Rees, R. (1996) *Our Ecological Footprint, Reducing Human Impact on Earth*. Gabriola Island BC: New Society Publishers

Wall, G. (1997) 'Is ecotourism sustainable?' *Environmental Management* 21(4), 483–491

Wall, G. and McDonald, M. (2007) 'Improving bus service quality and information in Winchester'. *Transport Policy* 14, 165–179

Wallace, A. (1993) *Walking: Literature and English Culture*. Oxford: Clarendon Press

Walsh, C., Jakeman, P., Moles, R. and O'Regan, B. (2008) 'A comparison of carbon dioxide emissions associated with motorized transport modes and cycling in Ireland'. *Transportation Research Part D* 13, 392–399

Walsh, M. (2000) *Making Connections. The Long Distance Bus Industry in the USA*. Aldershot: Ashgate

Walton, J.K. (2009) 'Prospect in tourism history: evolution, state of play and future developments'. *Tourism Management* 30(6), 783–793

Wang, G., Macera, C.A., Scudder-Soucie, B., Schmid, T., Pratt, M. and Buchner, D. (2004) 'Cost effectiveness of a bicycle/pedestrian trail development in health prevention.' *Preventive Medicine* 38, 237–242

Warde, A. (2005) 'Consumption and theories of practice'. *Journal of Consumer Culture* 5(2), 131–153

Warnken, J. and Byrnes, T. (2004) 'Impacts of tourboats in marine environments'. In R. Buckley (ed) *Environmental Impacts of Ecotourism*. Wallingford: CABI Publishing, 99–124

Watts, L. (2008) 'The art and craft of train travel'. *Social and Cultural Geography* 9(6), 711–726

Watts, L. (2009) *An Ethnographer's Guide To: Making A Train Journey*. Lancaster: Centre for Mobility Research

Wearing, S. (2001) 'Exploring socio-cultural impacts on local communities'. In D.B. Weaver (ed) *The Encyclopaedia of Ecotourism*. Wallingford: CABI Publishing, 395–410

Weaver, D. (2005) 'Comprehensive and minimalist dimensions of ecotourism'. *Annals of Tourism Research* 32(2), 439–455

Weaver, D. (2006) *Sustainable Tourism: Theory and Practice*. Oxford: Elsevier, Butterworth-Heinemann

Weaver, D. (2007) 'Towards sustainable mass tourism: Paradigm shift or paradigm nudge?' *Tourism Recreation Research* 32, 65–69

Weaver, D.B. (2009) 'Reflections on Sustainable Tourism and Paradigm Change'. In S. Gössling, C.M. Hall and D.B. Weaver (eds) *Sustainable Tourism Futures, Perspectives on Systems, Restructuring and Innovations*. London: Routledge, 19–33

Weinberger, C. (2009) *The Development of Cycling Tourism in (Lower) Austria*. Available on: www.toerismevlaanderen.be/doc/UPL-200005 (accessed 20.11.09)

Wendel-Vos, G.C.W. Schmit, A.J., De Niet, R., Boshuizen, H.C., Saris, W.H.M. and Kromhout, D. (2004) 'Factors of the physical environment associated with walking and bicycling'. *Medicine and Science in Sports Exercise* 36(4), 725–730

Wheeller, B. (1993) 'Sustaining the ego'. *Journal of Sustainable Tourism* 1(2), 121–129

Wikiloc (2009) *Wikiloc*. Available on: www.wikiloc.com/wikiloc/hom.co (accessed 21.11.09)

Williams, S. (1995) *Outdoor Recreation and the Urban Environment*. London: Routledge

Willig, C. (2003) 'Discourse analysis'. In A.J. Smith (ed) *Qualitative Psychology: A practical guide to research methods*. London: Sage, 159–183

Woehler, K.H. (2004) 'The rediscovery of slowness, or leisure time as one's own and as self aggrandizement in the tourism and leisure industry'. In K. Weiemair and C. Mathies (eds) *The Tourism and Leisure Industry Shaping the Future*. New York, Haworth Press, 83–92

World Commission on Environment and Development (1987) *Our Common Future*. Available on: www.ourcommonfuture.org (accessed 12.09.09)

World Economic Forum (2009) *Towards a Low Carbon Travel and Tourism Sector, World Economic Forum, Geneva*. Available on: http://www.unwto.org/media/news/en/pdf/LowCarbonTravelTourism.pdf (accessed 16.09.09)

World Health Organization (2004) *Obesity: Preventing and Managing the Global Epidemic*. Geneva: World Health Organization

World Tourism Organization (2002) *Voluntary Initiatives for Sustainable Tourism. Worldwide Inventory and Comparative Analysis of 104 Eco-labels, Awards and Self-commitments*. Madrid: World Tourism Organization

World Tourism Organization (2003) *Climate Change and Tourism: Proceedings of the 1st International Conference on Climate Change and Tourism*. Djerba, Tunisia, 9–11 April

World Tourism Organization (2007) *Climate Change and Tourism: Responding to Global Challenges*. Available on: http://www.unwto.org/climate/support/en/pdf/summary_davos_e.pdf

World Tourism Organization (2008) *World Overview and Tourism Topics, 2006 Edition*. Madrid: World Tourism Organization

World Tourism Organization (2009) *Sustainable Development of Tourism: Concepts and Definitions*. Available on: http://www.unwto.org/frameset/ frame_sustainable.html (accessed 22.10.09)

World Travel and Tourism Council (2009) *The Longer Term Outlook For Travel And Tourism Is Still Bright*. Available on: www.org/eng/Tourism_News/Press_Releases _2009 (accessed 12.11.09)

World Wildlife Fund-UK (2002) *Holiday Footprinting. A Practical Tool For Responsible Tourism.* Godalming: WWF-UK

Wylie, J. (2005) 'A single day's walking: Narrative self and landscape on the South West Coastal Path'. *Royal Geographical Society* 30, 234–247

Wynne, J.R. (2008) 'Spatial narratives and experiential learning: Walking tourism as culture work'. In *The American Sociological Association Annual Meeting, Sheraton Boston and The Boston Marriott, Copley Place, Boston MA*, 31 July

Yeoman, I., Lennon, J., Blake, A., Galt, M., Greenwood, C. and McMahon-Beattie, U. (2007) 'Oil depletion: What does this mean for Scottish tourism?' *Tourism Management* 25(5), 1354–1365

Zehr, S.C. (2000) 'Public representations of scientific uncertainty about global climate change'. *Public Understanding of Science* 9, 85–103

Zhao, W. and Brent Ritchie, J.R. (2007) 'Tourism and poverty alleviation: an integrative research framework'. *Current Issues in Tourism* 10(2&3), 119–143

Index